MznLnx

Missing Links Exam Preps

Exam Prep for

Principles of Managerial Finance

Gitman, 10th Edition

The MznLnx Exam Prep is your link from the texbook and lecture to your exams.
The MznLnx Exam Preps are unauthorized and comprehensive reviews of your textbooks.

MznLnx

Rico
Publications

Exam Prep for Principles of Managerial Finance
10th Edition
Gitman

Publisher: Raymond Houge
Assistant Editor: Michael Rouger
Text and Cover Designer: Lisa Buckner
Marketing Manager: Sara Swagger
Project Manager, Editorial Production: Jerry Emerson
Art Director: Vernon Lowerui

Product Manager: Dave Mason
Editorial Assitant: Rachel Guzmanji
Pedagogy: Debra Long
Cover Image: Jim Reed/Getty Images
Text and Cover Printer: City Printing, Inc.
Compositor: Media Mix, Inc.

For more information about our products, contact us at:
Dave.Mason@RicoPublications.com

For permission to use material from this text or product, submit a request online to:
Dave.Mason@RicoPublications.com

Printed in the United States
ISBN:

Contents

TO THE STUDENT

COMPREHENSIVE

The *MznLnx* Exam Prep series is designed to help you pass your exams. Editors at MznLnx review your textbooks and then prepare these practice exams to help you master the textbook material. Unlike study guides, workbooks, and practice tests provided by the texbook publisher and textbook authors, *MznLnx* gives you ***all*** of the material in each chapter in exam form, not just samples, so you can be sure to nail your exam.

MECHANICAL

The MznLnx Exam Prep series creates exams that will help you learn the subject matter as well as test you on your understanding. Each question is designed to help you master the concept. Just working through the exams, you gain an understanding of the subject--its a simple mechanical process that produces success.

INTEGRATED STUDY GUIDE AND REVIEW

MznLnx is not just a set of exams designed to test you, its also a comprehensive review of the subject content. Each exam question is also a review of the concept, making sure that you will get the answer correct without having to go to other sources of material. You learn as you go! Its the easiest way to pass an exam.

HUMOR

Studying can be tedious and dry. MznLnx's instructional design includes moderate humor within the exam questions on occassion, to break the tedium and revitalize the brain

1. A _________ is a profit that results from investments into a capital asset, such as stocks, bonds or real estate, which exceeds the purchase price. It is the difference between a higher selling price and a lower purchase price, resulting in a financial gain for the seller. Conversely, a capital loss arises if the proceeds from the sale of a capital asset are less than the purchase price.

a. Capital gains tax
b. Capital gain
c. Tax brackets
d. Payroll tax

2. The _________ is the market for securities, where companies and governments can raise longterm funds. The _________ includes the stock market and the bond market. Financial regulators, such as the U.S. Securities and Exchange Commission, oversee the _________s in their designated countries to ensure that investors are protected against fraud.

a. Spot rate
b. Capital market
c. Delta neutral
d. Forward market

3. The institution most often referenced by the word '_________' is a public or publicly traded _________, the shares of which are traded on a public stock exchange (e.g., the New York Stock Exchange or Nasdaq in the United States) where shares of stock of _________s are bought and sold by and to the general public. Most of the largest businesses in the world are publicly traded _________s. However, the majority of _________s are said to be closely held, privately held or close _________s, meaning that no ready market exists for the trading of shares.

a. Federal Home Loan Mortgage Corporation
b. Protect
c. Depository Trust Company
d. Corporation

4. _________ is the provision of resources (such as granting a loan) by one party to another party where that second party does not reimburse the first party immediately, thereby generating a debt, and instead arranges either to repay or return those resources (or material(s) of equal value) at a later date. The first party is called a creditor, also known as a lender, while the second party is called a debtor, also known as a borrower.

Movements of financial capital are normally dependent on either _________ or equity transfers.

a. Clearing house
b. Comparable
c. Warrant
d. Credit

5. In finance, the _________ is the global financial market for short-term borrowing and lending. It provides short-term liquidity funding for the global financial system. The _________ is where short-term obligations such as Treasury bills, commercial paper and bankers' acceptances are bought and sold.

a. Debt-for-equity swap
b. Cramdown
c. Consumer debt
d. Money market

6. In finance, the value of an option consists of two components, its intrinsic value and its _________. Time value is simply the difference between option value and intrinsic value. _________ is also known as theta, extrinsic value, or instrumental value.

a. Debt buyer
b. Conservatism
c. Global Squeeze
d. Time value

7. Simply put, _________ is the value of money figuring in a given amount of interest for a given amount of time. For example 100 dollars of todays money held for a year at 5 percent interest is worth 105 dollars, therefore 100 dollars paid now or 105 dollars paid exactly one year from now is the same amount of payment of money with that given intersest at that given amount of time. This notion dates at least to Martín de Azpilcueta of the School of Salamanca.

All of the standard calculations for _________ derive from the most basic algebraic expression for the present value of a future sum, 'discounted' to the present by an amount equal to the _________. For example, a sum of FV to be received in one year is discounted (at the rate of interest r) to give a sum of PV at present: PV = FV -- rÂ·PV = FV/(1+r).

a. Zero-coupon bond
b. Current account
c. Coefficient of variation
d. Time value of money

8. In finance, _________ refers to the way a corporation finances its assets through some combination of equity, debt, or hybrid securities. A firm's _________ is then the composition or 'structure' of its liabilities. For example, a firm that sells $20 billion in equity and $80 billion in debt is said to be 20% equity-financed and 80% debt-financed.

a. Book building
b. Rights issue
c. Market for corporate control
d. Capital structure

9. In the United States, the Financial Industry Regulatory Authority (FINRA) is a self-regulatory organization (SRO) under the Securities Exchange Act of 1934, successor to the _________, Inc.

FINRA is responsible for regulatory oversight of all securities firms that do business with the public; professional training, testing and licensing of registered persons; arbitration and mediation; market regulation by contract for The NASDAQ Stock Market, Inc., the American Stock Exchange LLC, and the International Securities Exchange, LLC; and industry utilities, such as Trade Reporting Facilities and other over-the-counter operations.

a. 529 plan
b. 7-Eleven
c. 4-4-5 Calendar
d. National Association of Securities Dealers

10. A _________ is a fungible, negotiable instrument representing financial value. They are broadly categorized into debt securities (such as banknotes, bonds and debentures), and equity securities; e.g., common stocks. The company or other entity issuing the _________ is called the issuer.

a. Tracking stock
b. Securities lending
c. Security
d. Book entry

11. _________ refer to services provided by the finance industry.

The finance industry encompasses a broad range of organizations that deal with the management of money. Among these organizations are banks, credit card companies, insurance companies, consumer finance companies, stock brokerages, investment funds and some government sponsored enterprises.

a. Cost of carry
b. Delta hedging
c. Financial instruments
d. Financial services

12. In the commercial and legal parlance of most countries, a _________ or simply a partnership, refers to an association of persons or an unincorporated company with the following major features:

- Created by agreement, proof of existence and estoppel.
- Formed by two or more persons
- The owners are all personally liable for any legal actions and debts the company may face

It is a partnership in which partners share equally in both responsibility and liability.

Partnerships have certain default characteristics relating to both the relationship between the individual partners and (b) the relationship between the partnership and the outside world. The former can generally be overridden by agreement between the partners, whereas the latter generally cannot be.

The assets of the business are owned on behalf of the other partners, and they are each personally liable, jointly and severally, for business debts, taxes or tortious liability.

a. First Prudential Markets
b. The Depository Trust ' Clearing Corporation
c. General partnership
d. Federal Home Loan Mortgage Corporation

13. A _________ is a type of business entity in which partners (owners) share with each other the profits or losses of the business undertaking in which all have invested. _________s are often favored over corporations for taxation purposes, as the _________ structure does not generally incur a tax on profits before it is distributed to the partners (i.e. there is no dividend tax levied.) However, depending on the _________ structure and the jurisdiction in which it operates, owners of a _________ may be exposed to greater personal liability than they would as shareholders of a corporation.

a. Fiduciary
b. National Securities Markets Improvement Act of 1996
c. Clayton Antitrust Act
d. Partnership

14. A sole _________, or simply _________ is a type of business entity which legally has no separate existence from its owner. Hence, the limitations of liability enjoyed by a corporation and limited liability partnerships do not apply to sole proprietors. All debts of the business are debts of the owner.

a. Product life cycle
b. Just-in-time
c. Free cash flow
d. Proprietorship

15. In the most general sense, a _________ is anything that is a hindrance, or puts individuals at a disadvantage.

Before we discuss the financial terms, we should note that a _________ can also have a much more important slang meaning.

This is best described in an example.

a. McFadden Act
b. Liability
c. Limited liability
d. Covenant

16. _________ is a form of corporation equity ownership represented in the securities. It is dangerous in comparison to preferred shares and some other investment options, in that in the event of bankruptcy, _________ investors receive their funds after preferred stockholders, bondholders, creditors, etc. On the other hand, common shares on average perform better than preferred shares or bonds over time.

a. Common stock
b. Stop-limit order
c. Stock market bubble
d. Stock split

17. A _________ is a payment made by a corporation to its shareholder members. When a corporation earns a profit or surplus, that money can be put to two uses: it can either be re-invested in the business (called retained earnings), or it can be paid to the shareholders as a _________. Many corporations retain a portion of their earnings and pay the remainder as a _________.

a. Special dividend
b. Dividend yield
c. Dividend puzzle
d. Dividend

18. _________ is a concept whereby a person's financial liability is limited to a fixed sum, most commonly the value of a person's investment in a company or partnership with _________. A shareholder in a limited company is not personally liable for any of the debts of the company, other than for the value of his investment in that company. The same is true for the members of a _________ partnership and the limited partners in a limited partnership.

a. Personal property
b. Sarbanes-Oxley Act
c. Beneficial owner
d. Limited liability

19. A mutual shareholder or _________ is an individual or company (including a corporation) that legally owns one or more shares of stock in a joint stock company. A company's shareholders collectively own that company. Thus, the typical goal of such companies is to enhance shareholder value.

a. Stockholder
b. Stock market bubble
c. Trading curb
d. Limit order

20. A _________ or chief executive is one of the highest-ranking corporate officer (executive) or administrator in charge of total management. An individual selected as President and _________ of a corporation, company, organization, or agency, reports to the board of directors. In internal communication and press releases, many companies capitalize the term and those of other high positions, even when they are not proper nouns.

a. Portfolio manager
b. Chief executive officer
c. Purchasing manager
d. Stockbroker

21. A _________ in the law of the vast majority of United States jurisdictions is a legal form of business company that provides limited liability to its owners. It is a hybrid business entity having certain characteristics of both a corporation and a partnership or sole proprietorship (depending on how many owners there are.) The primary characteristic an _________ shares with a corporation is limited liability, and the primary characteristic it shares with a partnership is the availability of pass-through income taxation.

a. Financial endowment
b. Pension fund
c. Fund of funds
d. Limited liability company

22. A _________ has elements of partnerships and corporations. In an _________ one partner is not responsible or liable for another partner's misconduct or negligence. This is an important difference from that of a limited partnership.

a. Limited liability partnership
b. Citrix Systems
c. KPMG
d. Governmental Accounting Standards Board

23. A _________ is a form of partnership similar to a general partnership, except that in addition to one or more general partners (GPs), there are one or more limited partners (_________s). It is a partnership in which only one partner is required to be a general partner.

The GPs are, in all major respects, in the same legal position as partners in a conventional firm, i.e. they have management control, share the right to use partnership property, share the profits of the firm in predefined proportions, and have joint and several liability for the debts of the partnership.

a. Fund of funds
b. Limited partnership
c. Leverage
d. Limited liability company

24. An _________ is a corporation that makes a valid election to be taxed under Subchapter S of Chapter 1 of the Internal Revenue Code.

In general, _________s do not pay any income taxes. Instead, the corporation's income or losses are divided among and passed through to its shareholders.

a. 4-4-5 Calendar
b. 7-Eleven
c. 529 plan
d. S corporation

25. A _________ is an expenditure creating future benefits. A _________ is incurred when a business spends money either to buy fixed assets or to add to the value of an existing fixed asset with a useful life that extends beyond the taxable year. Capex are used by a company to acquire or upgrade physical assets such as equipment, property, or industrial buildings.

a. 4-4-5 Calendar
b. Weighted average cost of capital
c. Cost of capital
d. Capital expenditure

26. A _________, securities analyst, research analyst, equity analyst, or investment analyst is a person who performs financial analysis for external or internal clients as a core part of the job.

An analyst studies companies and other entities to arrive at the estimate of their financial value. It is normally done by analyzing financial reports, aided by follow-up interviews with company representatives and industry experts.

a. Portfolio manager
b. Stockbroker
c. Purchasing manager
d. Financial analyst

27. The _________ of a stock is a measure of the price paid for a share relative to the annual income or profit earned by the firm per share. It is a financial ratio used for valuation: a higher _________ means that investors are paying more for each unit of income, so the stock is more expensive compared to one with lower _________.

The _________ has units of years, which can be interpreted as 'number of years of earnings to pay back purchase price'.

a. P/E ratio
b. Return of capital
c. Quick ratio
d. Sustainable growth rate

28. _________ is the financing of long-term infrastructure and industrial projects based upon a complex financial structure where project debt and equity are used to finance the project, rather than the balance sheets of project sponsors. Usually, a _________ structure involves a number of equity investors, known as sponsors, as well as a syndicate of banks that provide loans to the operation. The loans are most commonly non-recourse loans, which are secured by the project assets and paid entirely from project cash flow, rather than from the general assets or creditworthiness of the project sponsors, a decision in part supported by financial modeling.

a. Duration gap
b. Standard of deferred payment
c. FATF Blacklist
d. Project finance

29. _________ is a type of credit that does not have a fixed number of payments, in contrast to installment credit. Examples of _________s used by consumers include credit cards. Corporate _________ facilities are typically used to provide liquidity for a company's day-to-day operations.

a. Revolving credit
b. Commercial finance
c. Reverse stock split
d. Package loan

30. Accrual, in accounting, describes the accounting method known as _________, whereby revenues and expenses are recognized when they are accrued, i.e. accumulated (earned or incurred), regardless when the actual cash is received or paid out.

E.g. a company delivers a product to a customer who will pay for it 30 days later in the next fiscal year starting a week after the delivery. The company recognizes the proceeds as a revenue in its current income statement still for the fiscal year of the delivery, even though it will get paid in cash during the following accounting period.

a. AAB
b. ABN Amro
c. A Random Walk Down Wall Street
d. Accrual basis

31. _________ is the balance of the amounts of cash being received and paid by a business during a defined period of time, sometimes tied to a specific project. Measurement of _________ can be used

- to evaluate the state or performance of a business or project.
- to determine problems with liquidity. Being profitable does not necessarily mean being liquid. A company can fail because of a shortage of cash, even while profitable.
- to generate project rate of returns. The time of _________s into and out of projects are used as inputs to financial models such as internal rate of return, and net present value.
- to examine income or growth of a business when it is believed that accrual accounting concepts do not represent economic realities. Alternately, _________ can be used to 'validate' the net income generated by accrual accounting.

_________ as a generic term may be used differently depending on context, and certain _________ definitions may be adapted by analysts and users for their own uses. Common terms include operating _________ and free _________.

_________s can be classified into:

1. Operational _________s: Cash received or expended as a result of the company's core business activities.
2. Investment _________s: Cash received or expended through capital expenditure, investments or acquisitions.
3. Financing _________s: Cash received or expended as a result of financial activities, such as interests and dividends.

All three together - the net _________ - are necessary to reconcile the beginning cash balance to the ending cash balance. Loan draw downs or equity injections, that is just shifting of capital but no expenditure as such, are not considered in the net _________.

a. Shareholder value
b. Real option
c. Corporate finance
d. Cash flow

32. _________ can be regarded as an outcome of mental processes (cognitive process) leading to the selection of a course of action among several alternatives. Every _________ process produces a final choice. The output can be an action or an opinion of choice.

a. 7-Eleven
b. 529 plan
c. 4-4-5 Calendar
d. Decision making

33. _________ are the earnings returned on the initial investment amount.

In the US, the Financial Accounting Standards Board (FASB) requires companies' income statements to report _________ for each of the major categories of the income statement: continuing operations, discontinued operations, extraordinary items, and net income.

The _________ formula does not include preferred dividends for categories outside of continued operations and net income.

a. Average accounting return
b. Earnings per share
c. Inventory turnover
d. Assets turnover

34. The _________ is a private, not-for-profit organization whose primary purpose is to develop generally accepted accounting principles (GAAP) within the United States in the public's interest. The Securities and Exchange Commission (SEC) designated the _________ as the organization responsible for setting accounting standards for public companies in the U.S. It was created in 1973, replacing the Accounting Principles Board and the Committee on Accounting Procedure of the American Institute of Certified Public Accountants. The _________'s mission is 'to establish and improve standards of financial accounting and reporting for the guidance and education of the public, including issuers, auditors, and users of financial information.'

The _________ is not a governmental body.

a. PlaNet Finance
b. Credit karma
c. FASB
d. MRU Holdings

35. _________ is the difference between price and the costs of bringing to market whatever it is that is accounted as an enterprise (whether by harvest, extraction, manufacture, or purchase) in terms of the component costs of delivered goods and/or services and any operating or other expenses.

A key difficulty in measuring profit is in defining costs. Pure economic monetary profits can be zero or negative even in competitive equilibrium when accounted monetized costs exceed monetized price.

a. AAB
b. A Random Walk Down Wall Street
c. Economic profit
d. Accounting profit

36. In economics, _________ is the process by which a firm determines the price and output level that returns the greatest profit. There are several approaches to this problem. The total revenue--total cost method relies on the fact that profit equals revenue minus cost, and the marginal revenue--marginal cost method is based on the fact that total profit in a perfectly competitive market reaches its maximum point where marginal revenue equals marginal cost.

a. Profit maximization
b. 4-4-5 Calendar
c. Profit margin
d. Net profit margin

37. In business and finance, a _________ (also referred to as equity _________) of stock means a _________ of ownership in a corporation (company.) In the plural, stocks is often used as a synonym for _________s especially in the United States, but it is less commonly used that way outside of North America.

In the United Kingdom, South Africa, and Australia, stock can also refer to completely different financial instruments such as government bonds or, less commonly, to all kinds of marketable securities.

a. Bucket shop
b. Procter ' Gamble
c. Margin
d. Share

38. In the United States, _________ are overnight borrowings by banks to maintain their bank reserves at the Federal Reserve. Banks keep reserves at Federal Reserve Banks to meet their reserve requirements and to clear financial transactions. Transactions in the _________ market enable depository institutions with reserve balances in excess of reserve requirements to lend reserves to institutions with reserve deficiencies.

a. 4-4-5 Calendar
b. Federal funds rate
c. Regulation T
d. Federal funds

39. _________ in technical analysis is typical price multiplied by volume, a kind of approximation to the dollar value of a day's trading.

_________ index (Money flowl) is an oscillator calculated over an N-day period, ranging from 0 to 100, showing _________ on up days as a percentage of the total of up and down days.

The calculations are as follows. The typical price for each day is the average of high, low and close,

>

_________ is the product of typical price and the volume on that day.

>

a. Money flow
b. Technical analysis
c. Support and resistance
d. Dow theory

40. A _________ is the price of a single share of a no. of saleable stocks of the company. Once the stock is purchased, the owner becomes a shareholder of the company that issued the share.

a. Whisper numbers
b. Share price
c. Stock split
d. Trading curb

41. In corporate finance, _________ is an estimate of true economic profit after making corrective adjustments to GAAP accounting, including deducting the opportunity cost of equity capital. GAAP is estimated to ignore US$300 billion in shareholder opportunity costs. _________ can be measured as Net Operating Profit After Taxes(or NOPAT) less the money cost of capital.

a. ABN Amro
b. AAB
c. Economic value added
d. A Random Walk Down Wall Street

42. _________ refers to the additional value of a commodity over the cost of commodities used to produce it from the previous stage of production. An example is the price of gasoline at the pump over the price of the oil in it. In national accounts used in macroeconomics, it refers to the contribution of the factors of production, i.e., land, labor, and capital goods, to raising the value of a product and corresponds to the incomes received by the owners of these factors.

a. Value added
b. Supply shock
c. Demand shock
d. Deregulation

43. In Modern Portfolio Theory, the _________ is the graphical representation of the Capital Asset Pricing Model. It displays the expected rate of return for an overall market as a function of systematic (non-diversifiable) risk (beta.)

The Y-Intercept (beta=0) of the _________ is equal to the risk-free interest rate.

a. Rebalancing
b. Certificate in Investment Performance Measurement
c. Divestment
d. Security market line

44. An _________ is an economic concept that relates to the cost incurred by an entity (such as organizations) associated with problems such as divergent management-shareholder objectives and information asymmetry. The costs consist of two main sources:

1. The costs inherently associated with using an agent (e.g., the risk that agents will use organizational resource for their own benefit) and
2. The costs of techniques used to mitigate the problems associated with using an agent (e.g., the costs of producing financial statements or the use of stock options to align executive interests to shareholder interests.)

Though effects of _________ are present in any agency relationship, the term is most used in business contexts.

The information asymmetry that exists between shareholders and the Chief Executive Officer is generally considered to be a classic example of a principal-agent problem. The agent (the manager) is working on behalf of the principal (the shareholders), who does not observe the actions of the agent.

a. AAB
b. ABN Amro
c. A Random Walk Down Wall Street
d. Agency cost

45. In political science and economics, the _________ or agency dilemma treats the difficulties that arise under conditions of incomplete and asymmetric information when a principal hires an agent. Various mechanisms may be used to try to align the interests of the agent with those of the principal, such as piece rates/commissions, profit sharing, efficiency wages, performance measurement (including financial statements), the agent posting a bond, or fear of firing. The _________ is found in most employer/employee relationships, for example, when stockholders hire top executives of corporations.

a. 529 plan
b. 7-Eleven
c. Principal-agent problem
d. 4-4-5 Calendar

46. In economics, business, and accounting, a _________ is the value of money that has been used up to produce something, and hence is not available for use anymore. In business, the _________ may be one of acquisition, in which case the amount of money expended to acquire it is counted as _________. In this case, money is the input that is gone in order to acquire the thing.

a. Marginal cost
b. Sliding scale fees
c. Fixed costs
d. Cost

47. The U.S. _________ is an independent agency of the United States government which holds primary responsibility for enforcing the federal securities laws and regulating the securities industry, the nation's stock and options exchanges, and other electronic securities markets. The SEC was created by section 4 of the SEC of 1934 (now codified as 15 U.S.C. Â§ 78d and commonly referred to as the 1934 Act.)

a. 4-4-5 Calendar
b. 529 plan
c. Securities and Exchange Commission
d. 7-Eleven

48. An _________ is a contract written by a seller that conveys to the buyer the right -- but not the obligation -- to buy (in the case of a call _________) or to sell (in the case of a put _________) a particular asset, such as a piece of property such as, among others, a futures contract. In return for granting the _________, the seller collects a payment (the premium) from the buyer.

For example, buying a call _________ provides the right to buy a specified quantity of a security at a set strike price at some time on or before expiration, while buying a put _________ provides the right to sell.

a. Annuity
b. Amortization
c. Option
d. AT'T Mobility LLC

49. In business, a _________ is the purchase of one company (the target) by another (the acquirer or bidder). In the UK the term refers to the acquisition of a public company whose shares are listed on a stock exchange, in contrast to the acquisition of a private company.

Before a bidder makes an offer for another company, it usually first informs that company's board of directors.

a. 529 plan
b. 4-4-5 Calendar
c. Stock swap
d. Takeover

50. In economics, a _________ is a mechanism that allows people to easily buy and sell (trade) financial securities (such as stocks and bonds), commodities (such as precious metals or agricultural goods), and other fungible items of value at low transaction costs and at prices that reflect the efficient-market hypothesis.

_________s have evolved significantly over several hundred years and are undergoing constant innovation to improve liquidity.

Both general markets (where many commodities are traded) and specialized markets (where only one commodity is traded) exist.

a. Financial market
b. Cost of carry
c. Secondary market
d. Delta hedging

51. In the United States, a _________ is an offering of securities that are not registered with the Securities and Exchange Commission (SEC.) Such offerings exploit an exemption offered by the Securities Act of 1933 that comes with several restrictions, including a prohibition against general solicitation. This exemption allows companies to avoid quarterly reporting requirements and many of the legal liabilities associated with the Sarbanes-Oxley Act.

a. Private placement
b. 529 plan
c. 7-Eleven
d. 4-4-5 Calendar

52. _________, is when a company issues common stock or shares to the public for the first time. They are often issued by smaller, younger companies seeking capital to expand, but can also be done by large privately-owned companies looking to become publicly traded.

In an _________ the issuer may obtain the assistance of an underwriting firm, which helps it determine what type of security to issue (common or preferred), best offering price and time to bring it to market.

a. Asian Financial Crisis
b. Insolvency
c. Interest
d. Initial public offering

53. _________ is the term used to describe deposits residing in banks that are located outside the borders of the country that issues the currency the deposit is denominated in. For example a deposit denominated in US dollars residing in a Japanese bank is a _________ deposit, or more specifically a Eurodollar deposit.

Key points are the location of the bank and the denomination of the currency, not the nationality of the bank or the owner of the deposit/loan.

a. ABN Amro
b. Eurocurrency
c. A Random Walk Down Wall Street
d. AAB

54. _________ are securities that can be easily converted into cash. Such securities will generally have highly liquid markets allowing the security to be sold at a reasonable price very quickly.This is a usual feature in real estate .

a. Book entry
b. Securities lending
c. Tracking stock
d. Marketable

55. The _________ is that part of the capital markets that deals with the issuance of new securities. Companies, governments or public sector institutions can obtain funding through the sale of a new stock or bond issue. This is typically done through a syndicate of securities dealers.

a. Peer group analysis
b. Volatility clustering
c. Primary market
d. Sector rotation

56. In economics, the concept of the _________ refers to the decision-making time frame of a firm in which at least one factor of production is fixed. Costs which are fixed in the _________ have no impact on a firms decisions. For example a firm can raise output by increasing the amount of labour through overtime.

a. 4-4-5 Calendar
b. 529 plan
c. Short-run
d. Long-run

57. The _________ is a daily reference rate based on the interest rates at which banks borrow unsecured funds from banks in the London wholesale money market (or interbank market.) It is roughly comparable to the U.S. Federal funds rate.

During 1984 it became apparent that an increasing number of banks were trading actively in a variety of relatively new market instruments, notably interest rate swaps, foreign currency options and forward rate agreements.

a. London Interbank Offered Rate
b. Fixed interest
c. Risk-free interest rate
d. Shanghai Interbank Offered Rate

58. A _________ is a money deposit at a banking institution that cannot be withdrawn for a certain 'term' or period of time. When the term is over it can be withdrawn or it can be held for another term. Generally speaking, the longer the term the better the yield on the money.

a. Private money
b. Certificate of deposit
c. Basel Accord
d. Time deposit

59. _________ refers to a business or organization attempting to acquire goods or services to accomplish the goals of the enterprise. Though there are several organizations that attempt to set standards in the _________ process, processes can vary greatly between organizations. Typically the word '_________' is not used interchangeably with the word 'procurement', since procurement typically includes Expediting, Supplier Quality, and Traffic and Logistics (T'L) in addition to _________.

a. 7-Eleven
b. 4-4-5 Calendar
c. Purchasing
d. 529 plan

60. In finance, a _________ is a debt security, in which the authorized issuer owes the holders a debt and, depending on the terms of the _________, is obliged to pay interest (the coupon) and/or to repay the principal at a later date, termed maturity.

Thus a _________ is a loan: the issuer is the borrower, the _________ holder is the lender, and the coupon is the interest. _________s provide the borrower with external funds to finance long-term investments, or, in the case of government _________s, to finance current expenditure.

a. Puttable bond
b. Bond
c. Catastrophe bonds
d. Convertible bond

61. A _________ is a bond issued by a corporation. The term is usually applied to longer-term debt instruments, generally with a maturity date falling at least a year after their issue date. (The term 'commercial paper' is sometimes used for instruments with a shorter maturity.)

a. Brady bonds
b. Government bond
c. Serial bond
d. Corporate bond

62. The coupon or _________ of a bond is the amount of interest paid per year expressed as a percentage of the face value of the bond.

For example if you hold $10,000 nominal of a bond described as a 4.5% loan stock, you will receive $450 in interest each year (probably in two installments of $225 each.)

Not all bonds have coupons.

a. Zero-coupon bond
b. Coupon rate
c. Revenue bonds
d. Puttable bond

63. In economic models, the _________ time frame assumes no fixed factors of production. Firms can enter or leave the marketplace, and the cost (and availability) of land, labor, raw materials, and capital goods can be assumed to vary. In contrast, in the short-run time frame, certain factors are assumed to be fixed, because there is not sufficient time for them to change.

a. 4-4-5 Calendar
b. 529 plan
c. Long-run
d. Short-run

64. The _________ is a stock exchange based in New York City, New York. It is the largest stock exchange in the world by dollar value of its listed companies securities. As of October 2008, the combined capitalization of all domestic _________ listed companies was $10.1 trillion.

a. 7-Eleven
b. 529 plan
c. 4-4-5 Calendar
d. New York Stock Exchange

65. _________, in finance and accounting, means stated value or face value. From this comes the expressions at par (at the _________), over par (over _________) and under par (under _________.)

The term '_________' has several meanings depending on context and geography.

a. Par value
b. FIDC
c. Global Squeeze
d. Sinking fund

66. _________ is typically a higher ranking stock than voting shares, and its terms are negotiated between the corporation and the investor.

_________ usually carry no voting rights, but may carry superior priority over common stock in the payment of dividends and upon liquidation. _________ may carry a dividend that is paid out prior to any dividends to common stock holders.

a. Trade-off theory
b. Follow-on offering
c. Second lien loan
d. Preferred stock

67. A _________, securities exchange or (in Europe) bourse is a corporation or mutual organization which provides 'trading' facilities for stock brokers and traders, to trade stocks and other securities. _________s also provide facilities for the issue and redemption of securities as well as other financial instruments and capital events including the payment of income and dividends. The securities traded on a _________ include: shares issued by companies, unit trusts and other pooled investment products and bonds.

a. Stock Exchange
b. 7-Eleven
c. 529 plan
d. 4-4-5 Calendar

68. A _________ is a private or public market for the trading of company stock and derivatives of company stock at an agreed price; these are securities listed on a stock exchange as well as those only traded privately.

The size of the world _________ is estimated at about $36.6 trillion US at the beginning of October 2008 . The world derivatives market has been estimated at about $480 trillion face or nominal value, 12 times the size of the entire world economy.

a. Adolph Coors
b. Andrew Tobias
c. Anton Gelonkin
d. Stock market

69. _________ or financing is to provide capital (funds), which means money for a project, a person, a business or any other private or public institutions.

Those funds can be allocated for either short term or long term purposes. The health fund is a new way of _________ private healthcare centers.

a. Funding
b. Proxy fight
c. Product life cycle
d. Synthetic CDO

70. _________ is a fee paid on borrowed assets. It is the price paid for the use of borrowed money , or, money earned by deposited funds . Assets that are sometimes lent with _________ include money, shares, consumer goods through hire purchase, major assets such as aircraft, and even entire factories in finance lease arrangements.

a. Insolvency
b. A Random Walk Down Wall Street
c. AAB
d. Interest

71. An _________ is the price a borrower pays for the use of money they do not own, and the return a lender receives for deferring the use of funds, by lending it to the borrower. _________s are normally expressed as a percentage rate over the period of one year.

_________s targets are also a vital tool of monetary policy and are used to control variables like investment, inflation, and unemployment.

a. AAB
b. Interest rate
c. ABN Amro
d. A Random Walk Down Wall Street

72. _________ offer, asking price is a price a seller of a good is willing to accept for that particular good.

In bid and ask, the term _________ is used in contrast to the term bid price. The difference between the _________ and the bid price is called the spread.

a. Interest rate parity
b. A Random Walk Down Wall Street
c. AAB
d. Ask price

73. A _________ is the highest price that a buyer (i.e., bidder) is willing to pay for a good. It is usually referred to simply as the 'bid.'

In bid and ask, the _________ stands in contrast to the ask price or 'offer', and the difference between the two is called the bid/ask spread.

An unsolicited bid or offer is when a person or company receives a bid even though they are not looking to sell.

a. Mid price
b. Settlement date
c. Political risk
d. Bid price

74. A _________ is an international bond that is denominated in a currency not native to the country where it is issued. It can be categorised according to the currency in which it is issued. London is one of the centers of the _________ market, but _________s may be traded throughout the world - for example in Singapore or Tokyo.

a. Education production function
b. Interest rate option
c. Eurobond
d. Economic entity

75. _________ is an economic model based on price, utility and quantity in a market. It predicts that in a competitive market, price will function to equalize the quantity demanded by consumers, and the quantity supplied by producers, resulting in an economic equilibrium of price and quantity. Similarly, an increase in the number of workers tends to result in lower wages and vice-versa.

a. Price channel
b. Supply and demand
c. Rural credit cooperatives
d. Loan participation

76. _________ refers to a tax levied by various jurisdictions on the profits made by companies or associations. It is a tax on the value of the corporation's profits.

The measure of taxable profits varies from country to country.

a. Proxy fight
b. Corporate tax
c. Trade finance
d. First-mover advantage

77. _________ is the increase in the amount of the goods and services produced by an economy over time. It is conventionally measured as the percent rate of increase in real gross domestic product, or real GDP. Growth is usually calculated in real terms, i.e. inflation-adjusted terms, in order to net out the effect of inflation on the price of the goods and services produced.

a. A Random Walk Down Wall Street
b. ABN Amro
c. AAB
d. Economic Growth

78. Under the United States Internal Revenue Code, the type of income is defined by its character. _________ is usually characterized as income other than capital gain. _________ can consist of income from wages, salaries, tips, commissions, bonuses, and other types of compensation from employment, interest, dividends, or net income from a sole proprietorship, partnership or LLC.

a. A Random Walk Down Wall Street
b. AAB
c. ABN Amro
d. Ordinary income

79. _________, refers to consumption opportunity gained by an entity within a specified time frame, which is generally expressed in monetary terms. However, for households and individuals, '_________ is the sum of all the wages, salaries, profits, interests payments, rents and other forms of earnings received... in a given period of time.' For firms, _________ generally refers to net-profit: what remains of revenue after expenses have been subtracted.

a. Income
b. Annual report
c. OIBDA
d. Accrual

80. _________ is the imposition of two or more taxes on the same income (in the case of income taxes), asset (in the case of capital taxes), or financial transaction (in the case of sales taxes.) It refers to two distinct situations:

- taxation of dividend income without relief or credit for taxes paid by the company paying the dividend on the income from which the dividend is paid. This arises in the so-called 'classical' system of corporate taxation, used in the United States.
- taxation by two or more countries of the same income, asset or transaction, for example income paid by an entity of one country to a resident of a different country. The double liability is often mitigated by tax treaties between countries.

It is not unusual for a business or individual who is resident in one country to make a taxable gain (earnings, profits) in another. This person may find that he is obliged by domestic laws to pay tax on that gain locally and pay again in the country in which the gain was made. Since this is inequitable, many nations make bilateral _________ agreements with each other.

a. 4-4-5 Calendar
b. 7-Eleven
c. 529 plan
d. Double taxation

1. An _________ is a document a company presents at an annual general meeting for approval by its shareholders, or a charitable organization presents its trustees. The report is made up of reports, which may include the following:

- Chairman's report
- CEO's report
- Auditor's report on corporate governance
- Mission statement
- Corporate governance statement of compliance
- Statement of directors' responsibilities
- Invitation to the company's AGM

as well as financial statements including:

- Auditor's report on the financial statements
- Balance sheet
- Statement of retained earnings
- Income statement
- Cash flow statement
- Notes to the financial statements
- Accounting policies

Other information deemed relevant to stakeholders may be included, such as a report on operations for manufacturing firms. In the case of larger companies, it is usually a sleek, colorful, high gloss publication.

The details provided in the report are of use to investors to understand the company's financial position and future direction.

a. Annual report
b. Accrued liabilities
c. Outstanding balance
d. Amortization schedule

2. _________, refers to consumption opportunity gained by an entity within a specified time frame, which is generally expressed in monetary terms. However, for households and individuals, '_________ is the sum of all the wages, salaries, profits, interests payments, rents and other forms of earnings received... in a given period of time.' For firms, _________ generally refers to net-profit: what remains of revenue after expenses have been subtracted.

a. Income
b. Accrual
c. OIBDA
d. Annual report

3. An _________ is a financial statement for companies that indicates how Revenue is transformed into net income The purpose of the _________ is to show managers and investors whether the company made or lost money during the period being reported.

The important thing to remember about an _________ is that it represents a period of time.

a. AAB
b. A Random Walk Down Wall Street
c. Income statement
d. ABN Amro

4. In financial accounting, a _________ or statement of cash flows is a financial statement that shows a company's flow of cash. The money coming into the business is called cash inflow, and money going out from the business is called cash outflow. The statement shows how changes in balance sheet and income accounts affect cash and cash equivalents, and breaks the analysis down to operating, investing, and financing activities.

a. 7-Eleven
b. 529 plan
c. 4-4-5 Calendar
d. Cash flow statement

5. _________ is the balance of the amounts of cash being received and paid by a business during a defined period of time, sometimes tied to a specific project. Measurement of _________ can be used

- to evaluate the state or performance of a business or project.
- to determine problems with liquidity. Being profitable does not necessarily mean being liquid. A company can fail because of a shortage of cash, even while profitable.
- to generate project rate of returns. The time of _________s into and out of projects are used as inputs to financial models such as internal rate of return, and net present value.
- to examine income or growth of a business when it is believed that accrual accounting concepts do not represent economic realities. Alternately, _________ can be used to 'validate' the net income generated by accrual accounting.

_________ as a generic term may be used differently depending on context, and certain _________ definitions may be adapted by analysts and users for their own uses. Common terms include operating _________ and free _________.

_________s can be classified into:

1. Operational _________s: Cash received or expended as a result of the company's core business activities.
2. Investment _________s: Cash received or expended through capital expenditure, investments or acquisitions.
3. Financing _________s: Cash received or expended as a result of financial activities, such as interests and dividends.

All three together - the net _________ - are necessary to reconcile the beginning cash balance to the ending cash balance. Loan draw downs or equity injections, that is just shifting of capital but no expenditure as such, are not considered in the net _________.

a. Shareholder value
b. Real option
c. Cash flow
d. Corporate finance

6. In finance, _________, also known as return on investment is the ratio of money gained or lost on an investment relative to the amount of money invested. The amount of money gained or lost may be referred to as interest, profit/loss, gain/loss, or net income/loss. The money invested may be referred to as the asset, capital, principal, or the cost basis of the investment.

a. Stock or scrip dividends
b. Doctrine of the Proper Law
c. Composiition of Creditors
d. Rate of return

7. The role of the _________ is to issue accounting standards in the United Kingdom. It is recognised for that purpose under the Companies Act 1985. It took over the task of setting accounting standards from the Accounting Standards Committee (ASC) in 1990.

a. ABN Amro
b. A Random Walk Down Wall Street
c. AAB
d. Accounting Standards Board

8. _________ is the field of accountancy concerned with the preparation of financial statements for decision makers, such as stockholders, suppliers, banks, employees, government agencies, owners, and other stakeholders. The fundamental need for _________ is to reduce principal-agent problem by measuring and monitoring agents' performance and reporting the results to interested users.

_________ is used to prepare accounting information for people outside the organization or not involved in the day to day running of the company.

a. 7-Eleven
b. 4-4-5 Calendar
c. 529 plan
d. Financial Accounting

9. The _________ is a private, not-for-profit organization whose primary purpose is to develop generally accepted accounting principles (GAAP) within the United States in the public's interest. The Securities and Exchange Commission (SEC) designated the _________ as the organization responsible for setting accounting standards for public companies in the U.S. It was created in 1973, replacing the Accounting Principles Board and the Committee on Accounting Procedure of the American Institute of Certified Public Accountants. The _________'s mission is 'to establish and improve standards of financial accounting and reporting for the guidance and education of the public, including issuers, auditors, and users of financial information.'

The _________ is not a governmental body.

a. KPMG
b. World Congress of Accountants
c. Federal Deposit Insurance Corporation
d. Financial Accounting Standards Board

10. _________ is the standard framework of guidelines for financial accounting used in the United States of America. It includes the standards, conventions, and rules accountants follow in recording and summarizing transactions, and in the preparation of financial statements. _________ are now issued by the Financial Accounting Standards Board (FASB).

a. Revenue
b. Net income
c. Depreciation
d. Generally accepted accounting principles

11. A _________ is a fungible, negotiable instrument representing financial value. They are broadly categorized into debt securities (such as banknotes, bonds and debentures), and equity securities; e.g., common stocks. The company or other entity issuing the _________ is called the issuer.

a. Security
b. Book entry
c. Securities lending
d. Tracking stock

12. The U.S. _________ is an independent agency of the United States government which holds primary responsibility for enforcing the federal securities laws and regulating the securities industry, the nation's stock and options exchanges, and other electronic securities markets. The SEC was created by section 4 of the SEC of 1934 (now codified as 15 U.S.C. Â§ 78d and commonly referred to as the 1934 Act.)

a. Securities and Exchange Commission
b. 529 plan
c. 7-Eleven
d. 4-4-5 Calendar

13. The institution most often referenced by the word '_________' is a public or publicly traded _________, the shares of which are traded on a public stock exchange (e.g., the New York Stock Exchange or Nasdaq in the United States) where shares of stock of _________s are bought and sold by and to the general public. Most of the largest businesses in the world are publicly traded _________s. However, the majority of _________s are said to be closely held, privately held or close _________s, meaning that no ready market exists for the trading of shares.

a. Federal Home Loan Mortgage Corporation
b. Depository Trust Company
c. Protect
d. Corporation

14. _________ are formal records of a business' financial activities.

_________ provide an overview of a business' financial condition in both short and long term. There are four basic _________:

1. **Balance sheet**: also referred to as statement of financial position or condition, reports on a company's assets, liabilities, and net equity as of a given point in time.
2. **Income statement**: also referred to as Profit and Loss statement (or a 'P'L'), reports on a company's income, expenses, and profits over a period of time.
3. **Statement of retained earnings**: explains the changes in a company's retained earnings over the reporting period.
4. **Statement of cash flows**: reports on a company's cash flow activities, particularly its operating, investing and financing activities.

a. Statement on Auditing Standards No. 70: Service Organizations
b. Statement of retained earnings
c. Notes to the Financial Statements
d. Financial statements

15. A mutual shareholder or _________ is an individual or company (including a corporation) that legally owns one or more shares of stock in a joint stock company. A company's shareholders collectively own that company. Thus, the typical goal of such companies is to enhance shareholder value.

a. Limit order
b. Trading curb
c. Stockholder
d. Stock market bubble

16. In economics, business, and accounting, a _________ is the value of money that has been used up to produce something, and hence is not available for use anymore. In business, the _________ may be one of acquisition, in which case the amount of money expended to acquire it is counted as _________. In this case, money is the input that is gone in order to acquire the thing.

a. Sliding scale fees
b. Marginal cost
c. Fixed costs
d. Cost

17. In accounting, _________ or sales profit is the difference between revenue and the cost of making a product or providing a service, before deducting overhead, payroll, taxation, and interest payments. Note that this is different than operating profit.

Net sales are calculated:

Net sales = Sales - Sales returns and allowances

_________ is found by deducting the cost of goods sold:

_________ = Net sales - Cost of goods sold

_________ should not be confused with net income:

Net income = _________ - Total operating expenses

Cost of goods sold is calculated differently for merchandising business than for a manufacturer.

a. Cash flow
b. Real option
c. Gross profit
d. Gross income

18. An _________, operating expenditure, operational expense, operational expenditure or OPEX is an on-going cost for running a product, business, or system. Its counterpart, a capital expenditure (CAPEX), is the cost of developing or providing non-consumable parts for the product or system. For example, the purchase of a photocopier is the CAPEX, and the annual paper and toner cost is the OPEX.

a. Operating expense
b. AAB
c. A Random Walk Down Wall Street
d. ABN Amro

19. _________ is the difference between price and the costs of bringing to market whatever it is that is accounted as an enterprise (whether by harvest, extraction, manufacture, or purchase) in terms of the component costs of delivered goods and/or services and any operating or other expenses.

A key difficulty in measuring profit is in defining costs. Pure economic monetary profits can be zero or negative even in competitive equilibrium when accounted monetized costs exceed monetized price.

a. A Random Walk Down Wall Street
b. Economic profit
c. AAB
d. Accounting profit

20. _________, in bookkeeping, refers to assets, liabilities, income, and expenses recorded on individual pages of the so called book of final entry or ledger. Changes in _________ value are made by chronologically posting debit (DR) and credit (CR) entries to its page. Examples of _________s are cash, _________s receivable, mortgages, loans, land and buildings, common stock, sales, services provided, wages, and payroll overhead.

a. Option
b. Alpha
c. Accretion
d. Account

21. _________ is a file or account that contains money that a person or company owes to suppliers, but hasn't paid yet (a form of debt.) When you receive an invoice you add it to the file, and then you remove it when you pay. Thus, the A/P is a form of credit that suppliers offer to their purchasers by allowing them to pay for a product or service after it has already been received.

a. Outstanding balance
b. Accrual
c. Accounts payable
d. Earnings before interest, taxes, depreciation and amortization

22. _________ is one of a series of accounting transactions dealing with the billing of customers who owe money to a person, company or organization for goods and services that have been provided to the customer. In most business entities this is typically done by generating an invoice and mailing or electronically delivering it to the customer, who in turn must pay it within an established timeframe called credit or payment terms.

An example of a common payment term is Net 30, meaning payment is due in the amount of the invoice 30 days from the date of invoice.

a. Impaired asset
b. Income
c. Accounting methods
d. Accounts receivable

23. In business and accounting, _________s are everything of value that is owned by a person or company. The balance sheet of a firm records the monetary value of the _________s owned by the firm. The two major _________ classes are tangible _________s and intangible _________s.

a. Asset
b. Accounts payable
c. EBITDA
d. Income

24. In financial accounting, a _________ or statement of financial position is a summary of a person's or organization's balances. Assets, liabilities and ownership equity are listed as of a specific date, such as the end of its financial year. A _________ is often described as a snapshot of a company's financial condition.

a. Financial statements
b. Statement of retained earnings
c. Statement on Auditing Standards No. 70: Service Organizations
d. Balance sheet

25. In accounting, a _________ is an asset on the balance sheet which is expected to be sold or otherwise used up in the near future, usually within one year, or one business cycle - whichever is longer. Typical _________s include cash, cash equivalents, accounts receivable, inventory, the portion of prepaid accounts which will be used within a year, and short-term investments.

On the balance sheet, assets will typically be classified into _________s and long-term assets.

a. Current asset
b. Write-off
c. Historical cost
d. Long-term liabilities

26. In accounting, _________ are considered liabilities of the business that are to be settled in cash within the fiscal year or the operating cycle, whichever period is longer.

For example accounts payable for goods, services or supplies that were purchased for use in the operation of the business and payable within a normal period of time would be _________.

Bonds, mortgages and loans that are payable over a term exceeding one year would be fixed liabilities.

a. Closing entries
b. Gross sales
c. Net income
d. Current liabilities

27. _________ is that which is owed; usually referencing assets owed, but the term can cover other obligations. In the case of assets, _________ is a means of using future purchasing power in the present before a summation has been earned. Some companies and corporations use _________ as a part of their overall corporate finance strategy.

a. Cross-collateralization
b. Debt
c. Credit cycle
d. Partial Payment

28. A _________ is a payment made by a corporation to its shareholder members. When a corporation earns a profit or surplus, that money can be put to two uses: it can either be re-invested in the business (called retained earnings), or it can be paid to the shareholders as a _________. Many corporations retain a portion of their earnings and pay the remainder as a _________.

a. Dividend yield
b. Dividend puzzle
c. Dividend
d. Special dividend

29. In financial and business accounting, _________ is a measure of a firm's profitability that excludes interest and income tax expenses.

EBIT = Operating Revenue - Operating Expenses (OPEX) + Non-operating Income

Operating Income = Operating Revenue - Operating Expenses

Operating income is the difference between operating revenues and operating expenses, but it is also sometimes used as a synonym for EBIT and operating profit. This is true if the firm has no non-operating income.

a. ABN Amro
b. A Random Walk Down Wall Street
c. AAB
d. Earnings before interest and taxes

30. _________ are the earnings returned on the initial investment amount.

In the US, the Financial Accounting Standards Board (FASB) requires companies' income statements to report _________ for each of the major categories of the income statement: continuing operations, discontinued operations, extraordinary items, and net income.

The _________ formula does not include preferred dividends for categories outside of continued operations and net income.

a. Inventory turnover
b. Assets turnover
c. Average accounting return
d. Earnings per share

31. _________ plant, and equipment, is a term used in accountancy for assets and property which cannot easily be converted into cash. This can be compared with current assets such as cash or bank accounts, which are described as liquid assets. In most cases, only tangible assets are referred to as fixed.

a. Petty cash
b. Remittance advice
c. Percentage of Completion
d. Fixed asset

32. _________ is a fee paid on borrowed assets. It is the price paid for the use of borrowed money , or, money earned by deposited funds . Assets that are sometimes lent with _________ include money, shares, consumer goods through hire purchase, major assets such as aircraft, and even entire factories in finance lease arrangements.

a. Insolvency
b. Interest
c. AAB
d. A Random Walk Down Wall Street

33. _________ relates to the cost of borrowing money. It is the price that a lender charges a borrower for the use of the lender's money. _________ is different from OPEX and CAPEX, for it relates to the capital structure of a company.

a. ABN Amro
b. A Random Walk Down Wall Street
c. Interest expense
d. AAB

34. In economic models, the _________ time frame assumes no fixed factors of production. Firms can enter or leave the marketplace, and the cost (and availability) of land, labor, raw materials, and capital goods can be assumed to vary. In contrast, in the short-run time frame, certain factors are assumed to be fixed, because there is not sufficient time for them to change.

a. 529 plan
b. 4-4-5 Calendar
c. Short-run
d. Long-run

35. _________ are securities that can be easily converted into cash. Such securities will generally have highly liquid markets allowing the security to be sold at a reasonable price very quickly.This is a usual feature in real estate .

a. Book entry
b. Securities lending
c. Tracking stock
d. Marketable

36. In business and finance accounting, _________ is equal to the gross profit minus overheads minus interest payable plus/minus one off items for a given time period (usually: accounting period.)

A common synonym for '_________' when discussing financial statements (which include a balance sheet and an income statement) is the bottom line. This term results from the traditional appearance of an income statement which shows all allocated revenues and expenses over a specified time period with the resulting summation on the bottom line of the report.

a. Gross sales
b. Salvage value
c. Deferred
d. Net profit

37. _________ is a measure of a company's earning power from ongoing operations, equal to earnings before the deduction of interest payments and income taxes.

To accountants, economic profit, or EP, is a single-period metric to determine the value created by a company in one period - usually a year. It is the net profit after tax less the equity charge, a risk-weighted cost of capital.

a. Economic profit
b. A Random Walk Down Wall Street
c. AAB
d. Operating profit

38. The phrase _________ refers to the aspect of corporate strategy, corporate finance and management dealing with the buying, selling and combining of different companies that can aid, finance, or help a growing company in a given industry grow rapidly without having to create another business entity.

An acquisition, also known as a takeover, is the buying of one company (the 'target') by another. An acquisition may be friendly or hostile.

a. 529 plan
b. Mergers and acquisitions
c. 4-4-5 Calendar
d. 7-Eleven

39. In probability theory and statistics, _________ indicates the strength and direction of a linear relationship between two random variables. That is in contrast with the usage of the term in colloquial speech, which denotes any relationship, not necessarily linear. In general statistical usage, _________ or co-relation refers to the departure of two random variables from independence.

a. Correlation
b. Geometric mean
c. Probability distribution
d. Variance

40. In business and finance, a _________ (also referred to as equity _________) of stock means a _________ of ownership in a corporation (company.) In the plural, stocks is often used as a synonym for _________s especially in the United States, but it is less commonly used that way outside of North America.

In the United Kingdom, South Africa, and Australia, stock can also refer to completely different financial instruments such as government bonds or, less commonly, to all kinds of marketable securities.

a. Bucket shop
b. Procter ' Gamble
c. Share
d. Margin

41. Accrual, in accounting, describes the accounting method known as _________, whereby revenues and expenses are recognized when they are accrued, i.e. accumulated (earned or incurred), regardless when the actual cash is received or paid out.

E.g. a company delivers a product to a customer who will pay for it 30 days later in the next fiscal year starting a week after the delivery. The company recognizes the proceeds as a revenue in its current income statement still for the fiscal year of the delivery, even though it will get paid in cash during the following accounting period.

a. AAB
b. A Random Walk Down Wall Street
c. ABN Amro
d. Accrual basis

42. _________ is a form of corporation equity ownership represented in the securities. It is dangerous in comparison to preferred shares and some other investment options, in that in the event of bankruptcy, _________ investors receive their funds after preferred stockholders, bondholders, creditors, etc. On the other hand, common shares on average perform better than preferred shares or bonds over time.

a. Stop-limit order
b. Common stock
c. Stock market bubble
d. Stock split

43. _________ is a term used in accounting, economics and finance to spread the cost of an asset over the span of several years.

In simple words we can say that _________ is the reduction in the value of an asset due to usage, passage of time, wear and tear, technological outdating or obsolescence, depletion or other such factors.

In accounting, _________ is a term used to describe any method of attributing the historical or purchase cost of an asset across its useful life, roughly corresponding to normal wear and tear.

a. Deferred financing costs
b. Depreciation
c. Matching principle
d. Bottom line

44. The _________ is a private, not-for-profit organization whose primary purpose is to develop generally accepted accounting principles (GAAP) within the United States in the public's interest. The Securities and Exchange Commission (SEC) designated the _________ as the organization responsible for setting accounting standards for public companies in the U.S. It was created in 1973, replacing the Accounting Principles Board and the Committee on Accounting Procedure of the American Institute of Certified Public Accountants. The _________'s mission is 'to establish and improve standards of financial accounting and reporting for the guidance and education of the public, including issuers, auditors, and users of financial information.'

The _________ is not a governmental body.

a. Credit karma
b. PlaNet Finance
c. MRU Holdings
d. FASB

45. _________ is typically a higher ranking stock than voting shares, and its terms are negotiated between the corporation and the investor.

_________ usually carry no voting rights, but may carry superior priority over common stock in the payment of dividends and upon liquidation. _________ may carry a dividend that is paid out prior to any dividends to common stock holders.

a. Second lien loan
b. Preferred stock
c. Trade-off theory
d. Follow-on offering

46. In accounting, _________ refers to the portion of net income which is retained by the corporation rather than distributed to its owners as dividends. Similarly, if the corporation makes a loss, then that loss is retained and called variously retained losses, accumulated losses or accumulated deficit. _________ and losses are cumulative from year to year with losses offsetting earnings.

a. Retained earnings
b. Matching principle
c. Generally Accepted Accounting Principles
d. Historical cost

47. The _________ is one of the basic financial statements as per Generally Accepted Accounting Principles, and it explains the changes in a company's retained earnings over the reporting period. It breaks down changes affecting the account, such as profits or losses from operations, dividends paid, and any other items charged or credited to retained earnings. A retained earnings statement is required by Generally Accepted Accounting Principles (GAAP) whenever comparative balance sheets and income statements are presented.

a. Financial statements
b. Notes to the Financial Statements
c. Statement of retained earnings
d. Statement on Auditing Standards No. 70: Service Organizations

48. A _________ is an equity investment option offered directly from the underlying company. The investor does not receive quarterly dividends directly as cash; instead, the investor's dividends are directly reinvested in the underlying equity. It should be noted that the investor still must pay tax annually on his or her dividend income, whether it is received or reinvested.

a. Dividend payout ratio
b. Dividend puzzle
c. Dividend decision
d. Dividend reinvestment plan

49. In finance, a _________ or accounting ratio is a ratio of two selected numerical values taken from an enterprise's financial statements. There are many standard ratios used to try to evaluate the overall financial condition of a corporation or other organization. They may be used by managers within a firm, by current and potential shareholders (owners) of a firm, and by a firm's creditors. Security analysts use these to compare the strengths and weaknesses in various companies.

a. Price/cash flow ratio
b. Return on capital employed
c. Sustainable growth rate
d. Financial ratio

50. _________ is the process of comparing the cost, time or quality of what one organization does against what another organization does. The result is often a business case for making changes in order to make improvements.

Also referred to as 'best practice _________' or 'process _________', it is a process used in management and particularly strategic management, in which organizations evaluate various aspects of their processes in relation to best practice, usually within their own sector.

a. 4-4-5 Calendar
b. 7-Eleven
c. 529 plan
d. Benchmarking

51. In economics, _________ is a rise in the general level of prices of goods and services in an economy over a period of time. The term '_________' once referred to increases in the money supply (monetary _________); however, economic debates about the relationship between money supply and price levels have led to its primary use today in describing price _________. _________ can also be described as a decline in the real value of money--a loss of purchasing power in the medium of exchange which is also the monetary unit of account.

a. A Random Walk Down Wall Street
b. ABN Amro
c. AAB
d. Inflation

52. In finance, the Acid-test or _________ or liquid ratio measures the ability of a company to use its near cash or quick assets to immediately extinguish or retire its current liabilities. Quick assets include those current assets that presumably can be quickly converted to cash at close to their book values.

Generally, the acid test ratio should be 1:1 or better, however this varies widely by industry.

a. P/E ratio
b. Quick ratio
c. Financial ratio
d. Net assets

53. The _________ is a financial ratio that measures whether or not a firm has enough resources to pay its debts over the next 12 months. It compares a firm's current assets to its current liabilities. It is expressed as follows:

$$\text{Current ratio} = \frac{\text{Current Assets}}{\text{Current Liabilities}}$$

For example, if WXY Company's current assets are $50,000,000 and its current liabilities are $40,000,000, then its _________ would be $50,000,000 divided by $40,000,000, which equals 1.25.

a. Sustainable growth rate
b. Debt service coverage ratio
c. PEG ratio
d. Current ratio

54. _________ is a measure of the ability of a debtor to pay their debts as and when they fall due. It is usually expressed as a ratio or a percentage of current liabilities.

For a corporation with a published balance sheet there are various ratios used to calculate a measure of liquidity.

a. Invested capital
b. Operating leverage
c. Operating profit margin
d. Accounting liquidity

55. _________ is a list for goods and materials held available in stock by a business. It is also used for a list of the contents of a household and for a list for testamentary purposes of the possessions of someone who has died. In accounting _________ is considered an asset.

a. AAB
b. A Random Walk Down Wall Street
c. ABN Amro
d. Inventory

56. The _________ is an equation that equals the cost of goods sold divided by the average inventory. Average inventory equals beginning inventory plus ending inventory divided by 2.

The formula for _________:

$$\text{Inventory Turnover} = \frac{\text{Cost of Goods Sold}}{\text{Average Inventory}}$$

The formula for average inventory:

$$\text{Average Inventory} = \frac{\text{Beginning inventory+Ending inventory}}{2}$$

A low turnover rate may point to overstocking, obsolescence, or deficiencies in the product line or marketing effort.

a. Inventory turnover
b. Operating leverage
c. Earnings yield
d. Information ratio

57. _________ is a financial ratio that measures the efficiency of a company's use of its assets in generating sales revenue or sales income to the company.

$$Asset\ Turnover = \frac{Sales}{AverageTotalAssets}$$

- 'Sales' is the value of 'Net Sales' or 'Sales' from the company's income statement
- 'Average Total Assets' is the value of 'Total assets' from the company's balance sheet in the beginning and the end of the fiscal period divided by 2.

- Assets turnover

.

a. Earnings yield
b. Asset turnover
c. Inventory turnover
d. Average accounting return

58. The term _________ has three unrelated technical definitions, and is also used in a variety of non-technical ways.

- In financial economics, it refers to any asset used to make money, as opposed to assets used for personal enjoyment or consumption. This is an important distinction because two people can disagree sharply about the value of personal assets, one person might think a sports car is more valuable than a pickup truck, another person might have the opposite taste. But if an asset is held for the purpose of making money, taste has nothing to do with it, only differences of opinion about how much money the asset will produce. With the further assumption that people agree on the probability distribution of future cash flows, it is possible to have an objective _________ pricing model. Even without the assumption of agreement, it is possible to set rational limits on _________ value.
- In governmental accounting, it is defined as any asset used in operations with an initial useful life extending beyond one reporting period. Generally, government managers have a 'stewardship' duty to maintain _________s under their control. See International Public Sector Accounting Standards for details.
- In US tax accounting, it is defined as any property other than a list of exceptions. The main exceptions are anything held for sale, and any real estate or depreciable property used in business. Almost everything you own and use for personal purposes, pleasure or investment is a _________. If something is a _________ for tax purposes, gains or losses on sale or disposition are capital gains or capital losses. For individuals, however, capital losses on property held for personal use are generally not deductible. See the IRS publication Tax Facts about Capital Gains and Losses for details.

A well-known financial accounting textbook advises that the term be avoided except in tax accounting because it is used in so many different senses, not all of them well-defined. For example it is often used as a synonym for fixed assets or for investments in securities.

A common non-technical usage occurs when people ask that employees or the environment or something else be treated as a _________.

a. Settlement date
b. Solvency
c. Political risk
d. Capital asset

59. In finance, the _________ is used to determine a theoretically appropriate required rate of return of an asset, if that asset is to be added to an already well-diversified portfolio, given that asset's non-diversifiable risk. The model takes into account the asset's sensitivity to non-diversifiable risk (also known as systemic risk or market risk), often represented by the quantity beta (β) in the financial industry, as well as the expected return of the market and the expected return of a theoretical risk-free asset.

The model was introduced by Jack Treynor (1961, 1962), William Sharpe (1964), John Lintner (1965a,b) and Jan Mossin (1966) independently, building on the earlier work of Harry Markowitz on diversification and modern portfolio theory.

a. Cox-Ingersoll-Ross model
b. Hull-White model
c. Random walk hypothesis
d. Capital asset pricing model

60. _________ is a financial ratio that indicates the percentage of a company's assets are provided via debt. It is the ratio of total debt (the sum of current liabilities and long-term liabilities) and total assets (the sum of current assets, fixed assets, and other assets such as 'goodwill'.)

>

or alternatively:

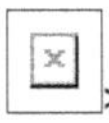

>

For example, a company with $2 million in total assets and $500,000 in total liabilities would have a _________ of 25%

Like all financial ratios, a company's _________ should be compared with their industry average or other competing firms.

a. Cash management
b. Capitalization rate
c. Cash concentration
d. Debt ratio

61. In finance, _________ occurs when a debtor has not met its legal obligations according to the debt contract, e.g. it has not made a scheduled payment, or has violated a loan covenant (condition) of the debt contract. _________ may occur if the debtor is either unwilling or unable to pay their debt. This can occur with all debt obligations including bonds, mortgages, loans, and promissory notes.

a. Credit crunch
b. Debt validation
c. Default
d. Vendor finance

62. _________ is the risk of loss due to a debtor's non-payment of a loan or other line of credit (either the principal or interest (coupon) or both)

Most lenders employ their own models (credit scorecards) to rank potential and existing customers according to risk, and then apply appropriate strategies. With products such as unsecured personal loans or mortgages, lenders charge a higher price for higher risk customers and vice versa. With revolving products such as credit cards and overdrafts, risk is controlled through careful setting of credit limits.

a. Transaction risk
b. Liquidity risk
c. Credit risk
d. Market risk

63. In finance, the _________ between two currencies specifies how much one currency is worth in terms of the other. For example an _________ of 102 Japanese yen to the United States dollar means that JPY 102 is worth the same as USD 1. The foreign exchange market is one of the largest markets in the world.

a. A Random Walk Down Wall Street
b. AAB
c. ABN Amro
d. Exchange rate

64. _________ is a form of risk that arises from the change in price of one currency against another. Whenever investors or companies have assets or business operations across national borders, they face _________ if their positions are not hedged.

- Transaction risk is the risk that exchange rates will change unfavourably over time. It can be hedged against using forward currency contracts;
- Translation risk is an accounting risk, proportional to the amount of assets held in foreign currencies. Changes in the exchange rate over time will render a report inaccurate, and so assets are usually balanced by borrowings in that currency.

The exchange risk associated with a foreign denominated instrument is a key element in foreign investment. This risk flows from differential monetary policy and growth in real productivity, which results in differential inflation rates.

a. Market risk
b. Tracking error
c. Currency risk
d. Credit risk

65. _________ is a type of risk faced by investors, corporations, and governments. It is a risk that can be understood and managed with proper aforethought and investment.

Broadly, _________ refers to the complications businesses and governments may face as a result of what are commonly referred to as political decisions--or 'any political change that alters the expected outcome and value of a given economic action by changing the probability of achieving business objectives.' .

a. Mid price
b. Single-index model
c. Capital asset
d. Political risk

66. In finance, _________ is the process of estimating the potential market value of a financial asset or liability. they can be done on assets (for example, investments in marketable securities such as stocks, options, business enterprises, or intangible assets such as patents and trademarks) or on liabilities (e.g., Bonds issued by a company.) _________s are required in many contexts including investment analysis, capital budgeting, merger and acquisition transactions, financial reporting, taxable events to determine the proper tax liability, and in litigation.

a. Procter ' Gamble
b. Margin
c. Share
d. Valuation

67. _________ is the planning process used to determine whether a firm's long term investments such as new machinery, replacement machinery, new plants, new products, and research development projects are worth pursuing. It is budget for major capital, or investment, expenditures.

Many formal methods are used in _________, including the techniques such as

- Net present value
- Profitability index
- Internal rate of return
- Modified Internal Rate of Return
- Equivalent annuity

These methods use the incremental cash flows from each potential investment, or project. Techniques based on accounting earnings and accounting rules are sometimes used - though economists consider this to be improper - such as the accounting rate of return, and 'return on investment.' Simplified and hybrid methods are used as well, such as payback period and discounted payback period.

a. Shareholder value
b. Financial distress
c. Preferred stock
d. Capital budgeting

68. In finance, _________ refers to the way a corporation finances its assets through some combination of equity, debt, or hybrid securities. A firm's _________ is then the composition or 'structure' of its liabilities. For example, a firm that sells $20 billion in equity and $80 billion in debt is said to be 20% equity-financed and 80% debt-financed.

a. Rights issue
b. Market for corporate control
c. Book building
d. Capital structure

69. In finance, _________ (or gearing) is borrowing money to supplement existing funds for investment in such a way that the potential positive or negative outcome is magnified and/or enhanced. It generally refers to using borrowed funds, or debt, so as to attempt to increase the returns to equity. Deleveraging is the action of reducing borrowings.

a. Leverage
b. Limited partnership
c. Financial endowment
d. Pension fund

70. Times interest earned (TIE) or _________ is a measure of a company's ability to honor its debt payments. It may be calculated as either EBIT or EBITDA divided by the total interest payable.

$$\text{Times-Interest-Earned} = \frac{\text{EBIT or EBITDA}}{\text{Interest Charges}}$$

- Financial ratio
- Financial leverage
- EBIT
- EBITDA
- Debt service coverage ratio

Interest Charges = Traditionally 'charges' refers to interest expense found on the income statement.

Times Interest Earned or Interest Coverage is a great tool when measuring a company's ability to meet its debt obligations.

a. Information ratio
b. Assets turnover
c. Earnings per share
d. Interest coverage ratio

71. _________ or interest coverage ratio is a measure of a company's ability to honor its debt payments. It may be calculated as either EBIT or EBITDA divided by the total interest payable.

$$\text{Times-Interest-Earned} = \frac{\text{EBIT or EBITDA}}{\text{Interest Charges}}$$

- Financial ratio
- Financial leverage
- EBIT
- EBITDA
- Debt service coverage ratio

Interest Charges = Traditionally 'charges' refers to interest expense found on the income statement.

_________ or Interest Coverage is a great tool when measuring a company's ability to meet its debt obligations.

a. Return of capital
b. Cash conversion cycle
c. Times interest earned
d. Net assets

72. _________ is a financial ratio used to assess the profitability of a firm's core activities, excluding fixed costs.

The general calculation is

$$\text{Gross profit margin} = \frac{\text{Revenue} - \text{Cost of Sales}}{\text{Revenue}}$$

The _________ is related to the net profit margin, which assesses the profitability of an organization after including fixed costs.

Indicates the relationship between net sales revenue and the cost of goods sold.

a. Gross profit margin
b. Second lien loan
c. Tender offer
d. Gross profit

73. In finance, a _________ is collateral that the holder of a position in securities, options, or futures contracts has to deposit to cover the credit risk of his counterparty (most often his broker.) This risk can arise if the holder has done any of the following:

- borrowed cash from the counterparty to buy securities or options,
- sold securities or options short, or
- entered into a futures contract.

The collateral can be in the form of cash or securities, and it is deposited in a _________ account. On U.S. futures exchanges, '_________' was formally called performance bond.

_________ buying is buying securities with cash borrowed from a broker, using other securities as collateral.

a. Procter ' Gamble
b. Margin
c. Credit
d. Share

74. _________, Net Margin, Net _________ or Net Profit Ratio all refer to a measure of profitability. It is calculated using a formula and written as a percentage or a number.

$$\text{Net profit margin} = \frac{\text{Net profit after taxes}}{\text{Net Sales}}$$

The _________ is mostly used for internal comparison.

a. 4-4-5 Calendar
b. Net profit margin
c. Profit maximization
d. Profit margin

75. In business, operating margin, operating income margin, _________ or return on sales (ROS) is the ratio of operating income (operating profit in the UK) divided by net sales, usually presented in percent.

>

(Relevant figures in italics)

>

It is a measurement of what proportion of a company's revenue is left over, before taxes and other indirect costs (such as rent, bonus, interest, etc.), after paying for variable costs of production as wages, raw materials, etc. A good operating margin is needed for a company to be able to pay for its fixed costs, such as interest on debt.

a. Average rate of return
b. Operating profit margin
c. Operating leverage
d. Interest coverage ratio

76. Profit margin, net margin, _________ or net profit ratio all refer to a measure of profitability. It is calculated by finding the net profit as a percentage of the revenue.

>

The profit margin is mostly used for internal comparison.

a. Profit maximization
b. 4-4-5 Calendar
c. Profit margin
d. Net profit margin

77. The _________ of a stock is a measure of the price paid for a share relative to the annual income or profit earned by the firm per share. It is a financial ratio used for valuation: a higher _________ means that investors are paying more for each unit of income, so the stock is more expensive compared to one with lower _________.

The _________ has units of years, which can be interpreted as 'number of years of earnings to pay back purchase price'.

a. Sustainable growth rate
b. Quick ratio
c. Return of capital
d. P/E ratio

78. A _________ is a documented investigation of a Market that is used to inform a firm's planning activities particularly around decision of: inventory, purchase, work force expansion/contraction, facility expansion, purchases of capital equipment, promotional activities, and many other aspects of a company.

Not all managers are asked to conduct a _________, but all managers must make decisions using _________ data and understand how the data was derived. So all managers need a reasonable understanding of the tools most used for making sales forecasts and analyzing markets.

a. 7-Eleven
b. 4-4-5 Calendar
c. 529 plan
d. Market analysis

79. The _________ is the current method of accelerated asset depreciation required by the United States income tax code. Under _________, all assets are divided into classes which dictate the number of years over which an asset's cost will be recovered.

Prior to the Accelerated Cost Recovery System (ACRS), most capital purchases were depreciated using a straight line technique, that allowed for the depreciation of the asset over its useful life.

a. 4-4-5 Calendar
b. Modified Accelerated Cost Recovery System
c. 529 plan
d. 7-Eleven

80. _________ is the price at which an asset would trade in a competitive Walrasian auction setting. _________ is often used interchangeably with open _________, fair value or fair _________, although these terms have distinct definitions in different standards, and may differ in some circumstances.

International Valuation Standards defines _________ as 'the estimated amount for which a property should exchange on the date of valuation between a willing buyer and a willing seller in an arm'e;s-length transaction after proper marketing wherein the parties had each acted knowledgeably, prudently, and without compulsion.'

_________ is a concept distinct from market price, which is 'e;the price at which one can transact'e;, while _________ is 'e;the true underlying value'e; according to theoretical standards.

a. Market value
b. Wrap account
c. Debt restructuring
d. T-Model

1. _________ is the balance of the amounts of cash being received and paid by a business during a defined period of time, sometimes tied to a specific project. Measurement of _________ can be used

- to evaluate the state or performance of a business or project.
- to determine problems with liquidity. Being profitable does not necessarily mean being liquid. A company can fail because of a shortage of cash, even while profitable.
- to generate project rate of returns. The time of _________s into and out of projects are used as inputs to financial models such as internal rate of return, and net present value.
- to examine income or growth of a business when it is believed that accrual accounting concepts do not represent economic realities. Alternately, _________ can be used to 'validate' the net income generated by accrual accounting.

_________ as a generic term may be used differently depending on context, and certain _________ definitions may be adapted by analysts and users for their own uses. Common terms include operating _________ and free _________.

_________s can be classified into:

1. Operational _________s: Cash received or expended as a result of the company's core business activities.
2. Investment _________s: Cash received or expended through capital expenditure, investments or acquisitions.
3. Financing _________s: Cash received or expended as a result of financial activities, such as interests and dividends.

All three together - the net _________ - are necessary to reconcile the beginning cash balance to the ending cash balance. Loan draw downs or equity injections, that is just shifting of capital but no expenditure as such, are not considered in the net _________.

a. Real option
b. Cash flow
c. Corporate finance
d. Shareholder value

2. _________ is a term used in accounting, economics and finance to spread the cost of an asset over the span of several years.

In simple words we can say that _________ is the reduction in the value of an asset due to usage, passage of time, wear and tear, technological outdating or obsolescence, depletion or other such factors.

In accounting, _________ is a term used to describe any method of attributing the historical or purchase cost of an asset across its useful life, roughly corresponding to normal wear and tear.

a. Deferred financing costs
b. Matching principle
c. Bottom line
d. Depreciation

3. _________ is the task of determining how a business will afford to achieve its strategic goals and objectives. Usually, a company creates a Financial Plan immediately after the vision and objectives have been set. The Financial Plan describes each of the activities, resources, equipment and materials that are needed to achieve these objectives, as well as the timeframes involved.

a. Management by exception
b. Corporate Transparency
c. Performance measurement
d. Financial planning

4. The term _________ is a term applied to practices that are perfunctory, or seek to satisfy the minimum requirements or to conform to a convention or doctrine. It has different meanings in different fields.

In accounting, _________ earnings are those earnings of companies in addition to actual earnings calculated under the Generally Accepted Accounting Principles (GAAP) in their quarterly and yearly financial reports.

a. Pro forma
b. Deferred financing costs
c. Long-term liabilities
d. Deferred income

5. In financial accounting, a _________ or statement of cash flows is a financial statement that shows a company's flow of cash. The money coming into the business is called cash inflow, and money going out from the business is called cash outflow. The statement shows how changes in balance sheet and income accounts affect cash and cash equivalents, and breaks the analysis down to operating, investing, and financing activities.

a. 4-4-5 Calendar
b. 7-Eleven
c. 529 plan
d. Cash flow statement

6. _________ means regulating, adapting or settling in a variety of contexts:

In commercial law, _________ means the settlement of a loss incurred on insured goods. The calculation of the amounts of compensation to be paid by or to the several interests is a complicated matter. It involves much detail and arithmetic, and requires a full and accurate knowledge of the principles of the subject.

a. Intelligent investor
b. Equity method
c. Asset recovery
d. Adjustment

7. _________, refers to consumption opportunity gained by an entity within a specified time frame, which is generally expressed in monetary terms. However, for households and individuals, '_________ is the sum of all the wages, salaries, profits, interests payments, rents and other forms of earnings received... in a given period of time.' For firms, _________ generally refers to net-profit: what remains of revenue after expenses have been subtracted.

a. Income
b. OIBDA
c. Annual report
d. Accrual

8. An _________ is a financial statement for companies that indicates how Revenue is transformed into net income The purpose of the _________ is to show managers and investors whether the company made or lost money during the period being reported.

The important thing to remember about an _________ is that it represents a period of time.

a. AAB
b. A Random Walk Down Wall Street
c. ABN Amro
d. Income statement

9. In corporate finance, _________ is a cash flow available for distribution among all the security holders of a company. They include equity holders, debt holders, preferred stock holders, convertible security holders, and so on.

Note that the first three lines above are calculated for you on the standard Statement of Cash Flows.

a. Safety stock
b. Funding
c. Forfaiting
d. Free cash flow

10. In financial accounting, _________ , cash flow provided by operations or cash flow from operating activities, refers to the amount of cash a company generates from the revenues it brings in, excluding costs associated with long-term investment on capital items or investment in securities.

_________ = Cash generated from operations less taxation and interest paid, investment income received and less dividends paid gives rise to _________s per International Financial Reporting Standards.

To calculate cash generated from operations, one must calculate cash generated from customers and cash paid to suppliers.

a. A Random Walk Down Wall Street
b. Appreciation
c. Other Comprehensive Basis of Accounting
d. Operating cash flow

11. In business, _________ is income that a company receives from its normal business activities, usually from the sale of goods and services to customers. Some companies also receive _________ from interest, dividends or royalties paid to them by other companies. _________ may refer to business income in general, or it may refer to the amount, in a monetary unit, received during a period of time, as in 'Last year, Company X had _________ of $32 million.'

In many countries, including the UK, _________ is referred to as turnover.

a. Revenue
b. Bottom line
c. Matching principle
d. Furniture, Fixtures and Equipment

12. The phrase _________ refers to the aspect of corporate strategy, corporate finance and management dealing with the buying, selling and combining of different companies that can aid, finance, or help a growing company in a given industry grow rapidly without having to create another business entity.

An acquisition, also known as a takeover, is the buying of one company (the 'target') by another. An acquisition may be friendly or hostile.

a. 529 plan
b. 7-Eleven
c. 4-4-5 Calendar
d. Mergers and acquisitions

13. In business and accounting, _________s are everything of value that is owned by a person or company. The balance sheet of a firm records the monetary value of the _________s owned by the firm. The two major _________ classes are tangible _________s and intangible _________s.

a. Accounts payable
b. Income
c. EBITDA
d. Asset

14. In probability theory and statistics, _________ indicates the strength and direction of a linear relationship between two random variables. That is in contrast with the usage of the term in colloquial speech, which denotes any relationship, not necessarily linear. In general statistical usage, _________ or co-relation refers to the departure of two random variables from independence.

a. Correlation
b. Geometric mean
c. Probability distribution
d. Variance

15. The _________ is the current method of accelerated asset depreciation required by the United States income tax code. Under _________, all assets are divided into classes which dictate the number of years over which an asset's cost will be recovered.

Prior to the Accelerated Cost Recovery System (ACRS), most capital purchases were depreciated using a straight line technique, that allowed for the depreciation of the asset over its useful life.

a. 4-4-5 Calendar
b. 7-Eleven
c. 529 plan
d. Modified Accelerated Cost Recovery System

16. Depreciation methods that provide for a higher depreciation charge in the first year of an asset's life and gradually decreasing charges in subsequent years are called accelerated depreciation methods. This may be a more realistic reflection of an asset's actual expected benefit from the use of the asset: many assets are most useful when they are new. One popular accelerated method is the declining-balance method. Under this method the Book Value is multiplied by a fixed rate.

The most common rate used is double the straight-line rate. For this reason, this technique is referred to as the _________. To illustrate, suppose a business has an asset with $1,000 Original Cost, $100 Salvage Value, and 5 years useful life. First, calculate straight-line depreciation rate. Since the asset has 5 years useful life, the straight-line depreciation rate equals (100% / 5) 20% per year. With _________, as the name suggests, double that rate, or 40% depreciation rate is used.

a. The Goodyear Tire ' Rubber Company
b. Database auditing
c. Doctrine of the Proper Law
d. Double-declining-balance method

17. The institution most often referenced by the word '_________' is a public or publicly traded _________, the shares of which are traded on a public stock exchange (e.g., the New York Stock Exchange or Nasdaq in the United States) where shares of stock of _________s are bought and sold by and to the general public. Most of the largest businesses in the world are publicly traded _________s. However, the majority of _________s are said to be closely held, privately held or close _________s, meaning that no ready market exists for the trading of shares.

a. Corporation
b. Protect
c. Federal Home Loan Mortgage Corporation
d. Depository Trust Company

18. In finance, _________ refers to the way a corporation finances its assets through some combination of equity, debt, or hybrid securities. A firm's _________ is then the composition or 'structure' of its liabilities. For example, a firm that sells $20 billion in equity and $80 billion in debt is said to be 20% equity-financed and 80% debt-financed.

a. Rights issue
b. Capital structure
c. Market for corporate control
d. Book building

19. _________ or financing is to provide capital (funds), which means money for a project, a person, a business or any other private or public institutions.

Those funds can be allocated for either short term or long term purposes. The health fund is a new way of _________ private healthcare centers.

a. Proxy fight
b. Product life cycle
c. Funding
d. Synthetic CDO

20. In accounting, a _________ is an asset on the balance sheet which is expected to be sold or otherwise used up in the near future, usually within one year, or one business cycle - whichever is longer. Typical _________s include cash, cash equivalents, accounts receivable, inventory, the portion of prepaid accounts which will be used within a year, and short-term investments.

On the balance sheet, assets will typically be classified into _________s and long-term assets.

a. Write-off
b. Historical cost
c. Long-term liabilities
d. Current asset

21. _________ plant, and equipment, is a term used in accountancy for assets and property which cannot easily be converted into cash. This can be compared with current assets such as cash or bank accounts, which are described as liquid assets. In most cases, only tangible assets are referred to as fixed.

a. Remittance advice
b. Percentage of Completion
c. Petty cash
d. Fixed asset

22. In economic models, the _________ time frame assumes no fixed factors of production. Firms can enter or leave the marketplace, and the cost (and availability) of land, labor, raw materials, and capital goods can be assumed to vary. In contrast, in the short-run time frame, certain factors are assumed to be fixed, because there is not sufficient time for them to change.

a. 529 plan
b. Short-run
c. 4-4-5 Calendar
d. Long-run

23. _________ is the difference between price and the costs of bringing to market whatever it is that is accounted as an enterprise (whether by harvest, extraction, manufacture, or purchase) in terms of the component costs of delivered goods and/or services and any operating or other expenses.

A key difficulty in measuring profit is in defining costs. Pure economic monetary profits can be zero or negative even in competitive equilibrium when accounted monetized costs exceed monetized price.

a. A Random Walk Down Wall Street
b. Accounting profit
c. AAB
d. Economic profit

24. In economics, the concept of the _________ refers to the decision-making time frame of a firm in which at least one factor of production is fixed. Costs which are fixed in the _________ have no impact on a firms decisions. For example a firm can raise output by increasing the amount of labour through overtime.

a. Short-run
b. Long-run
c. 529 plan
d. 4-4-5 Calendar

25. In general usage, a _________ can be a budget, a plan for spending and saving future income. This plan allocates future income to various types of expenses, such as rent or utilities, and also reserves some income for short-term and long-term savings. A _________ can also be an investment plan, which allocates savings to various assets or projects expected to produce future income, such as a new business or product line, shares in an existing business, or real estate.

a. Credit repair software
b. Title loan
c. Financial plan
d. Promissory note

26. Working capital requirements of a business should be monitored at all times to ensure that there are sufficient funds available to meet short-term expenses.

The _________ is basically a detailed plan that shows all expected sources and uses of cash

a. Rate of return
b. Loans and interest, in Judaism
c. Mitigating Control
d. Cash budget

27. The _________ is one of the measures of national income and input for a given country's economy. _________ is defined as the total cost of all finished goods and services produced within the country in a stipulated period of time (usually a 365-day year.) It is sometimes regarded as the sum of profits added at every level of production (the intermediate stages) of all final goods and services produced within a country in a stipulated timeframe, and it is rarely given a monetary value.

a. Macroeconomics
b. Gross domestic product
c. Recession
d. Behavioral finance

28. _________ is a financial transaction whereby a business sells its accounts receivable (i.e., invoices) at a discount. _________ differs from a bank loan in three main ways. First, the emphasis is on the value of the receivables (essentially a financial asset), not the firm's credit worthiness.

a. Debt-for-equity swap
b. Credit card balance transfer
c. Financial Literacy Month
d. Factoring

29. _________, in bookkeeping, refers to assets, liabilities, income, and expenses recorded on individual pages of the so called book of final entry or ledger. Changes in _________ value are made by chronologically posting debit (DR) and credit (CR) entries to its page. Examples of _________s are cash, _________s receivable, mortgages, loans, land and buildings, common stock, sales, services provided, wages, and payroll overhead.

a. Alpha
b. Accretion
c. Option
d. Account

30. _________ is one of a series of accounting transactions dealing with the billing of customers who owe money to a person, company or organization for goods and services that have been provided to the customer. In most business entities this is typically done by generating an invoice and mailing or electronically delivering it to the customer, who in turn must pay it within an established timeframe called credit or payment terms.

An example of a common payment term is Net 30, meaning payment is due in the amount of the invoice 30 days from the date of invoice.

a. Income
b. Accounts receivable
c. Accounting methods
d. Impaired asset

31. _________ is a fee paid on borrowed assets. It is the price paid for the use of borrowed money , or, money earned by deposited funds . Assets that are sometimes lent with _________ include money, shares, consumer goods through hire purchase, major assets such as aircraft, and even entire factories in finance lease arrangements.

a. A Random Walk Down Wall Street
b. AAB
c. Insolvency
d. Interest

32. _________ refers to a business or organization attempting to acquire goods or services to accomplish the goals of the enterprise. Though there are several organizations that attempt to set standards in the _________ process, processes can vary greatly between organizations. Typically the word '_________' is not used interchangeably with the word 'procurement', since procurement typically includes Expediting, Supplier Quality, and Traffic and Logistics (T'L) in addition to _________.

a. 7-Eleven
b. 529 plan
c. 4-4-5 Calendar
d. Purchasing

33. The _________ is the rate that a company is expected to pay to finance its assets. WACC is the minimum return that a company must earn on existing asset base to satisfy its creditors, owners, and other providers of capital.

Companies raise money from a number of sources: common equity, preferred equity, straight debt, convertible debt, exchangeable debt, warrants, options, pension liabilities, executive stock options, governmental subsidies, and so on.

a. 4-4-5 Calendar
b. Capital intensity
c. Cost of capital
d. Weighted average cost of capital

34. _________ is a file or account that contains money that a person or company owes to suppliers, but hasn't paid yet (a form of debt.) When you receive an invoice you add it to the file, and then you remove it when you pay. Thus, the A/P is a form of credit that suppliers offer to their purchasers by allowing them to pay for a product or service after it has already been received.

a. Earnings before interest, taxes, depreciation and amortization
b. Accrual
c. Outstanding balance
d. Accounts payable

35. A _________ is a payment made by a corporation to its shareholder members. When a corporation earns a profit or surplus, that money can be put to two uses: it can either be re-invested in the business (called retained earnings), or it can be paid to the shareholders as a _________. Many corporations retain a portion of their earnings and pay the remainder as a _________.

a. Special dividend
b. Dividend yield
c. Dividend puzzle
d. Dividend

36. _________ is the study of how the variation (uncertainty) in the output of a mathematical model can be apportioned, qualitatively or quantitatively, to different sources of variation in the input of a model .

In more general terms uncertainty and sensitivity analyses investigate the robustness of a study when the study includes some form of mathematical modelling. While uncertainty analysis studies the overall uncertainty in the conclusions of the study, _________ tries to identify what source of uncertainty weights more on the study's conclusions.

a. Proxy fight
b. Golden parachute
c. Synthetic CDO
d. Sensitivity analysis

37. _________ are formal records of a business' financial activities.

_________ provide an overview of a business' financial condition in both short and long term. There are four basic _________:

1. **Balance sheet**: also referred to as statement of financial position or condition, reports on a company's assets, liabilities, and net equity as of a given point in time.
2. **Income statement**: also referred to as Profit and Loss statement (or a 'P'L'), reports on a company's income, expenses, and profits over a period of time.
3. **Statement of retained earnings**: explains the changes in a company's retained earnings over the reporting period.
4. **Statement of cash flows**: reports on a company's cash flow activities, particularly its operating, investing and financing activities.

a. Financial statements
b. Notes to the Financial Statements
c. Statement on Auditing Standards No. 70: Service Organizations
d. Statement of retained earnings

38. In economics, business, and accounting, a _________ is the value of money that has been used up to produce something, and hence is not available for use anymore. In business, the _________ may be one of acquisition, in which case the amount of money expended to acquire it is counted as _________. In this case, money is the input that is gone in order to acquire the thing.

a. Sliding scale fees
b. Fixed costs
c. Cost
d. Marginal cost

39. _________ are expenses that change in proportion to the activity of a business. In other words, _________ are the sum of marginal costs. It can also be considered normal costs. Along with fixed costs, _________ make up the two components of total cost. Direct Costs, however, are costs that can be associated with a particular cost object.

a. Transaction cost
b. Variable costs
c. Cost accounting
d. Fixed costs

40. In the theory of capital structure, _________ is the phrase used to describe funds that firms obtain from outside of the firm. It is contrasted to internal financing which consists mainly of profits retained by the firm for investment. There are many kinds of _________.

a. Asset-backed commercial paper
b. Ownership equity
c. External financing
d. Adjustment

41. In financial accounting, a _________ or statement of financial position is a summary of a person's or organization's balances. Assets, liabilities and ownership equity are listed as of a specific date, such as the end of its financial year. A _________ is often described as a snapshot of a company's financial condition.

a. Balance sheet
b. Statement on Auditing Standards No. 70: Service Organizations
c. Financial statements
d. Statement of retained earnings

1. _________ measures the nominal future sum of money that a given sum of money is 'worth' at a specified time in the future assuming a certain interest rate rate of return; it is the present value multiplied by the accumulation function.

The value does not include corrections for inflation or other factors that affect the true value of money in the future. This is used in time value of money calculations.

a. Future-oriented
b. Present value of costs
c. Discounted cash flow
d. Future value

2. _________ is a fee paid on borrowed assets. It is the price paid for the use of borrowed money , or, money earned by deposited funds . Assets that are sometimes lent with _________ include money, shares, consumer goods through hire purchase, major assets such as aircraft, and even entire factories in finance lease arrangements.

a. AAB
b. Insolvency
c. Interest
d. A Random Walk Down Wall Street

3. _________ is the value on a given date of a future payment or series of future payments, discounted to reflect the time value of money and other factors such as investment risk. _________ calculations are widely used in business and economics to provide a means to compare cash flows at different times on a meaningful 'like to like' basis.

The most commonly applied model of the time value of money is compound interest.

a. Net present value
b. Present value of benefits
c. Negative gearing
d. Present value

4. In finance, the value of an option consists of two components, its intrinsic value and its _________. Time value is simply the difference between option value and intrinsic value. _________ is also known as theta, extrinsic value, or instrumental value.

a. Debt buyer
b. Conservatism
c. Global Squeeze
d. Time value

5. Simply put, _________ is the value of money figuring in a given amount of interest for a given amount of time. For example 100 dollars of todays money held for a year at 5 percent interest is worth 105 dollars, therefore 100 dollars paid now or 105 dollars paid exactly one year from now is the same amount of payment of money with that given intersest at that given amount of time. This notion dates at least to Martín de Azpilcueta of the School of Salamanca.

All of the standard calculations for _________ derive from the most basic algebraic expression for the present value of a future sum, 'discounted' to the present by an amount equal to the _________. For example, a sum of FV to be received in one year is discounted (at the rate of interest r) to give a sum of PV at present: PV = FV -- rÂ·PV = FV/(1+r).

a. Zero-coupon bond
b. Coefficient of variation
c. Time value of money
d. Current account

6. _________ is the concept of adding accumulated interest back to the principal, so that interest is earned on interest from that moment on. The act of declaring interest to be principal is called compounding (i.e., interest is compounded.) A loan, for example, may have its interest compounded every month: in this case, a loan with $100 principal and 1% interest per month would have a balance of $101 at the end of the first month.

a. Penny stock
b. Compound interest
c. 4-4-5 Calendar
d. Risk management

7. In finance, _________ is the process of estimating the potential market value of a financial asset or liability. they can be done on assets (for example, investments in marketable securities such as stocks, options, business enterprises, or intangible assets such as patents and trademarks) or on liabilities (e.g., Bonds issued by a company.) _________s are required in many contexts including investment analysis, capital budgeting, merger and acquisition transactions, financial reporting, taxable events to determine the proper tax liability, and in litigation.

a. Procter ' Gamble
b. Margin
c. Valuation
d. Share

8. A '_________' is a 'Charge' that is paid to obtain the right to delay a payment. Essentially, the payer purchases the right to make a given payment in the future instead of in the Present. The '_________', or 'Charge' that must be paid to delay the payment, is simply the difference between what the payment amount would be if it were paid in the present and what the payment amount would be paid if it were paid in the future.

a. Risk modeling
b. Risk aversion
c. Value at risk
d. Discount

9. _________ mature in one year or less. Like zero-coupon bonds, they do not pay interest prior to maturity; instead they are sold at a discount of the par value to create a positive yield to maturity. Many regard _________ as the least risky investment available to U.S. investors.

a. Treasury securities
b. Treasury Inflation Protected Securities
c. 4-4-5 Calendar
d. Treasury bills

10. _________ is the provision of resources (such as granting a loan) by one party to another party where that second party does not reimburse the first party immediately, thereby generating a debt, and instead arranges either to repay or return those resources (or material(s) of equal value) at a later date. The first party is called a creditor, also known as a lender, while the second party is called a debtor, also known as a borrower.

Movements of financial capital are normally dependent on either _________ or equity transfers.

a. Clearing house
b. Comparable
c. Warrant
d. Credit

11. An _________ can be defined as a contract which provides an income stream in return for an initial payment.

An immediate _________ is an _________ for which the time between the contract date and the date of the first payment is not longer than the time interval between payments. A common use for an immediate _________ is to provide a pension to a retired person or persons.

a. Intrinsic value
b. Amortization
c. AT'T Inc.
d. Annuity

12. _________ is the balance of the amounts of cash being received and paid by a business during a defined period of time, sometimes tied to a specific project. Measurement of _________ can be used

- to evaluate the state or performance of a business or project.
- to determine problems with liquidity. Being profitable does not necessarily mean being liquid. A company can fail because of a shortage of cash, even while profitable.
- to generate project rate of returns. The time of _________s into and out of projects are used as inputs to financial models such as internal rate of return, and net present value.
- to examine income or growth of a business when it is believed that accrual accounting concepts do not represent economic realities. Alternately, _________ can be used to 'validate' the net income generated by accrual accounting.

_________ as a generic term may be used differently depending on context, and certain _________ definitions may be adapted by analysts and users for their own uses. Common terms include operating _________ and free _________.

_________s can be classified into:

1. Operational _________s: Cash received or expended as a result of the company's core business activities.
2. Investment _________s: Cash received or expended through capital expenditure, investments or acquisitions.
3. Financing _________s: Cash received or expended as a result of financial activities, such as interests and dividends.

All three together - the net _________ - are necessary to reconcile the beginning cash balance to the ending cash balance. Loan draw downs or equity injections, that is just shifting of capital but no expenditure as such, are not considered in the net _________.

a. Real option
b. Corporate finance
c. Shareholder value
d. Cash flow

13. In corporate finance, _________ is a cash flow available for distribution among all the security holders of a company. They include equity holders, debt holders, preferred stock holders, convertible security holders, and so on.

Note that the first three lines above are calculated for you on the standard Statement of Cash Flows.

a. Funding
b. Safety stock
c. Forfaiting
d. Free cash flow

14. In financial accounting, _________ , cash flow provided by operations or cash flow from operating activities, refers to the amount of cash a company generates from the revenues it brings in, excluding costs associated with long-term investment on capital items or investment in securities.

_________ = Cash generated from operations less taxation and interest paid, investment income received and less dividends paid gives rise to _________s per International Financial Reporting Standards.

To calculate cash generated from operations, one must calculate cash generated from customers and cash paid to suppliers.

a. A Random Walk Down Wall Street
b. Appreciation
c. Other Comprehensive Basis of Accounting
d. Operating cash flow

15. In economics, business, and accounting, a _________ is the value of money that has been used up to produce something, and hence is not available for use anymore. In business, the _________ may be one of acquisition, in which case the amount of money expended to acquire it is counted as _________. In this case, money is the input that is gone in order to acquire the thing.

a. Fixed costs
b. Marginal cost
c. Sliding scale fees
d. Cost

16. The _________ is an expected return that the provider of capital plans to earn on their investment.

Capital (money) used for funding a business should earn returns for the capital providers who risk their capital. For an investment to be worthwhile, the expected return on capital must be greater than the _________.

a. Cost of capital
b. 4-4-5 Calendar
c. Capital intensity
d. Weighted average cost of capital

17. The _________ is an interest rate a central bank charges depository institutions that borrow reserves from it.

The term _________ has two meanings:

- the same as interest rate; the term 'discount' does not refer to the meaning of the word, but to the purpose of using the quantity, such as computations of present value, e.g. net present value / discounted cash flow

- the annual effective _________, which is the annual interest divided by the capital including that interest; this rate is lower than the interest rate; it corresponds to using the value after a year as the nominal value, and seeing the initial value as the nominal value minus a discount; it is used for Treasury Bills and similar financial instruments

The annual effective _________ is the annual interest divided by the capital including that interest, which is the interest rate divided by 100% plus the interest rate. It is the annual discount factor to be applied to the future cash flow, to find the discount, subtracted from a future value to find the value one year earlier.

For example, suppose there is a government bond that sells for $95 and pays $100 in a year's time.

a. Fisher equation
b. Black-Scholes
c. Stochastic volatility
d. Discount rate

18. _________ or net present worth (NPW) is defined as the total present value (PV) of a time series of cash flows. It is a standard method for using the time value of money to appraise long-term projects. Used for capital budgeting, and widely throughout economics, it measures the excess or shortfall of cash flows, in present value terms, once financing charges are met.

a. Tax shield
b. Negative gearing
c. Net present value
d. Present value of costs

19. _________ or economic opportunity loss is the value of the next best alternative foregone as the result of making a decision. _________ analysis is an important part of a company's decision-making processes but is not treated as an actual cost in any financial statement. The next best thing that a person can engage in is referred to as the _________ of doing the best thing and ignoring the next best thing to be done.

a. AAB
b. Opportunity cost
c. ABN Amro
d. A Random Walk Down Wall Street

20. In finance, _________, also known as return on investment is the ratio of money gained or lost on an investment relative to the amount of money invested. The amount of money gained or lost may be referred to as interest, profit/loss, gain/loss, or net income/loss. The money invested may be referred to as the asset, capital, principal, or the cost basis of the investment.

a. Composiition of Creditors
b. Stock or scrip dividends
c. Rate of return
d. Doctrine of the Proper Law

21. An _________ is the price a borrower pays for the use of money they do not own, and the return a lender receives for deferring the use of funds, by lending it to the borrower. _________s are normally expressed as a percentage rate over the period of one year.

_________s targets are also a vital tool of monetary policy and are used to control variables like investment, inflation, and unemployment.

a. AAB
b. A Random Walk Down Wall Street
c. ABN Amro
d. Interest rate

22. _________ is the planning process used to determine whether a firm's long term investments such as new machinery, replacement machinery, new plants, new products, and research development projects are worth pursuing. It is budget for major capital, or investment, expenditures.

Many formal methods are used in _________, including the techniques such as

- Net present value
- Profitability index
- Internal rate of return
- Modified Internal Rate of Return
- Equivalent annuity

These methods use the incremental cash flows from each potential investment, or project. Techniques based on accounting earnings and accounting rules are sometimes used - though economists consider this to be improper - such as the accounting rate of return, and 'return on investment.' Simplified and hybrid methods are used as well, such as payback period and discounted payback period.

a. Financial distress
b. Shareholder value
c. Preferred stock
d. Capital budgeting

23. In financial accounting, a _________ or statement of cash flows is a financial statement that shows a company's flow of cash. The money coming into the business is called cash inflow, and money going out from the business is called cash outflow. The statement shows how changes in balance sheet and income accounts affect cash and cash equivalents, and breaks the analysis down to operating, investing, and financing activities.

a. 4-4-5 Calendar
b. Cash flow statement
c. 7-Eleven
d. 529 plan

24. _________ is a life of security. It may also refer to the final payment date of a loan or other financial instrument, at which point all remaining interest and principal is due to be paid.

1, 3, 6 months _________ band can be calculated by using 30-day per month periods.

a. Primary market
b. Replacement cost
c. False billing
d. Maturity

25. A _________ is an annuity in which the periodic payments begin on a fixed date and continue indefinitely. It is sometimes referred to as a perpetual annuity. Fixed coupon payments on permanently invested (irredeemable) sums of money are prime examples of these. Scholarships paid perpetually from an endowment fit the definition of _________.

a. Current yield
b. Stochastic volatility
c. LIBOR market model
d. Perpetuity

26. The _________, effective annual interest rate, Annual Equivalent Rate (AER) or simply effective rate is the interest rate on a loan or financial product restated from the nominal interest rate as an interest rate with annual compound interest. It is used to compare the annual interest between loans with different compounding terms (daily, monthly, annually, or other.)

The _________ differs in two important respects from the annual percentage rate (APR):

1. the _________ generally does not incorporate one-time charges such as front-end fees;
2. the _________ is (generally) not defined by legal or regulatory authorities (as APR is in many jurisdictions.)

By contrast, the 'effective APR' is used as a legal term, where front-fees and other costs can be included, as defined by local law.

Annual Percentage Yield or effective annual yield is the analogous concept used for savings or investment products, such as a certificate of deposit.

a. A Random Walk Down Wall Street
b. AAB
c. ABN Amro
d. Effective interest rate

27. The terms _________ , nominal _________, and effective _________ describe the interest rate for a whole year (annualized), rather than just a monthly fee/rate, as applied on a loan, mortgage, credit card, etc. Those terms have formal, legal definitions in some countries or legal jurisdictions, but in general:

- The nominal _________ is the simple-interest rate (for a year.)
- The effective _________ is the fee+compound interest rate (calculated across a year.)

The nominal _________ is calculated as: the rate, for a payment period, multiplied by the number of payment periods in a year. However, the exact legal definition of 'effective _________' can vary greatly in each jurisdiction, depending on the type of fees included, such as participation fees, loan origination fees, monthly service charges, or late fees. The effective _________ has been called the 'mathematically-true' interest rate for each year. The computation for the effective _________, as the fee+compound interest rate, can also vary depending on whether the up-front fees, such as origination or participation fees, are added to the entire amount, or treated as a short-term loan due in the first payment.

a. AAB
b. A Random Walk Down Wall Street
c. ABN Amro
d. Annual percentage rate

28. _________ expresses an annual rate of interest taking into account the effect of compounding, usually for deposit or investment products (such as a certificate of deposit.) It is analogous to the Annual percentage rate (APR), which is used for loans. In some jurisdictions, the use and definition of _________ may be regulated by a government agency, in which case it would generally be capitalized.

a. ABN Amro
b. AAB
c. A Random Walk Down Wall Street
d. Annual percentage yield

29. In finance, the term _________ describes the amount in cash that returns to the owners of a security. Normally it does not include the price variations, at the difference of the total return. _________ applies to various stated rates of return on stocks (common and preferred, and convertible), fixed income instruments (bonds, notes, bills, strips, zero coupon), and some other investment type insurance products (e.g. annuities.)

a. 4-4-5 Calendar
b. Macaulay duration
c. Yield to maturity
d. Yield

30. _________ is the process of decreasing an amount over a period of time. The word comes from Middle English amortisen to kill, alienate in mortmain, from Anglo-French amorteser, alteration of amortir, from Vulgar Latin admortire to kill, from Latin ad- + mort-, mors death. Particular instances of the term include:

- _________ (business), the allocation of a lump sum amount to different time periods, particularly for loans and other forms of finance, including related interest or other finance charges.
  - _________ schedule, a table detailing each periodic payment on a loan (typically a mortgage), as generated by an _________ calculator.
  - Negative _________, an _________ schedule where the loan amount actually increases through not paying the full interest
- Amortized analysis, analyzing the execution cost of algorithms over a sequence of operations.
- _________ of capital expenditures of certain assets under accounting rules, particularly intangible assets, in a manner analogous to depreciation.
- _________ (tax law)

_________ is also used in the context of zoning regulations and describes the time in which a property owner has to relocate when the property's use constitutes a preexisting nonconforming use under zoning regulations.

- Depreciation

.

a. Intrinsic value
b. Amortization
c. AT'T Inc.
d. Option

31. An _________ is a table detailing each periodic payment on a amortizing loan (typically a mortgage), as generated by an amortization calculator.

While a portion of every payment is applied towards both the interest and the principal balance of the loan, the exact amount applied to principal each time varies (with the remainder going to interest.) An _________ reveals the specific monetary amount put towards interest, as well as the specific put towards the Principal balance, with each payment.

a. Amortization schedule
b. Adjusting entries
c. Adjusted basis
d. Annual report

32. In business and finance, a _________ (also referred to as equity _________) of stock means a _________ of ownership in a corporation (company.) In the plural, stocks is often used as a synonym for _________s especially in the United States, but it is less commonly used that way outside of North America.

In the United Kingdom, South Africa, and Australia, stock can also refer to completely different financial instruments such as government bonds or, less commonly, to all kinds of marketable securities.

a. Bucket shop
b. Margin
c. Procter ' Gamble
d. Share

33. A _________ is the price of a single share of a no. of saleable stocks of the company. Once the stock is purchased, the owner becomes a shareholder of the company that issued the share.

a. Share price

b. Whisper numbers

c. Stock split

d. Trading curb

1. The term _________ has three unrelated technical definitions, and is also used in a variety of non-technical ways.

- In financial economics, it refers to any asset used to make money, as opposed to assets used for personal enjoyment or consumption. This is an important distinction because two people can disagree sharply about the value of personal assets, one person might think a sports car is more valuable than a pickup truck, another person might have the opposite taste. But if an asset is held for the purpose of making money, taste has nothing to do with it, only differences of opinion about how much money the asset will produce. With the further assumption that people agree on the probability distribution of future cash flows, it is possible to have an objective _________ pricing model. Even without the assumption of agreement, it is possible to set rational limits on _________ value.
- In governmental accounting, it is defined as any asset used in operations with an initial useful life extending beyond one reporting period. Generally, government managers have a 'stewardship' duty to maintain _________s under their control. See International Public Sector Accounting Standards for details.
- In US tax accounting, it is defined as any property other than a list of exceptions. The main exceptions are anything held for sale, and any real estate or depreciable property used in business. Almost everything you own and use for personal purposes, pleasure or investment is a _________. If something is a _________ for tax purposes, gains or losses on sale or disposition are capital gains or capital losses. For individuals, however, capital losses on property held for personal use are generally not deductible. See the IRS publication Tax Facts about Capital Gains and Losses for details.

A well-known financial accounting textbook advises that the term be avoided except in tax accounting because it is used in so many different senses, not all of them well-defined. For example it is often used as a synonym for fixed assets or for investments in securities.

A common non-technical usage occurs when people ask that employees or the environment or something else be treated as a _________.

a. Capital asset
b. Solvency
c. Political risk
d. Settlement date

2. In finance, the _________ is used to determine a theoretically appropriate required rate of return of an asset, if that asset is to be added to an already well-diversified portfolio, given that asset's non-diversifiable risk. The model takes into account the asset's sensitivity to non-diversifiable risk (also known as systemic risk or market risk), often represented by the quantity beta (β) in the financial industry, as well as the expected return of the market and the expected return of a theoretical risk-free asset.

The model was introduced by Jack Treynor (1961, 1962), William Sharpe (1964), John Lintner (1965a,b) and Jan Mossin (1966) independently, building on the earlier work of Harry Markowitz on diversification and modern portfolio theory.

a. Hull-White model
b. Capital asset pricing model
c. Cox-Ingersoll-Ross model
d. Random walk hypothesis

3. In probability theory and statistics, _________ indicates the strength and direction of a linear relationship between two random variables. That is in contrast with the usage of the term in colloquial speech, which denotes any relationship, not necessarily linear. In general statistical usage, _________ or co-relation refers to the departure of two random variables from independence.

a. Variance
b. Geometric mean
c. Probability distribution
d. Correlation

4. A _________ is a fungible, negotiable instrument representing financial value. They are broadly categorized into debt securities (such as banknotes, bonds and debentures), and equity securities; e.g., common stocks. The company or other entity issuing the _________ is called the issuer.

a. Securities lending
b. Tracking stock
c. Book entry
d. Security

5. In Modern Portfolio Theory, the _________ is the graphical representation of the Capital Asset Pricing Model. It displays the expected rate of return for an overall market as a function of systematic (non-diversifiable) risk (beta.)

The Y-Intercept (beta=0) of the _________ is equal to the risk-free interest rate.

a. Divestment
b. Certificate in Investment Performance Measurement
c. Security market line
d. Rebalancing

6. _________ is the study of how the variation (uncertainty) in the output of a mathematical model can be apportioned, qualitatively or quantitatively, to different sources of variation in the input of a model .

In more general terms uncertainty and sensitivity analyses investigate the robustness of a study when the study includes some form of mathematical modelling. While uncertainty analysis studies the overall uncertainty in the conclusions of the study, _________ tries to identify what source of uncertainty weights more on the study's conclusions.

a. Golden parachute
b. Proxy fight
c. Synthetic CDO
d. Sensitivity analysis

7. In business and accounting, _________s are everything of value that is owned by a person or company. The balance sheet of a firm records the monetary value of the _________s owned by the firm. The two major _________ classes are tangible _________s and intangible _________s.

a. EBITDA
b. Income
c. Accounts payable
d. Asset

8. In finance, _________ is the process of estimating the potential market value of a financial asset or liability. they can be done on assets (for example, investments in marketable securities such as stocks, options, business enterprises, or intangible assets such as patents and trademarks) or on liabilities (e.g., Bonds issued by a company.) _________s are required in many contexts including investment analysis, capital budgeting, merger and acquisition transactions, financial reporting, taxable events to determine the proper tax liability, and in litigation.

a. Procter ' Gamble
b. Share
c. Margin
d. Valuation

9. In finance, _________ occurs when a debtor has not met its legal obligations according to the debt contract, e.g. it has not made a scheduled payment, or has violated a loan covenant (condition) of the debt contract. _________ may occur if the debtor is either unwilling or unable to pay their debt. This can occur with all debt obligations including bonds, mortgages, loans, and promissory notes.

a. Credit crunch
b. Debt validation
c. Default
d. Vendor finance

10. _________ is the risk of loss due to a debtor's non-payment of a loan or other line of credit (either the principal or interest (coupon) or both)

Most lenders employ their own models (credit scorecards) to rank potential and existing customers according to risk, and then apply appropriate strategies. With products such as unsecured personal loans or mortgages, lenders charge a higher price for higher risk customers and vice versa. With revolving products such as credit cards and overdrafts, risk is controlled through careful setting of credit limits.

a. Liquidity risk
b. Transaction risk
c. Market risk
d. Credit risk

11. In finance, the _________ between two currencies specifies how much one currency is worth in terms of the other. For example an _________ of 102 Japanese yen to the United States dollar means that JPY 102 is worth the same as USD 1. The foreign exchange market is one of the largest markets in the world.

a. A Random Walk Down Wall Street
b. AAB
c. ABN Amro
d. Exchange rate

12. _________ is a form of risk that arises from the change in price of one currency against another. Whenever investors or companies have assets or business operations across national borders, they face _________ if their positions are not hedged.

- Transaction risk is the risk that exchange rates will change unfavourably over time. It can be hedged against using forward currency contracts;
- Translation risk is an accounting risk, proportional to the amount of assets held in foreign currencies. Changes in the exchange rate over time will render a report inaccurate, and so assets are usually balanced by borrowings in that currency.

The exchange risk associated with a foreign denominated instrument is a key element in foreign investment. This risk flows from differential monetary policy and growth in real productivity, which results in differential inflation rates.

a. Tracking error
b. Credit risk
c. Currency risk
d. Market risk

13. _________ is a type of risk faced by investors, corporations, and governments. It is a risk that can be understood and managed with proper aforethought and investment.

Broadly, _________ refers to the complications businesses and governments may face as a result of what are commonly referred to as political decisions--or 'any political change that alters the expected outcome and value of a given economic action by changing the probability of achieving business objectives.' .

a. Mid price
b. Single-index model
c. Capital asset
d. Political risk

14. _________ is the planning process used to determine whether a firm's long term investments such as new machinery, replacement machinery, new plants, new products, and research development projects are worth pursuing. It is budget for major capital, or investment, expenditures.

Many formal methods are used in _________, including the techniques such as

- Net present value
- Profitability index
- Internal rate of return
- Modified Internal Rate of Return
- Equivalent annuity

These methods use the incremental cash flows from each potential investment, or project. Techniques based on accounting earnings and accounting rules are sometimes used - though economists consider this to be improper - such as the accounting rate of return, and 'return on investment.' Simplified and hybrid methods are used as well, such as payback period and discounted payback period.

a. Capital budgeting
b. Financial distress
c. Shareholder value
d. Preferred stock

15. _________ in finance is a risk management technique, related to hedging, that mixes a wide variety of investments within a portfolio. Because the fluctuations of a single security have less impact on a diverse portfolio, _________ minimizes the risk from any one investment.

A simple example of _________ is the following: On a particular island the entire economy consists of two companies: one that sells umbrellas and another that sells sunscreen.

a. 529 plan
b. 4-4-5 Calendar
c. Diversification
d. 7-Eleven

16. _________ is a fee paid on borrowed assets. It is the price paid for the use of borrowed money , or, money earned by deposited funds . Assets that are sometimes lent with _________ include money, shares, consumer goods through hire purchase, major assets such as aircraft, and even entire factories in finance lease arrangements.

a. A Random Walk Down Wall Street
b. AAB
c. Interest
d. Insolvency

17. The phrase _________ refers to the aspect of corporate strategy, corporate finance and management dealing with the buying, selling and combining of different companies that can aid, finance, or help a growing company in a given industry grow rapidly without having to create another business entity.

An acquisition, also known as a takeover, is the buying of one company (the 'target') by another. An acquisition may be friendly or hostile.

a. 7-Eleven
b. 529 plan
c. Mergers and acquisitions
d. 4-4-5 Calendar

18. _________ is normally any risk associated with any form of financing.

Depending on the nature of the investment, the type of 'investment' risk will vary. High risk investments have greater potential rewards, but you may lose your money instead by taking the risk for more money.

a. Liquidating dividend
b. Stock market index option
c. Revaluation
d. Financial risk

19. An _________ is the price a borrower pays for the use of money they do not own, and the return a lender receives for deferring the use of funds, by lending it to the borrower. _________s are normally expressed as a percentage rate over the period of one year.

_________s targets are also a vital tool of monetary policy and are used to control variables like investment, inflation, and unemployment.

a. ABN Amro
b. AAB
c. Interest rate
d. A Random Walk Down Wall Street

20. _________ is the risk (variability in value) borne by an interest-bearing asset, such as a loan or a bond, due to variability of interest rates. In general, as rates rise, the price of a fixed rate bond will fall, and vice versa. _________ is commonly measured by the bond's duration.

a. Interest rate risk
b. International Fisher effect
c. A Random Walk Down Wall Street
d. Official bank rate

21. _________ is a measure of the ability of a debtor to pay their debts as and when they fall due. It is usually expressed as a ratio or a percentage of current liabilities.

For a corporation with a published balance sheet there are various ratios used to calculate a measure of liquidity.

a. Operating leverage
b. Accounting liquidity
c. Operating profit margin
d. Invested capital

22. _________ arises from situations in which a party interested in trading an asset cannot do it because nobody in the market wants to trade that asset. _________ becomes particularly important to parties who are about to hold or currently hold an asset, since it affects their ability to trade.

Manifestation of _________ is very different from a drop of price to zero.

a. Credit risk
b. Liquidity risk
c. Currency risk
d. Tracking error

23. _________ is the risk that the value of an investment will decrease due to moves in market factors. The five standard _________ factors are:

- Equity risk, the risk that stock prices will change.
- Interest rate risk, the risk that interest rates will change.
- Currency risk, the risk that foreign exchange rates will change.
- Commodity risk, the risk that commodity prices (e.g. grains, metals) will change.

As with other forms of risk, _________ may be measured in a number of ways. Traditionally, this is done using a Value at Risk methodology. Value at risk is well established as a risk management technique, but it contains a number of limiting assumptions that constrain its accuracy.

a. Transaction risk
b. Currency risk
c. Market risk
d. Tracking error

24. Procter is a surname, and may also refer to:

- Bryan Waller Procter (pseud. Barry Cornwall), English poet
- Goodwin Procter, American law firm
- _________, consumer products multinational

.

a. Bucket shop
b. Valuation
c. Clearing house
d. Procter ' Gamble

25. _________ is a step in a risk management process. _________ is the determination of quantitative or qualitative value of risk related to a concrete situation and a recognized threat (also called hazard.) Quantitative _________ requires calculations of two components of risk: R, the magnitude of the potential loss L, and the probability p that the loss will occur.

a. 4-4-5 Calendar
b. 529 plan
c. Risk assessment
d. 7-Eleven

26. In probability theory and statistics, a _________ identifies either the probability of each value of an unidentified random variable (when the variable is discrete), or the probability of the value falling within a particular interval (when the variable is continuous.) The _________ describes the range of possible values that a random variable can attain and the probability that the value of the random variable is within any (measurable) subset of that range. The Normal distribution, often called the 'bell curve'

When the random variable takes values in the set of real numbers, the _________ is completely described by the cumulative distribution function, whose value at each real x is the probability that the random variable is smaller than or equal to x.

a. Probability distribution
b. Standard deviation
c. P-value
d. Correlation

27. In probability and statistics, the _________ of a collection of numbers is a measure of the dispersion of the numbers from their expected (mean) value. It can apply to a probability distribution, a random variable, a population or a data set. The _________ is usually denoted with the letter σ (lowercase sigma.)

a. Sample size
b. Kurtosis
c. Standard deviation
d. Mean

28. _________ is a mathematical science pertaining to the collection, analysis, interpretation or explanation, and presentation of data. It also provides tools for prediction and forecasting based on data. It is applicable to a wide variety of academic disciplines, from the natural and social sciences to the humanities, government and business.

a. Statistics
b. Mean
c. Covariance
d. Sample size

29. _________ is a concept in economics, finance, and psychology related to the behaviour of consumers and investors under uncertainty. _________ is the reluctance of a person to accept a bargain with an uncertain payoff rather than another bargain with a more certain, but possibly lower, expected payoff.

The inverse of a person's _________ is sometimes called their risk tolerance

a. Risk aversion
b. Risk premium
c. Risk adjusted return on capital
d. Discount factor

30. In probability theory and statistics, the _________ is a normalized measure of dispersion of a probability distribution. It is defined as the ratio of the standard deviation > to the mean >:

>

This is only defined for non-zero mean, and is most useful for variables that are always positive. It is also known as unitized risk.

a. Sample size
b. Random variables
c. Harmonic mean
d. Coefficient of variation

31. The institution most often referenced by the word '_________' is a public or publicly traded _________, the shares of which are traded on a public stock exchange (e.g., the New York Stock Exchange or Nasdaq in the United States) where shares of stock of _________s are bought and sold by and to the general public. Most of the largest businesses in the world are publicly traded _________s. However, the majority of _________s are said to be closely held, privately held or close _________s, meaning that no ready market exists for the trading of shares.

a. Protect
b. Depository Trust Company
c. Federal Home Loan Mortgage Corporation
d. Corporation

32. In finance, _________ refers to the way a corporation finances its assets through some combination of equity, debt, or hybrid securities. A firm's _________ is then the composition or 'structure' of its liabilities. For example, a firm that sells $20 billion in equity and $80 billion in debt is said to be 20% equity-financed and 80% debt-financed.

a. Book building
b. Market for corporate control
c. Capital structure
d. Rights issue

33. In finance, _________ is that risk which is common to an entire market and not to any individual entity or component thereof. It should be distinguished from systemic risk which is the risk that the entire financial system will collapse as a result of some catastrophic event.

Risks can be reduced in four main ways: Avoidance, Reduction, Retention and Transfer.

a. Primary market
b. Capital surplus
c. Systematic risk
d. Conglomerate merger

34. In finance, a _________ is a type of bond that can be converted into shares of stock in the issuing company, usually at some pre-announced ratio. It is a hybrid security with debt- and equity-like features. Although it typically has a low coupon rate, the holder is compensated with the ability to convert the bond to common stock, usually at a substantial discount to the stock's market value.

a. Corporate bond
b. Convertible bond
c. Bond fund
d. Gilts

35. The _________, in terms of finance and investing, describes how the expected return of a stock or portfolio is correlated to the return of the financial market as a whole.

An asset with a beta of 0 means that its price is not at all correlated with the market; that asset is independent. A positive beta means that the asset generally follows the market.

a. Perpetuity
b. Current yield
c. LIBOR market model
d. Beta coefficient

36.

In finance, the _________ can be the expected rate of return above the risk-free interest rate. When measuring risk, a common sense approach is to compare the risk-free return on T-bills and the very risky return on other investments. The difference between these two returns can be interpreted as a measure of the excess return on the average risky asset. This excess return is known as the _________.

a. Risk aversion
b. Risk modeling
c. Risk premium
d. Risk adjusted return on capital

37. _________ mature in one year or less. Like zero-coupon bonds, they do not pay interest prior to maturity; instead they are sold at a discount of the par value to create a positive yield to maturity. Many regard _________ as the least risky investment available to U.S. investors.

a. Treasury Inflation Protected Securities
b. Treasury securities
c. Treasury bills
d. 4-4-5 Calendar

38. A _________ is a bond issued by a corporation. The term is usually applied to longer-term debt instruments, generally with a maturity date falling at least a year after their issue date. (The term 'commercial paper' is sometimes used for instruments with a shorter maturity.)

a. Serial bond
b. Brady bonds
c. Government bond
d. Corporate bond

39. In economic models, the _________ time frame assumes no fixed factors of production. Firms can enter or leave the marketplace, and the cost (and availability) of land, labor, raw materials, and capital goods can be assumed to vary. In contrast, in the short-run time frame, certain factors are assumed to be fixed, because there is not sufficient time for them to change.

a. Short-run
b. 529 plan
c. Long-run
d. 4-4-5 Calendar

40. In finance, a _________ is a debt security, in which the authorized issuer owes the holders a debt and, depending on the terms of the _________, is obliged to pay interest (the coupon) and/or to repay the principal at a later date, termed maturity.

Thus a _________ is a loan: the issuer is the borrower, the _________ holder is the lender, and the coupon is the interest. _________s provide the borrower with external funds to finance long-term investments, or, in the case of government _________s, to finance current expenditure.

a. Puttable bond
b. Catastrophe bonds
c. Convertible bond
d. Bond

41. In economics, _________ is a rise in the general level of prices of goods and services in an economy over a period of time. The term '_________' once referred to increases in the money supply (monetary _________); however, economic debates about the relationship between money supply and price levels have led to its primary use today in describing price _________. _________ can also be described as a decline in the real value of money--a loss of purchasing power in the medium of exchange which is also the monetary unit of account.

a. A Random Walk Down Wall Street
b. AAB
c. Inflation
d. ABN Amro

42. In finance, _________, also known as return on investment is the ratio of money gained or lost on an investment relative to the amount of money invested. The amount of money gained or lost may be referred to as interest, profit/loss, gain/loss, or net income/loss. The money invested may be referred to as the asset, capital, principal, or the cost basis of the investment.

a. Composiition of Creditors
b. Doctrine of the Proper Law
c. Stock or scrip dividends
d. Rate of return

43. The _________ is the weighted-average most likely outcome in gambling, probability theory, economics or finance.

In gambling and probability theory, there is usually a discrete set of possible outcomes. In this case, _________ is a measure of the relative balance of win or loss weighted by their chances of occurring.

a. A Random Walk Down Wall Street
b. AAB
c. ABN Amro
d. Expected return

44. In business and finance, a _________ (also referred to as equity _________) of stock means a _________ of ownership in a corporation (company.) In the plural, stocks is often used as a synonym for _________s especially in the United States, but it is less commonly used that way outside of North America.

In the United Kingdom, South Africa, and Australia, stock can also refer to completely different financial instruments such as government bonds or, less commonly, to all kinds of marketable securities.

a. Procter ' Gamble
b. Bucket shop
c. Margin
d. Share

45. A _________ is the price of a single share of a no. of saleable stocks of the company. Once the stock is purchased, the owner becomes a shareholder of the company that issued the share.

a. Stock split
b. Whisper numbers
c. Trading curb
d. Share price

1. In finance, a _________ is a debt security, in which the authorized issuer owes the holders a debt and, depending on the terms of the _________, is obliged to pay interest (the coupon) and/or to repay the principal at a later date, termed maturity.

Thus a _________ is a loan: the issuer is the borrower, the _________ holder is the lender, and the coupon is the interest. _________s provide the borrower with external funds to finance long-term investments, or, in the case of government _________s, to finance current expenditure.

a. Catastrophe bonds
b. Convertible bond
c. Puttable bond
d. Bond

2. _________ is a fee paid on borrowed assets. It is the price paid for the use of borrowed money , or, money earned by deposited funds . Assets that are sometimes lent with _________ include money, shares, consumer goods through hire purchase, major assets such as aircraft, and even entire factories in finance lease arrangements.

a. Insolvency
b. A Random Walk Down Wall Street
c. AAB
d. Interest

3. An _________ is the price a borrower pays for the use of money they do not own, and the return a lender receives for deferring the use of funds, by lending it to the borrower. _________s are normally expressed as a percentage rate over the period of one year.

_________s targets are also a vital tool of monetary policy and are used to control variables like investment, inflation, and unemployment.

a. Interest rate
b. A Random Walk Down Wall Street
c. ABN Amro
d. AAB

4. _________ is the process of decreasing an amount over a period of time. The word comes from Middle English amortisen to kill, alienate in mortmain, from Anglo-French amorteser, alteration of amortir, from Vulgar Latin admortire to kill, from Latin ad- + mort-, mors death. Particular instances of the term include:

- _________ (business), the allocation of a lump sum amount to different time periods, particularly for loans and other forms of finance, including related interest or other finance charges.
  - _________ schedule, a table detailing each periodic payment on a loan (typically a mortgage), as generated by an _________ calculator.
  - Negative _________, an _________ schedule where the loan amount actually increases through not paying the full interest
- Amortized analysis, analyzing the execution cost of algorithms over a sequence of operations.
- _________ of capital expenditures of certain assets under accounting rules, particularly intangible assets, in a manner analogous to depreciation.
- _________ (tax law)

_________ is also used in the context of zoning regulations and describes the time in which a property owner has to relocate when the property's use constitutes a preexisting nonconforming use under zoning regulations.

- Depreciation

.

a. Intrinsic value
b. Option
c. AT'T Inc.
d. Amortization

5. An _________ is a table detailing each periodic payment on a amortizing loan (typically a mortgage), as generated by an amortization calculator.

While a portion of every payment is applied towards both the interest and the principal balance of the loan, the exact amount applied to principal each time varies (with the remainder going to interest.) An _________ reveals the specific monetary amount put towards interest, as well as the specific put towards the Principal balance, with each payment.

a. Adjusting entries
b. Adjusted basis
c. Annual report
d. Amortization schedule

6. _________ is the provision of resources (such as granting a loan) by one party to another party where that second party does not reimburse the first party immediately, thereby generating a debt, and instead arranges either to repay or return those resources (or material(s) of equal value) at a later date. The first party is called a creditor, also known as a lender, while the second party is called a debtor, also known as a borrower.

Movements of financial capital are normally dependent on either _________ or equity transfers.

a. Clearing house
b. Warrant
c. Comparable
d. Credit

7. _________ is a measure of the ability of a debtor to pay their debts as and when they fall due. It is usually expressed as a ratio or a percentage of current liabilities.

For a corporation with a published balance sheet there are various ratios used to calculate a measure of liquidity.

a. Operating profit margin
b. Accounting liquidity
c. Operating leverage
d. Invested capital

8. John Maynard Keynes developed the _________ of Interest in the General Theory of Employment Interest and Money. The primary consideration of the _________ is the demand for money as an asset, as a means for holding wealth. Interest rates, he argues, cannot be a reward for savings as such because, if a person hoards his savings in cash, keeping it under his mattress say, he will receive no interest, although he has nevertheless, refrained from consuming all his current income.

a. 4-4-5 Calendar
b. Liquidity preference
c. 7-Eleven
d. 529 plan

9. _________ is a term applied in many countries to a reference interest rate used by banks. The term originally indicated the rate of interest at which banks lent to favored customers, i.e., those with high credibility, though this is no longer always the case. Some variable interest rates may be expressed as a percentage above or below _________.

a. Time deposit
b. Reserve requirement
c. Credit bureau
d. Prime rate

10. In financial accounting, the term _________ is most commonly used to describe any part of shareholders' equity, except for basic share capital. Sometimes, the term is used instead of the term provision; such a use, however, is inconsistent with the terminology suggested by International Accounting Standards Board. For more information about provisions, see provision (accounting.)

a. Treasury stock
b. Reserve
c. Closing entries
d. FIFO and LIFO accounting

11. _________ is an economic model based on price, utility and quantity in a market. It predicts that in a competitive market, price will function to equalize the quantity demanded by consumers, and the quantity supplied by producers, resulting in an economic equilibrium of price and quantity. Similarly, an increase in the number of workers tends to result in lower wages and vice-versa.

a. Rural credit cooperatives
b. Loan participation
c. Price channel
d. Supply and demand

12. In economics, _________ is a rise in the general level of prices of goods and services in an economy over a period of time. The term '_________' once referred to increases in the money supply (monetary _________); however, economic debates about the relationship between money supply and price levels have led to its primary use today in describing price _________. _________ can also be described as a decline in the real value of money--a loss of purchasing power in the medium of exchange which is also the monetary unit of account.

a. A Random Walk Down Wall Street
b. AAB
c. Inflation
d. ABN Amro

13. _________ mature in one year or less. Like zero-coupon bonds, they do not pay interest prior to maturity; instead they are sold at a discount of the par value to create a positive yield to maturity. Many regard _________ as the least risky investment available to U.S. investors.

a. 4-4-5 Calendar
b. Treasury Inflation Protected Securities
c. Treasury bills
d. Treasury securities

14. The _________, interest yield, income yield, flat yield or running yield is a financial term used in reference to bonds and other fixed-interest securities such as gilts. It is the ratio of the annual interest payment and the bond's current price.

The _________ only therefore refers to the yield of the bond at the current moment. It does not reflect the total return over the life of the bond. In particular, it takes no account of reinvestment risk (the uncertainty about the rate at which future cashflows can be reinvested) or the fact that bonds usually mature at par value, which can be an important component of a bond's return.

a. Current yield
b. Perpetuity
c. Modified Internal Rate of Return
d. Stochastic volatility

15. In finance, the yield curve is the relation between the interest rate (or cost of borrowing) and the time to maturity of the debt for a given borrower in a given currency. For example, the current U.S. dollar interest rates paid on U.S. Treasury securities for various maturities are closely watched by many traders, and are commonly plotted on a graph such as the one on the right which is informally called 'the yield curve.' More formal mathematical descriptions of this relation are often called the _________.

The yield of a debt instrument is the annualized percentage increase in the value of the investment.

a. 529 plan
b. Term structure of interest rates
c. 4-4-5 Calendar
d. 7-Eleven

16. In finance, the term _________ describes the amount in cash that returns to the owners of a security. Normally it does not include the price variations, at the difference of the total return. _________ applies to various stated rates of return on stocks (common and preferred, and convertible), fixed income instruments (bonds, notes, bills, strips, zero coupon), and some other investment type insurance products (e.g. annuities.)

a. Macaulay duration
b. 4-4-5 Calendar
c. Yield to maturity
d. Yield

17. In finance, the _________ is the relation between the interest rate (or cost of borrowing) and the time to maturity of the debt for a given borrower in a given currency. For example, the current U.S. dollar interest rates paid on U.S. Treasury securities for various maturities are closely watched by many traders, and are commonly plotted on a graph such as the one on the right which is informally called 'the _________.' More formal mathematical descriptions of this relation are often called the term structure of interest rates.

The yield of a debt instrument is the annualized percentage increase in the value of the investment.

a. 4-4-5 Calendar
b. 7-Eleven
c. Yield curve
d. 529 plan

18. The _________ or redemption yield is the yield promised to the bondholder on the assumption that the bond or other fixed-interest security such as gilts will be held to maturity, that all coupon and principal payments will be made and coupon payments are reinvested at the bond's promised yield at the same rate as invested. It is a measure of the return of the bond. This technique in theory allows investors to calculate the fair value of different financial instruments.

a. Macaulay duration
b. 4-4-5 Calendar
c. Yield
d. Yield to maturity

19. _________ is a life of security. It may also refer to the final payment date of a loan or other financial instrument, at which point all remaining interest and principal is due to be paid.

1, 3, 6 months _________ band can be calculated by using 30-day per month periods.

a. Replacement cost
b. False billing
c. Primary market
d. Maturity

20. _________ are government bonds issued by the United States Department of the Treasury through the Bureau of the Public Debt. They are the debt financing instruments of the U.S. Federal government, and they are often referred to simply as Treasuries or Treasurys. There are four types of marketable _________: Treasury bills, Treasury notes, Treasury bonds, and Treasury Inflation Protected Securities (TIPS.)

a. Treasury Inflation Protected Securities
b. 4-4-5 Calendar
c. Treasury Inflation-Protected Securities
d. Treasury securities

21. A _________ is a fungible, negotiable instrument representing financial value. They are broadly categorized into debt securities (such as banknotes, bonds and debentures), and equity securities; e.g., common stocks. The company or other entity issuing the _________ is called the issuer.

a. Tracking stock
b. Book entry
c. Securities lending
d. Security

22.

In finance, the _________ can be the expected rate of return above the risk-free interest rate. When measuring risk, a common sense approach is to compare the risk-free return on T-bills and the very risky return on other investments. The difference between these two returns can be interpreted as a measure of the excess return on the average risky asset. This excess return is known as the _________.

a. Risk adjusted return on capital
b. Risk premium
c. Risk aversion
d. Risk modeling

23. In finance, _________ occurs when a debtor has not met its legal obligations according to the debt contract, e.g. it has not made a scheduled payment, or has violated a loan covenant (condition) of the debt contract. _________ may occur if the debtor is either unwilling or unable to pay their debt. This can occur with all debt obligations including bonds, mortgages, loans, and promissory notes.

a. Debt validation
b. Credit crunch
c. Vendor finance
d. Default

24. _________ is the risk of loss due to a debtor's non-payment of a loan or other line of credit (either the principal or interest (coupon) or both)

Most lenders employ their own models (credit scorecards) to rank potential and existing customers according to risk, and then apply appropriate strategies. With products such as unsecured personal loans or mortgages, lenders charge a higher price for higher risk customers and vice versa. With revolving products such as credit cards and overdrafts, risk is controlled through careful setting of credit limits.

a. Transaction risk
b. Market risk
c. Credit risk
d. Liquidity risk

25. In financial accounting, _________s are precautions for which the amount or probability of occurrence are not known. Typical examples are _________s for warranty costs and _________ for taxes the term reserve is used instead of term _________; such a use, however, is inconsistent with the terminology suggested by International Accounting Standards Board.

a. Momentum Accounting and Triple-Entry Bookkeeping
b. Petty cash
c. Money measurement concept
d. Provision

26. _________ (also trust indenture or deed of trust) is a legal document issued to lenders and describes key terms such as the interest rate, maturity date, convertibility, pledge, promises, representations, covenants, and other terms of the bond offering. When the Offering Memorandum is prepared in advance of marketing a Bond, the indenture will typically be summarised in the 'Description of Notes' section.

a. Court of Audit of Belgium
b. Bond indenture
c. Fair Labor Standards Act
d. McFadden Act

27. A _________ is a bond issued by a corporation. The term is usually applied to longer-term debt instruments, generally with a maturity date falling at least a year after their issue date. (The term 'commercial paper' is sometimes used for instruments with a shorter maturity.)

a. Government bond
b. Serial bond
c. Brady bonds
d. Corporate bond

28. The coupon or _________ of a bond is the amount of interest paid per year expressed as a percentage of the face value of the bond.

For example if you hold $10,000 nominal of a bond described as a 4.5% loan stock, you will receive $450 in interest each year (probably in two installments of $225 each.)

Not all bonds have coupons.

a. Zero-coupon bond
b. Puttable bond
c. Revenue bonds
d. Coupon rate

29. _________ is a financial transaction whereby a business sells its accounts receivable (i.e., invoices) at a discount. _________ differs from a bank loan in three main ways. First, the emphasis is on the value of the receivables (essentially a financial asset), not the firm's credit worthiness.

a. Debt-for-equity swap
b. Credit card balance transfer
c. Financial Literacy Month
d. Factoring

30. _________ is the standard framework of guidelines for financial accounting used in the United States of America. It includes the standards, conventions, and rules accountants follow in recording and summarizing transactions, and in the preparation of financial statements. _________ are now issued by the Financial Accounting Standards Board (FASB).

a. Generally accepted accounting principles
b. Revenue
c. Depreciation
d. Net income

31. A _________ is a property interest created by agreement or by operation of law over assets to secure the performance of an obligation, usually the payment of a debt. It gives the beneficiary of the _________ certain preferential rights in the disposition of secured assets. Such rights vary according to the type of _________, but in most cases, a holder of the _________ is entitled to seize, and usually sell, the property to discharge the debt that the _________ secures.

a. Security interest
b. Netting
c. FIDC
d. Retention ratio

32. _________, in bookkeeping, refers to assets, liabilities, income, and expenses recorded on individual pages of the so called book of final entry or ledger. Changes in _________ value are made by chronologically posting debit (DR) and credit (CR) entries to its page. Examples of _________s are cash, _________s receivable, mortgages, loans, land and buildings, common stock, sales, services provided, wages, and payroll overhead.

a. Option
b. Account
c. Accretion
d. Alpha

33. _________ is one of a series of accounting transactions dealing with the billing of customers who owe money to a person, company or organization for goods and services that have been provided to the customer. In most business entities this is typically done by generating an invoice and mailing or electronically delivering it to the customer, who in turn must pay it within an established timeframe called credit or payment terms.

An example of a common payment term is Net 30, meaning payment is due in the amount of the invoice 30 days from the date of invoice.

a. Accounting methods
b. Income
c. Impaired asset
d. Accounts receivable

34. A _________, in its most general sense, is a solemn promise to engage in or refrain from a specified action.

More specifically, a _________, in contrast to a contract, is a one-way agreement whereby the _________er is the only party bound by the promise. A _________ may have conditions and prerequisites that qualify the undertaking, including the actions of second or third parties, but there is no inherent agreement by such other parties to fulfill those requirements.

a. Federal Trade Commission Act
b. Partnership
c. Clayton Antitrust Act
d. Covenant

35. _________ is that which is owed; usually referencing assets owed, but the term can cover other obligations. In the case of assets, _________ is a means of using future purchasing power in the present before a summation has been earned. Some companies and corporations use _________ as a part of their overall corporate finance strategy.

a. Debt
b. Partial Payment
c. Cross-collateralization
d. Credit cycle

36. In economics, business, and accounting, a _________ is the value of money that has been used up to produce something, and hence is not available for use anymore. In business, the _________ may be one of acquisition, in which case the amount of money expended to acquire it is counted as _________. In this case, money is the input that is gone in order to acquire the thing.

a. Sliding scale fees
b. Marginal cost
c. Cost
d. Fixed costs

37. _________ or financing is to provide capital (funds), which means money for a project, a person, a business or any other private or public institutions.

Those funds can be allocated for either short term or long term purposes. The health fund is a new way of _________ private healthcare centers.

a. Proxy fight
b. Synthetic CDO
c. Product life cycle
d. Funding

38. In finance, a _________ is a type of bond that can be converted into shares of stock in the issuing company, usually at some pre-announced ratio. It is a hybrid security with debt- and equity-like features. Although it typically has a low coupon rate, the holder is compensated with the ability to convert the bond to common stock, usually at a substantial discount to the stock's market value.

a. Bond fund
b. Convertible bond
c. Corporate bond
d. Gilts

39. In finance, a _________ is a security that entitles the holder to buy stock of the company that issued it at a specified price, which is usually higher than the stock price at time of issue.

_________s are frequently attached to bonds or preferred stock as a sweetener, allowing the issuer to pay lower interest rates or dividends. They can be used to enhance the yield of the bond, and make them more attractive to potential buyers.

a. Credit
b. Clearing
c. Warrant
d. Clearing house

40. The _________ is a stock exchange based in New York City, New York. It is the largest stock exchange in the world by dollar value of its listed companies securities. As of October 2008, the combined capitalization of all domestic _________ listed companies was $10.1 trillion.

a. 4-4-5 Calendar
b. 7-Eleven
c. 529 plan
d. New York Stock Exchange

41. _________, in finance and accounting, means stated value or face value. From this comes the expressions at par (at the _________), over par (over _________) and under par (under _________.)

The term '_________' has several meanings depending on context and geography.

a. Sinking fund
b. Par value
c. FIDC
d. Global Squeeze

42. A _________, securities exchange or (in Europe) bourse is a corporation or mutual organization which provides 'trading' facilities for stock brokers and traders, to trade stocks and other securities. _________s also provide facilities for the issue and redemption of securities as well as other financial instruments and capital events including the payment of income and dividends. The securities traded on a _________ include: shares issued by companies, unit trusts and other pooled investment products and bonds.

a. 529 plan
b. 4-4-5 Calendar
c. 7-Eleven
d. Stock Exchange

43. In lending agreements, _________ is a borrower's pledge of specific property to a lender, to secure repayment of a loan. The _________ serves as protection for a lender against a borrower's risk of default - that is, a borrower failing to pay the principal and interest under the terms of a loan obligation. If a borrower does default on a loan (due to insolvency or other event), that borrower forfeits (gives up) the property pledged as _________ *ollateral* - and the lender then becomes the owner of the _________.

a. Refinancing risk
b. Future-oriented
c. Nominal value
d. Collateral

44. A _________ is defined as a certificate of agreement of loans which is given under the company's stamp and carries an undertaking that the _________ holder will get a fixed return (fixed on the basis of interest rates) and the principal amount whenever the _________ matures.

In finance, a _________ is a long-term debt instrument used by governments and large companies to obtain funds. It is defined as 'a debt secured only by the debtor's earning power, not by a lien on any specific asset.' It is similar to a bond except the securitization conditions are different.

a. Partial Payment
b. Collection agency
c. Collateral Management
d. Debenture

45. An _________ is a financial security used in aircraft finance, most commonly to take advantage of tax benefits in North America.

In a typical _________ transaction, a 'trust certificate' is sold to investors in order to finance the purchase of an aircraft by a trust managed on the investors' behalf. The trust then leases the aircraft to an airline, and the trustee routes payments through the trust to the investors.

a. A Random Walk Down Wall Street
b. ABN Amro
c. Equipment trust certificate
d. AAB

46. _________, refers to consumption opportunity gained by an entity within a specified time frame, which is generally expressed in monetary terms. However, for households and individuals, '_________ is the sum of all the wages, salaries, profits, interests payments, rents and other forms of earnings received... in a given period of time.' For firms, _________ generally refers to net-profit: what remains of revenue after expenses have been subtracted.

a. Accrual
b. OIBDA
c. Annual report
d. Income

47. In finance, a _________ (non-investment grade bond, speculative grade bond or junk bond) is a bond that is rated below investment grade at the time of purchase. These bonds have a higher risk of default or other adverse credit events, but typically pay higher yields than better quality bonds in order to make them attractive to investors.

a. Volatility
b. Sharpe ratio
c. High yield bond
d. Private equity

48. _________ is a combination of straight bond and embedded put option. The holder of the _________ has the right, but not the obligation, to demand early repayment of the principal. The put option is usually exercisable on specified dates.

a. Convertible bond
b. Puttable bond
c. Brady bonds
d. Callable bond

49. A _________ is a bond bought at a price lower than its face value, with the face value repaid at the time of maturity. It does not make periodic interest payments, or have so-called 'coupons,' hence the term _________. Investors earn return from the compounded interest all paid at maturity plus the difference between the discounted price of the bond and its par value.

a. Zero-coupon bond
b. Clean price
c. Bond fund
d. Corporate bond

50. A _________ is an international bond that is denominated in a currency not native to the country where it is issued. It can be categorised according to the currency in which it is issued. London is one of the centers of the _________ market, but _________s may be traded throughout the world - for example in Singapore or Tokyo.

a. Interest rate option
b. Economic entity
c. Eurobond
d. Education production function

51. _________ is the process of determining the fair price of a bond. As with any security or capital investment, the fair value of a bond is the present value of the stream of cash flows it is expected to generate. Hence, the price or value of a bond is determined by discounting the bond's expected cash flows to the present using the appropriate discount rate.

a. Bond fund
b. Collateralized debt obligations
c. Bond valuation
d. Catastrophe bonds

52. _________ is the planning process used to determine whether a firm's long term investments such as new machinery, replacement machinery, new plants, new products, and research development projects are worth pursuing. It is budget for major capital, or investment, expenditures.

Many formal methods are used in _________, including the techniques such as

- Net present value
- Profitability index
- Internal rate of return
- Modified Internal Rate of Return
- Equivalent annuity

These methods use the incremental cash flows from each potential investment, or project. Techniques based on accounting earnings and accounting rules are sometimes used - though economists consider this to be improper - such as the accounting rate of return, and 'return on investment.' Simplified and hybrid methods are used as well, such as payback period and discounted payback period.

a. Preferred stock
b. Shareholder value
c. Financial distress
d. Capital budgeting

53. _________ is the balance of the amounts of cash being received and paid by a business during a defined period of time, sometimes tied to a specific project. Measurement of _________ can be used

- to evaluate the state or performance of a business or project.
- to determine problems with liquidity. Being profitable does not necessarily mean being liquid. A company can fail because of a shortage of cash, even while profitable.
- to generate project rate of returns. The time of _________s into and out of projects are used as inputs to financial models such as internal rate of return, and net present value.
- to examine income or growth of a business when it is believed that accrual accounting concepts do not represent economic realities. Alternately, _________ can be used to 'validate' the net income generated by accrual accounting.

_________ as a generic term may be used differently depending on context, and certain _________ definitions may be adapted by analysts and users for their own uses. Common terms include operating _________ and free _________.

_________s can be classified into:

1. Operational _________s: Cash received or expended as a result of the company's core business activities.
2. Investment _________s: Cash received or expended through capital expenditure, investments or acquisitions.
3. Financing _________s: Cash received or expended as a result of financial activities, such as interests and dividends.

All three together - the net _________ - are necessary to reconcile the beginning cash balance to the ending cash balance. Loan draw downs or equity injections, that is just shifting of capital but no expenditure as such, are not considered in the net _________.

a. Shareholder value
b. Real option
c. Corporate finance
d. Cash flow

54. A '_________' is a 'Charge' that is paid to obtain the right to delay a payment. Essentially, the payer purchases the right to make a given payment in the future instead of in the Present. The '_________', or 'Charge' that must be paid to delay the payment, is simply the difference between what the payment amount would be if it were paid in the present and what the payment amount would be paid if it were paid in the future.

a. Risk modeling
b. Discount
c. Risk aversion
d. Value at risk

55. In financial accounting, a _________ or statement of cash flows is a financial statement that shows a company's flow of cash. The money coming into the business is called cash inflow, and money going out from the business is called cash outflow. The statement shows how changes in balance sheet and income accounts affect cash and cash equivalents, and breaks the analysis down to operating, investing, and financing activities.

a. 4-4-5 Calendar
b. 7-Eleven
c. Cash flow statement
d. 529 plan

56. The phrase _________ refers to the aspect of corporate strategy, corporate finance and management dealing with the buying, selling and combining of different companies that can aid, finance, or help a growing company in a given industry grow rapidly without having to create another business entity.

An acquisition, also known as a takeover, is the buying of one company (the 'target') by another. An acquisition may be friendly or hostile.

a. 529 plan
b. 7-Eleven
c. 4-4-5 Calendar
d. Mergers and acquisitions

57. In business and accounting, _________s are everything of value that is owned by a person or company. The balance sheet of a firm records the monetary value of the _________s owned by the firm. The two major _________ classes are tangible _________s and intangible _________s.

a. Income
b. EBITDA
c. Asset
d. Accounts payable

58. _________ is a form of corporation equity ownership represented in the securities. It is dangerous in comparison to preferred shares and some other investment options, in that in the event of bankruptcy, _________ investors receive their funds after preferred stockholders, bondholders, creditors, etc. On the other hand, common shares on average perform better than preferred shares or bonds over time.

a. Stock split
b. Stop-limit order
c. Stock market bubble
d. Common stock

59. In probability theory and statistics, _________ indicates the strength and direction of a linear relationship between two random variables. That is in contrast with the usage of the term in colloquial speech, which denotes any relationship, not necessarily linear. In general statistical usage, _________ or co-relation refers to the departure of two random variables from independence.

a. Variance
b. Probability distribution
c. Geometric mean
d. Correlation

60. In finance, _________ is the process of estimating the potential market value of a financial asset or liability. they can be done on assets (for example, investments in marketable securities such as stocks, options, business enterprises, or intangible assets such as patents and trademarks) or on liabilities (e.g., Bonds issued by a company.) _________s are required in many contexts including investment analysis, capital budgeting, merger and acquisition transactions, financial reporting, taxable events to determine the proper tax liability, and in litigation.

a. Share
b. Margin
c. Procter ' Gamble
d. Valuation

61. The term _________ has three unrelated technical definitions, and is also used in a variety of non-technical ways.

- In financial economics, it refers to any asset used to make money, as opposed to assets used for personal enjoyment or consumption. This is an important distinction because two people can disagree sharply about the value of personal assets, one person might think a sports car is more valuable than a pickup truck, another person might have the opposite taste. But if an asset is held for the purpose of making money, taste has nothing to do with it, only differences of opinion about how much money the asset will produce. With the further assumption that people agree on the probability distribution of future cash flows, it is possible to have an objective _________ pricing model. Even without the assumption of agreement, it is possible to set rational limits on _________ value.
- In governmental accounting, it is defined as any asset used in operations with an initial useful life extending beyond one reporting period. Generally, government managers have a 'stewardship' duty to maintain _________s under their control. See International Public Sector Accounting Standards for details.
- In US tax accounting, it is defined as any property other than a list of exceptions. The main exceptions are anything held for sale, and any real estate or depreciable property used in business. Almost everything you own and use for personal purposes, pleasure or investment is a _________. If something is a _________ for tax purposes, gains or losses on sale or disposition are capital gains or capital losses. For individuals, however, capital losses on property held for personal use are generally not deductible. See the IRS publication Tax Facts about Capital Gains and Losses for details.

A well-known financial accounting textbook advises that the term be avoided except in tax accounting because it is used in so many different senses, not all of them well-defined. For example it is often used as a synonym for fixed assets or for investments in securities.

A common non-technical usage occurs when people ask that employees or the environment or something else be treated as a _________.

a. Solvency
b. Settlement date
c. Political risk
d. Capital asset

62. In finance, the _________ is used to determine a theoretically appropriate required rate of return of an asset, if that asset is to be added to an already well-diversified portfolio, given that asset's non-diversifiable risk. The model takes into account the asset's sensitivity to non-diversifiable risk (also known as systemic risk or market risk), often represented by the quantity beta (β) in the financial industry, as well as the expected return of the market and the expected return of a theoretical risk-free asset.

The model was introduced by Jack Treynor (1961, 1962), William Sharpe (1964), John Lintner (1965a,b) and Jan Mossin (1966) independently, building on the earlier work of Harry Markowitz on diversification and modern portfolio theory.

a. Cox-Ingersoll-Ross model
b. Hull-White model
c. Capital asset pricing model
d. Random walk hypothesis

63. In finance, the _________ between two currencies specifies how much one currency is worth in terms of the other. For example an _________ of 102 Japanese yen to the United States dollar means that JPY 102 is worth the same as USD 1. The foreign exchange market is one of the largest markets in the world.

a. AAB
b. Exchange rate
c. ABN Amro
d. A Random Walk Down Wall Street

64. _________ is a form of risk that arises from the change in price of one currency against another. Whenever investors or companies have assets or business operations across national borders, they face _________ if their positions are not hedged.

- Transaction risk is the risk that exchange rates will change unfavourably over time. It can be hedged against using forward currency contracts;
- Translation risk is an accounting risk, proportional to the amount of assets held in foreign currencies. Changes in the exchange rate over time will render a report inaccurate, and so assets are usually balanced by borrowings in that currency.

The exchange risk associated with a foreign denominated instrument is a key element in foreign investment. This risk flows from differential monetary policy and growth in real productivity, which results in differential inflation rates.

a. Credit risk
b. Currency risk
c. Tracking error
d. Market risk

65. _________ is a type of risk faced by investors, corporations, and governments. It is a risk that can be understood and managed with proper aforethought and investment.

Broadly, _________ refers to the complications businesses and governments may face as a result of what are commonly referred to as political decisions--or 'any political change that alters the expected outcome and value of a given economic action by changing the probability of achieving business objectives.' .

a. Single-index model
b. Mid price
c. Capital asset
d. Political risk

66. An _________ is a contract written by a seller that conveys to the buyer the right -- but not the obligation -- to buy (in the case of a call _________) or to sell (in the case of a put _________) a particular asset, such as a piece of property such as, among others, a futures contract. In return for granting the _________, the seller collects a payment (the premium) from the buyer.

For example, buying a call _________ provides the right to buy a specified quantity of a security at a set strike price at some time on or before expiration, while buying a put _________ provides the right to sell.

a. Amortization
b. Annuity
c. AT'T Mobility LLC
d. Option

67. _________ is the risk (variability in value) borne by an interest-bearing asset, such as a loan or a bond, due to variability of interest rates. In general, as rates rise, the price of a fixed rate bond will fall, and vice versa. _________ is commonly measured by the bond's duration.

a. Interest rate risk
b. International Fisher effect
c. A Random Walk Down Wall Street
d. Official bank rate

68. The _________ is an interest rate a central bank charges depository institutions that borrow reserves from it.

The term _________ has two meanings:

- the same as interest rate; the term 'discount' does not refer to the meaning of the word, but to the purpose of using the quantity, such as computations of present value, e.g. net present value / discounted cash flow

- the annual effective _________, which is the annual interest divided by the capital including that interest; this rate is lower than the interest rate; it corresponds to using the value after a year as the nominal value, and seeing the initial value as the nominal value minus a discount; it is used for Treasury Bills and similar financial instruments

The annual effective _________ is the annual interest divided by the capital including that interest, which is the interest rate divided by 100% plus the interest rate. It is the annual discount factor to be applied to the future cash flow, to find the discount, subtracted from a future value to find the value one year earlier.

For example, suppose there is a government bond that sells for $95 and pays $100 in a year's time.

a. Black-Scholes
b. Discount rate
c. Fisher equation
d. Stochastic volatility

1. _________ is a form of corporation equity ownership represented in the securities. It is dangerous in comparison to preferred shares and some other investment options, in that in the event of bankruptcy, _________ investors receive their funds after preferred stockholders, bondholders, creditors, etc. On the other hand, common shares on average perform better than preferred shares or bonds over time.

a. Stock split
b. Stock market bubble
c. Stop-limit order
d. Common stock

2. _________ is an estimate of the fair value of corporations and their stocks, by using fundamental economic criteria. This theoretical valuation has to be perfected with market criteria, as the final purpose is to determine potential market prices.

a. 4-4-5 Calendar
b. Security Analysis
c. Stock valuation
d. Growth stocks

3. _________ is a type of private equity capital typically provided to early-stage, high-potential, growth companies in the interest of generating a return through an eventual realization event such as an IPO or trade sale of the company. _________ investments are generally made as cash in exchange for shares in the invested company. It is typical for _________ investors to identify and back companies in high technology industries such as biotechnology and ICT.

a. Venture capital
b. Tail risk
c. Treasury Inflation-Protected Securities
d. Probability distribution

4. _________ is that which is owed; usually referencing assets owed, but the term can cover other obligations. In the case of assets, _________ is a means of using future purchasing power in the present before a summation has been earned. Some companies and corporations use _________ as a part of their overall corporate finance strategy.

a. Debt
b. Partial Payment
c. Credit cycle
d. Cross-collateralization

5. In finance, _________ is the process of estimating the potential market value of a financial asset or liability. they can be done on assets (for example, investments in marketable securities such as stocks, options, business enterprises, or intangible assets such as patents and trademarks) or on liabilities (e.g., Bonds issued by a company.) _________s are required in many contexts including investment analysis, capital budgeting, merger and acquisition transactions, financial reporting, taxable events to determine the proper tax liability, and in litigation.

a. Procter ' Gamble
b. Margin
c. Share
d. Valuation

6. The _________ of a stock is a measure of the price paid for a share relative to the annual income or profit earned by the firm per share. It is a financial ratio used for valuation: a higher _________ means that investors are paying more for each unit of income, so the stock is more expensive compared to one with lower _________.

The _________ has units of years, which can be interpreted as 'number of years of earnings to pay back purchase price'.

a. Quick ratio
b. P/E ratio
c. Sustainable growth rate
d. Return of capital

7. _________ is the capital that a business raises by taking out a loan. It is a loan made to a company that is normally repaid at some future date. _________ differs from equity or share capital because subscribers to _________ do not become part owners of the business, but are merely creditors, and the suppliers of _________ usually receive a contractually fixed annual percentage return on their loan, and this is known as the coupon rate.

a. Financial assistance
b. Floating charge
c. Risk-return spectrum
d. Debt capital

8. _________, refers to consumption opportunity gained by an entity within a specified time frame, which is generally expressed in monetary terms. However, for households and individuals, '_________ is the sum of all the wages, salaries, profits, interests payments, rents and other forms of earnings received... in a given period of time.' For firms, _________ generally refers to net-profit: what remains of revenue after expenses have been subtracted.

a. Accrual
b. OIBDA
c. Annual report
d. Income

9. The phrase _________ refers to the aspect of corporate strategy, corporate finance and management dealing with the buying, selling and combining of different companies that can aid, finance, or help a growing company in a given industry grow rapidly without having to create another business entity.

An acquisition, also known as a takeover, is the buying of one company (the 'target') by another. An acquisition may be friendly or hostile.

a. 4-4-5 Calendar
b. 529 plan
c. 7-Eleven
d. Mergers and acquisitions

10. In business and accounting, _________s are everything of value that is owned by a person or company. The balance sheet of a firm records the monetary value of the _________s owned by the firm. The two major _________ classes are tangible _________s and intangible _________s.

a. Income
b. EBITDA
c. Accounts payable
d. Asset

11. In probability theory and statistics, _________ indicates the strength and direction of a linear relationship between two random variables. That is in contrast with the usage of the term in colloquial speech, which denotes any relationship, not necessarily linear. In general statistical usage, _________ or co-relation refers to the departure of two random variables from independence.

a. Geometric mean
b. Probability distribution
c. Variance
d. Correlation

12. In economics, business, and accounting, a _________ is the value of money that has been used up to produce something, and hence is not available for use anymore. In business, the _________ may be one of acquisition, in which case the amount of money expended to acquire it is counted as _________. In this case, money is the input that is gone in order to acquire the thing.

a. Fixed costs
b. Cost
c. Sliding scale fees
d. Marginal cost

13. _________ is a fee paid on borrowed assets. It is the price paid for the use of borrowed money , or, money earned by deposited funds . Assets that are sometimes lent with _________ include money, shares, consumer goods through hire purchase, major assets such as aircraft, and even entire factories in finance lease arrangements.

a. A Random Walk Down Wall Street
b. Interest
c. Insolvency
d. AAB

14. _________ is a life of security. It may also refer to the final payment date of a loan or other financial instrument, at which point all remaining interest and principal is due to be paid.

1, 3, 6 months _________ band can be calculated by using 30-day per month periods.

a. Primary market
b. False billing
c. Maturity
d. Replacement cost

15. _________ is typically a higher ranking stock than voting shares, and its terms are negotiated between the corporation and the investor.

_________ usually carry no voting rights, but may carry superior priority over common stock in the payment of dividends and upon liquidation. _________ may carry a dividend that is paid out prior to any dividends to common stock holders.

a. Preferred stock
b. Follow-on offering
c. Second lien loan
d. Trade-off theory

16. _________ is the maximum number of shares that a company can issue. This number is specified in the company's articles of association but can be changed by shareholder approval. A company usually authorizes a higher number of shares than required to be able to issue stock in the future.

a. Barcampbank
b. Market value
c. Shares authorized
d. Floating charge

17. _________, in finance and accounting, means stated value or face value. From this comes the expressions at par (at the _________), over par (over _________) and under par (under _________.)

The term '_________' has several meanings depending on context and geography.

a. Par value
b. FIDC
c. Global Squeeze
d. Sinking fund

18. A _________ is a right to acquire certain property in preference to any other person. It usually refers to property newly coming into existence. A right to acquire existing property in preference to any other person is usually referred to as a right of first refusal.

In practice, the most common form of _________ is the right of existing shareholders to acquire newly issued shares issued by a company in a rights issue, a usually but not always public offering.

a. Down payment
b. Pre-emption right
c. Fraud deterrence
d. Court of Audit of Belgium

19. A _________ or reacquired stock is stock which is bought back by the issuing company, reducing the amount of outstanding stock on the open market ('open market' including insiders' holdings.)

Stock repurchases are often used as a tax-efficient method to put cash into shareholders' hands, rather than pay dividends. Sometimes, companies do this when they feel that their stock is undervalued on the open market.

a. Trial balance
b. Current asset
c. Generally Accepted Accounting Principles
d. Treasury stock

20. In business and finance, a _________ (also referred to as equity _________) of stock means a _________ of ownership in a corporation (company.) In the plural, stocks is often used as a synonym for _________s especially in the United States, but it is less commonly used that way outside of North America.

In the United Kingdom, South Africa, and Australia, stock can also refer to completely different financial instruments such as government bonds or, less commonly, to all kinds of marketable securities.

a. Bucket shop
b. Share
c. Margin
d. Procter ' Gamble

21. A mutual shareholder or _________ is an individual or company (including a corporation) that legally owns one or more shares of stock in a joint stock company. A company's shareholders collectively own that company. Thus, the typical goal of such companies is to enhance shareholder value.

a. Trading curb
b. Stockholder
c. Limit order
d. Stock market bubble

22. A _________ is a statement required of a United States firm when soliciting shareholder votes. The firm needs to file a _________ with the U.S. Securities and Exchange Commission. This statement is useful in assessing how management is paid and potential conflict-of-interest issues with auditors.

a. 529 plan
b. 4-4-5 Calendar
c. 7-Eleven
d. Proxy statement

23. In business, a _________ is the purchase of one company (the target) by another (the acquirer or bidder). In the UK the term refers to the acquisition of a public company whose shares are listed on a stock exchange, in contrast to the acquisition of a private company.

Before a bidder makes an offer for another company, it usually first informs that company's board of directors.

a. 4-4-5 Calendar
b. Stock swap
c. Takeover
d. 529 plan

24. A _________ is a payment made by a corporation to its shareholder members. When a corporation earns a profit or surplus, that money can be put to two uses: it can either be re-invested in the business (called retained earnings), or it can be paid to the shareholders as a _________. Many corporations retain a portion of their earnings and pay the remainder as a _________.

a. Dividend
b. Special dividend
c. Dividend yield
d. Dividend puzzle

25. The _________ is a stock exchange based in New York City, New York. It is the largest stock exchange in the world by dollar value of its listed companies securities. As of October 2008, the combined capitalization of all domestic _________ listed companies was $10.1 trillion.

a. 529 plan
b. 7-Eleven
c. 4-4-5 Calendar
d. New York Stock Exchange

26. A _________ is an event that may occur when a corporation's stockholders develop opposition to some aspect of the corporate governance, often focusing on directorial and management positions. Corporate activists may attempt to persuade shareholders to use their proxy votes (i.e. votes by one individual or institution as the authorized representative of another) to install new management for any of a variety of reasons.

In a _________, incumbent directors and management have the odds stacked in their favor over those trying to force the corporate change.

a. Proxy fight
b. Procurement
c. Trade finance
d. Forfaiting

27. A _________ is a fungible, negotiable instrument representing financial value. They are broadly categorized into debt securities (such as banknotes, bonds and debentures), and equity securities; e.g., common stocks. The company or other entity issuing the _________ is called the issuer.

a. Tracking stock
b. Securities lending
c. Book entry
d. Security

28. The U.S. _________ is an independent agency of the United States government which holds primary responsibility for enforcing the federal securities laws and regulating the securities industry, the nation's stock and options exchanges, and other electronic securities markets. The SEC was created by section 4 of the SEC of 1934 (now codified as 15 U.S.C. Â§ 78d and commonly referred to as the 1934 Act.)

a. 7-Eleven
b. 529 plan
c. 4-4-5 Calendar
d. Securities and Exchange Commission

29. A _________, securities exchange or (in Europe) bourse is a corporation or mutual organization which provides 'trading' facilities for stock brokers and traders, to trade stocks and other securities. _________s also provide facilities for the issue and redemption of securities as well as other financial instruments and capital events including the payment of income and dividends. The securities traded on a _________ include: shares issued by companies, unit trusts and other pooled investment products and bonds.

a. Stock Exchange
b. 4-4-5 Calendar
c. 7-Eleven
d. 529 plan

30. _________ are those dividends paid out in form of additional stock shares of the issuing corporation or other corporation They are usually issued in proportion to shares owned (for example for every 100 shares of stock owned, 5% stock dividend will yield 5 extra shares). If this payment involves the issue of new shares, this is very similar to a stock split in that it increases the total number of shares while lowering the price of each share and does not change the market capitalization or the total value of the shares held

a. Database auditing
b. The Hong Kong Securities Institute
c. Time-based currency
d. Stock or scrip dividends

31. In finance, a _________ is a debt security, in which the authorized issuer owes the holders a debt and, depending on the terms of the _________, is obliged to pay interest (the coupon) and/or to repay the principal at a later date, termed maturity.

Thus a _________ is a loan: the issuer is the borrower, the _________ holder is the lender, and the coupon is the interest. _________s provide the borrower with external funds to finance long-term investments, or, in the case of government _________s, to finance current expenditure.

a. Catastrophe bonds
b. Puttable bond
c. Convertible bond
d. Bond

32. _________ (also trust indenture or deed of trust) is a legal document issued to lenders and describes key terms such as the interest rate, maturity date, convertibility, pledge, promises, representations, covenants, and other terms of the bond offering. When the Offering Memorandum is prepared in advance of marketing a Bond, the indenture will typically be summarised in the 'Description of Notes' section.

a. McFadden Act
b. Court of Audit of Belgium
c. Fair Labor Standards Act
d. Bond indenture

33. _________ is the difference between price and the costs of bringing to market whatever it is that is accounted as an enterprise (whether by harvest, extraction, manufacture, or purchase) in terms of the component costs of delivered goods and/or services and any operating or other expenses.

A key difficulty in measuring profit is in defining costs. Pure economic monetary profits can be zero or negative even in competitive equilibrium when accounted monetized costs exceed monetized price.

a. A Random Walk Down Wall Street
b. Economic profit
c. AAB
d. Accounting profit

34. A _________, in its most general sense, is a solemn promise to engage in or refrain from a specified action.

More specifically, a _________, in contrast to a contract, is a one-way agreement whereby the _________er is the only party bound by the promise. A _________ may have conditions and prerequisites that qualify the undertaking, including the actions of second or third parties, but there is no inherent agreement by such other parties to fulfill those requirements.

a. Partnership
b. Clayton Antitrust Act
c. Federal Trade Commission Act
d. Covenant

35. In law, _________ refers to the process by which a company (or part of a company) is brought to an end, and the assets and property of the company redistributed. _________ can also be referred to as winding-up or dissolution, although dissolution technically refers to the last stage of _________. The process of _________ also arises when customs, an authority or agency in a country responsible for collecting and safeguarding customs duties, determines the final computation or ascertainment of the duties or drawback accruing on an entry.

a. 4-4-5 Calendar
b. Debt settlement
c. 529 plan
d. Liquidation

36. In finance, a _________ is a type of bond that can be converted into shares of stock in the issuing company, usually at some pre-announced ratio. It is a hybrid security with debt- and equity-like features. Although it typically has a low coupon rate, the holder is compensated with the ability to convert the bond to common stock, usually at a substantial discount to the stock's market value.

a. Convertible bond
b. Bond fund
c. Corporate bond
d. Gilts

37. _________ is a measure of the ability of a debtor to pay their debts as and when they fall due. It is usually expressed as a ratio or a percentage of current liabilities.

For a corporation with a published balance sheet there are various ratios used to calculate a measure of liquidity.

a. Invested capital
b. Operating leverage
c. Operating profit margin
d. Accounting liquidity

38. A _________ is a documented investigation of a Market that is used to inform a firm's planning activities particularly around decision of: inventory, purchase, work force expansion/contraction, facility expansion, purchases of capital equipment, promotional activities, and many other aspects of a company.

Not all managers are asked to conduct a _________, but all managers must make decisions using _________ data and understand how the data was derived. So all managers need a reasonable understanding of the tools most used for making sales forecasts and analyzing markets.

a. 4-4-5 Calendar
b. 529 plan
c. 7-Eleven
d. Market analysis

39. _________ or net present worth (NPW) is defined as the total present value (PV) of a time series of cash flows. It is a standard method for using the time value of money to appraise long-term projects. Used for capital budgeting, and widely throughout economics, it measures the excess or shortfall of cash flows, in present value terms, once financing charges are met.

a. Present value of costs
b. Negative gearing
c. Tax shield
d. Net present value

40. In finance, _________, also known as return on investment is the ratio of money gained or lost on an investment relative to the amount of money invested. The amount of money gained or lost may be referred to as interest, profit/loss, gain/loss, or net income/loss. The money invested may be referred to as the asset, capital, principal, or the cost basis of the investment.

a. Stock or scrip dividends
b. Rate of return
c. Composiition of Creditors
d. Doctrine of the Proper Law

41. _________ is a process of analyzing possible future events by considering alternative possible outcomes (scenarios.) The analysis is designed to allow improved decision-making by allowing consideration of outcomes and their implications.

For example, in economics and finance, a financial institution might attempt to forecast several possible scenarios for the economy (e.g. rapid growth, moderate growth, slow growth) and it might also attempt to forecast financial market returns (for bonds, stocks and cash) in each of those scenarios.

a. Detection Risk
b. 4-4-5 Calendar
c. 529 plan
d. Scenario analysis

42. _________ is the study of how the variation (uncertainty) in the output of a mathematical model can be apportioned, qualitatively or quantitatively, to different sources of variation in the input of a model .

In more general terms uncertainty and sensitivity analyses investigate the robustness of a study when the study includes some form of mathematical modelling. While uncertainty analysis studies the overall uncertainty in the conclusions of the study, _________ tries to identify what source of uncertainty weights more on the study's conclusions.

a. Synthetic CDO
b. Sensitivity analysis
c. Proxy fight
d. Golden parachute

43. In financial mathematics and financial risk management, _________ is a widely used measure of the risk of loss on a specific portfolio of financial assets. For a given portfolio, probability and time horizon, VaR is defined as a threshold value such that the probability that the mark-to-market loss on the portfolio over the given time horizon exceeds this value (assuming normal markets and no trading) is the given probability level.

For example, if a portfolio of stocks has a one-day 5% VaR of $1 million, there is a 5% probability that the portfolio will fall in value by more than $1 million over a one day period, assuming markets are normal and there is no trading.

a. Value at risk
b. Discount factor
c. Risk modeling
d. Risk aversion

44. An _________ is a company whose main business is holding securities of other companies purely for investment purposes. The _________ invests money on behalf of its shareholders who in turn share in the profits and losses.

a. Unit investment trust
b. A Random Walk Down Wall Street
c. AAB
d. Investment company

45. _________ is the value on a given date of a future payment or series of future payments, discounted to reflect the time value of money and other factors such as investment risk. _________ calculations are widely used in business and economics to provide a means to compare cash flows at different times on a meaningful 'like to like' basis.

The most commonly applied model of the time value of money is compound interest.

a. Present value
b. Present value of benefits
c. Negative gearing
d. Net present value

46. _________, is when a company issues common stock or shares to the public for the first time. They are often issued by smaller, younger companies seeking capital to expand, but can also be done by large privately-owned companies looking to become publicly traded.

In an _________ the issuer may obtain the assistance of an underwriting firm, which helps it determine what type of security to issue (common or preferred), best offering price and time to bring it to market.

a. Insolvency
b. Initial public offering
c. Interest
d. Asian Financial Crisis

47. In the United States, a _________ is an offering of securities that are not registered with the Securities and Exchange Commission (SEC.) Such offerings exploit an exemption offered by the Securities Act of 1933 that comes with several restrictions, including a prohibition against general solicitation. This exemption allows companies to avoid quarterly reporting requirements and many of the legal liabilities associated with the Sarbanes-Oxley Act.

a. 7-Eleven
b. 529 plan
c. 4-4-5 Calendar
d. Private placement

48. The term _________, also known as a waiting period is a period extended from the time a company files a registration statement with the SEC until SEC staff declared the registration statement effective. During that period, the federal securities laws limited what information a company and related parties can release to the public.'

Under the rules of the Securities Act of 1933, as modified June 29, 2005, electronic communications, including electronic road shows and information located on or hyperlinked to an issuer's website are also governed. The rules changes of June 29, 2005 also included various changes which 'liberalize permitted offering activity and communications to allow more information' for certain qualifying organizations.

a. Leasing
b. Lien
c. Duty of loyalty
d. Quiet period

49. A _________ or bank is a financial institution whose primary activity is to act as a payment agent for customers and to borrow and lend money.

The first modern bank was founded in Italy in Genoa in 1406, its name was Banco di San Giorgio (Bank of St. George.)

Many other financial activities were added over time.

a. Banker
b. Black Sea Trade and Development Bank
c. Bought deal
d. 4-4-5 Calendar

50. The _________ on a company stock is the company's annual dividend payments divided by its market cap, or the dividend per share divided by the price per share. It is often expressed as a percentage.

Dividend payments on preferred shares are stipulated by the prospectus.

a. Dividend imputation
b. Dividend yield
c. Dividend reinvestment plan
d. Special dividend

51. In finance, the term _________ describes the amount in cash that returns to the owners of a security. Normally it does not include the price variations, at the difference of the total return. _________ applies to various stated rates of return on stocks (common and preferred, and convertible), fixed income instruments (bonds, notes, bills, strips, zero coupon), and some other investment type insurance products (e.g. annuities.)

a. Macaulay duration
b. 4-4-5 Calendar
c. Yield to maturity
d. Yield

52. The _________ is an American stock exchange. It is the largest electronic screen-based equity securities trading market in the United States. With approximately 3,200 companies, it has more trading volume per day than any other stock exchange in the world.

a. 7-Eleven
b. 529 plan
c. Nasdaq
d. 4-4-5 Calendar

53. _________ is the process of determining the fair price of a bond. As with any security or capital investment, the fair value of a bond is the present value of the stream of cash flows it is expected to generate. Hence, the price or value of a bond is determined by discounting the bond's expected cash flows to the present using the appropriate discount rate.

a. Bond valuation
b. Bond fund
c. Catastrophe bonds
d. Collateralized debt obligations

54. The _________ is the weighted-average most likely outcome in gambling, probability theory, economics or finance.

In gambling and probability theory, there is usually a discrete set of possible outcomes. In this case, _________ is a measure of the relative balance of win or loss weighted by their chances of occurring.

a. ABN Amro
b. A Random Walk Down Wall Street
c. AAB
d. Expected return

55. _________ is the price at which an asset would trade in a competitive Walrasian auction setting. _________ is often used interchangeably with open _________, fair value or fair _________, although these terms have distinct definitions in different standards, and may differ in some circumstances.

International Valuation Standards defines _________ as 'the estimated amount for which a property should exchange on the date of valuation between a willing buyer and a willing seller in an arm'e;s-length transaction after proper marketing wherein the parties had each acted knowledgeably, prudently, and without compulsion.'

_________ is a concept distinct from market price, which is 'e;the price at which one can transact'e;, while _________ is 'e;the true underlying value'e; according to theoretical standards.

a. Market value
b. Debt restructuring
c. Wrap account
d. T-Model

56. _________ means regulating, adapting or settling in a variety of contexts:

In commercial law, _________ means the settlement of a loss incurred on insured goods. The calculation of the amounts of compensation to be paid by or to the several interests is a complicated matter. It involves much detail and arithmetic, and requires a full and accurate knowledge of the principles of the subject.

a. Intelligent investor
b. Equity method
c. Asset recovery
d. Adjustment

57. In finance, the _________ asserts that financial markets are 'informationally efficient' e.g., stocks, bonds already reflect all known information. The _________ states that it is impossible to consistently outperform the market by using any information that the market already knows, except through luck. Information or news in the EMH is defined as anything that may affect prices that is unknowable in the present and thus appears randomly in the future.

a. Initial margin
b. Arbitrage
c. Efficient-market hypothesis
d. Issuer

58. _________ is a risk-adjusted measure of the so-called active return on an investment. It is the return in excess of the compensation for the risk borne, and thus commonly used to assess active managers' performances. Often, the return of a benchmark is subtracted in order to consider relative performance, which yields Jensen's _________.

a. Amortization
b. Option
c. Alpha
d. Annuity

59. _________ is a variant of the Discounted cash flow model, a method for valuing a stock or business. Often used to provide difficult-to-resolve valuation issues for litigation, tax planning, and business transactions that are currently off market.

It assumes that the company issues a dividend that has a current value of D that grows at a constant rate g. It also assumes that the required rate of return for the stock remains constant at k which is equal to the cost of equity for that company. It involves summing the infinite series which gives the value of price current P.

a. Gordon growth model
b. Securitization
c. Stock or scrip dividends
d. Special journals

60. In corporate finance, _________ is a cash flow available for distribution among all the security holders of a company. They include equity holders, debt holders, preferred stock holders, convertible security holders, and so on.

Note that the first three lines above are calculated for you on the standard Statement of Cash Flows.

a. Safety stock
b. Funding
c. Forfaiting
d. Free cash flow

61. _________ is the balance of the amounts of cash being received and paid by a business during a defined period of time, sometimes tied to a specific project. Measurement of _________ can be used

- to evaluate the state or performance of a business or project.
- to determine problems with liquidity. Being profitable does not necessarily mean being liquid. A company can fail because of a shortage of cash, even while profitable.
- to generate project rate of returns. The time of _________s into and out of projects are used as inputs to financial models such as internal rate of return, and net present value.
- to examine income or growth of a business when it is believed that accrual accounting concepts do not represent economic realities. Alternately, _________ can be used to 'validate' the net income generated by accrual accounting.

_________ as a generic term may be used differently depending on context, and certain _________ definitions may be adapted by analysts and users for their own uses. Common terms include operating _________ and free _________.

_________s can be classified into:

1. Operational _________s: Cash received or expended as a result of the company's core business activities.
2. Investment _________s: Cash received or expended through capital expenditure, investments or acquisitions.
3. Financing _________s: Cash received or expended as a result of financial activities, such as interests and dividends.

All three together - the net _________ - are necessary to reconcile the beginning cash balance to the ending cash balance. Loan draw downs or equity injections, that is just shifting of capital but no expenditure as such, are not considered in the net _________.

a. Real option
b. Corporate finance
c. Shareholder value
d. Cash flow

62. _________ is a process and a set of procedures used to estimate the economic value of an owner's interest in a business. Valuation is used by financial market participants to determine the price they are willing to pay or receive to consummate a sale of a business. In addition to estimating the selling price of a business, the same valuation tools are often used by business appraisers to resolve disputes related to estate and gift taxation, divorce litigation, allocate business purchase price among business assets, establish a formula for estimating the value of partners' ownership interest for buy-sell agreements, and many other business and legal purposes.

a. Federal Deposit Insurance Corporation Improvement Act
b. Family and Medical Leave Act
c. Covenant
d. Business Valuation

63. The institution most often referenced by the word '_________' is a public or publicly traded _________, the shares of which are traded on a public stock exchange (e.g., the New York Stock Exchange or Nasdaq in the United States) where shares of stock of _________s are bought and sold by and to the general public. Most of the largest businesses in the world are publicly traded _________s. However, the majority of _________s are said to be closely held, privately held or close _________s, meaning that no ready market exists for the trading of shares.

a. Depository Trust Company
b. Federal Home Loan Mortgage Corporation
c. Protect
d. Corporation

64. _________ is a measurement of corporate or economic size equal to the share price times the number of shares outstanding of a public company. As owning stock represents owning the company, including all its equity, capitalization could represent the public opinion of a company's net worth and is a determining factor in stock valuation. Likewise, the capitalization of stock markets or economic regions may be compared to other economic indicators.

a. Synthetic CDO
b. Market capitalization
c. Proxy fight
d. Just-in-time

65. The _________ is the rate that a company is expected to pay to finance its assets. WACC is the minimum return that a company must earn on existing asset base to satisfy its creditors, owners, and other providers of capital.

Companies raise money from a number of sources: common equity, preferred equity, straight debt, convertible debt, exchangeable debt, warrants, options, pension liabilities, executive stock options, governmental subsidies, and so on.

a. Weighted average cost of capital
b. Cost of capital
c. 4-4-5 Calendar
d. Capital intensity

66. _________ are costs incurred on the purchase of land, buildings, construction and equipment to be used in the production of goods or the rendering of services. In other words, the total cost needed to bring a project to a commercially operable status. However, _________ are not limited to the initial construction of a factory or other business.

a. Defined contribution plan
b. Capital outflow
c. Trade-off
d. Capital costs

67. The _________ is an expected return that the provider of capital plans to earn on their investment.

Capital (money) used for funding a business should earn returns for the capital providers who risk their capital. For an investment to be worthwhile, the expected return on capital must be greater than the _________.

a. Capital intensity
b. 4-4-5 Calendar
c. Weighted average cost of capital
d. Cost of capital

68. In economics and finance, _________ is the change in total cost that arises when the quantity produced changes by one unit. It is the cost of producing one more unit of a good. Mathematically, the _________ function is expressed as the first derivative of the total cost (TC) function with respect to quantity (Q). Note that the _________ may change with volume, and so at each level of production, the _________ is the cost of the next unit produced.

A typical _________ Curve

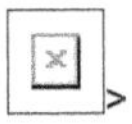

a. Cost accounting
b. Sliding scale fees
c. Marginal cost
d. Fixed costs

69. In accounting, _________ or *Carrying value* is the value of an asset according to its balance sheet account balance. For assets, the value is based on the original cost of the asset less any depreciation, amortization or impairment costs made against the asset. A company's _________ is its total assets minus intangible assets and liabilities.

a. Pro forma
b. Current liabilities
c. Retained earnings
d. Book value

70. _________ is the likely price of an asset when it is allowed insufficient time to sell on the open market, thereby reducing its exposure to potential buyers. _________ is typically lower than fair market value. Unlike cash or securities, certain illiquid assets, like real estate, often require a period of several months in order to obtain their fair market value in a sale, and will generally sell for a significantly lower price if a sale is forced to occur in a shorter time period.

a. REIT
b. Real estate investing
c. Tenancy
d. Liquidation value

71. _________ can be regarded as an outcome of mental processes (cognitive process) leading to the selection of a course of action among several alternatives. Every _________ process produces a final choice. The output can be an action or an opinion of choice.

a. 529 plan
b. 4-4-5 Calendar
c. 7-Eleven
d. Decision making

72. The term _________ has three unrelated technical definitions, and is also used in a variety of non-technical ways.

- In financial economics, it refers to any asset used to make money, as opposed to assets used for personal enjoyment or consumption. This is an important distinction because two people can disagree sharply about the value of personal assets, one person might think a sports car is more valuable than a pickup truck, another person might have the opposite taste. But if an asset is held for the purpose of making money, taste has nothing to do with it, only differences of opinion about how much money the asset will produce. With the further assumption that people agree on the probability distribution of future cash flows, it is possible to have an objective _________ pricing model. Even without the assumption of agreement, it is possible to set rational limits on _________ value.
- In governmental accounting, it is defined as any asset used in operations with an initial useful life extending beyond one reporting period. Generally, government managers have a 'stewardship' duty to maintain _________s under their control. See International Public Sector Accounting Standards for details.
- In US tax accounting, it is defined as any property other than a list of exceptions. The main exceptions are anything held for sale, and any real estate or depreciable property used in business. Almost everything you own and use for personal purposes, pleasure or investment is a _________. If something is a _________ for tax purposes, gains or losses on sale or disposition are capital gains or capital losses. For individuals, however, capital losses on property held for personal use are generally not deductible. See the IRS publication Tax Facts about Capital Gains and Losses for details.

A well-known financial accounting textbook advises that the term be avoided except in tax accounting because it is used in so many different senses, not all of them well-defined. For example it is often used as a synonym for fixed assets or for investments in securities.

A common non-technical usage occurs when people ask that employees or the environment or something else be treated as a _________.

a. Settlement date
b. Political risk
c. Capital asset
d. Solvency

73. In finance, the _________ is used to determine a theoretically appropriate required rate of return of an asset, if that asset is to be added to an already well-diversified portfolio, given that asset's non-diversifiable risk. The model takes into account the asset's sensitivity to non-diversifiable risk (also known as systemic risk or market risk), often represented by the quantity beta (β) in the financial industry, as well as the expected return of the market and the expected return of a theoretical risk-free asset.

The model was introduced by Jack Treynor (1961, 1962), William Sharpe (1964), John Lintner (1965a,b) and Jan Mossin (1966) independently, building on the earlier work of Harry Markowitz on diversification and modern portfolio theory.

a. Capital asset pricing model
b. Cox-Ingersoll-Ross model
c. Random walk hypothesis
d. Hull-White model

74. In finance, _________ occurs when a debtor has not met its legal obligations according to the debt contract, e.g. it has not made a scheduled payment, or has violated a loan covenant (condition) of the debt contract. _________ may occur if the debtor is either unwilling or unable to pay their debt. This can occur with all debt obligations including bonds, mortgages, loans, and promissory notes.

a. Credit crunch
b. Default
c. Debt validation
d. Vendor finance

75. _________ is the risk of loss due to a debtor's non-payment of a loan or other line of credit (either the principal or interest (coupon) or both)

Most lenders employ their own models (credit scorecards) to rank potential and existing customers according to risk, and then apply appropriate strategies. With products such as unsecured personal loans or mortgages, lenders charge a higher price for higher risk customers and vice versa. With revolving products such as credit cards and overdrafts, risk is controlled through careful setting of credit limits.

a. Transaction risk
b. Market risk
c. Liquidity risk
d. Credit risk

76. In finance, the _________ between two currencies specifies how much one currency is worth in terms of the other. For example an _________ of 102 Japanese yen to the United States dollar means that JPY 102 is worth the same as USD 1. The foreign exchange market is one of the largest markets in the world.

a. A Random Walk Down Wall Street
b. Exchange rate
c. ABN Amro
d. AAB

77. _________ is a form of risk that arises from the change in price of one currency against another. Whenever investors or companies have assets or business operations across national borders, they face _________ if their positions are not hedged.

- Transaction risk is the risk that exchange rates will change unfavourably over time. It can be hedged against using forward currency contracts;
- Translation risk is an accounting risk, proportional to the amount of assets held in foreign currencies. Changes in the exchange rate over time will render a report inaccurate, and so assets are usually balanced by borrowings in that currency.

The exchange risk associated with a foreign denominated instrument is a key element in foreign investment. This risk flows from differential monetary policy and growth in real productivity, which results in differential inflation rates.

a. Market risk
b. Credit risk
c. Tracking error
d. Currency risk

78. _________ is a type of risk faced by investors, corporations, and governments. It is a risk that can be understood and managed with proper aforethought and investment.

Broadly, _________ refers to the complications businesses and governments may face as a result of what are commonly referred to as political decisions--or 'any political change that alters the expected outcome and value of a given economic action by changing the probability of achieving business objectives.' .

a. Mid price
b. Capital asset
c. Single-index model
d. Political risk

79. _________ is the planning process used to determine whether a firm's long term investments such as new machinery, replacement machinery, new plants, new products, and research development projects are worth pursuing. It is budget for major capital, or investment, expenditures.

Many formal methods are used in _________, including the techniques such as

- Net present value
- Profitability index
- Internal rate of return
- Modified Internal Rate of Return
- Equivalent annuity

These methods use the incremental cash flows from each potential investment, or project. Techniques based on accounting earnings and accounting rules are sometimes used - though economists consider this to be improper - such as the accounting rate of return, and 'return on investment.' Simplified and hybrid methods are used as well, such as payback period and discounted payback period.

a. Capital budgeting
b. Shareholder value
c. Financial distress
d. Preferred stock

80. A '_________' is a 'Charge' that is paid to obtain the right to delay a payment. Essentially, the payer purchases the right to make a given payment in the future instead of in the Present. The '_________', or 'Charge' that must be paid to delay the payment, is simply the difference between what the payment amount would be if it were paid in the present and what the payment amount would be paid if it were paid in the future.

a. Risk aversion
b. Value at risk
c. Risk modeling
d. Discount

81. In financial accounting, _________ , cash flow provided by operations or cash flow from operating activities, refers to the amount of cash a company generates from the revenues it brings in, excluding costs associated with long-term investment on capital items or investment in securities.

_________ = Cash generated from operations less taxation and interest paid, investment income received and less dividends paid gives rise to _________s per International Financial Reporting Standards.

To calculate cash generated from operations, one must calculate cash generated from customers and cash paid to suppliers.

a. Appreciation
b. A Random Walk Down Wall Street
c. Operating cash flow
d. Other Comprehensive Basis of Accounting

82. An _________ can be defined as a contract which provides an income stream in return for an initial payment.

An immediate _________ is an _________ for which the time between the contract date and the date of the first payment is not longer than the time interval between payments. A common use for an immediate _________ is to provide a pension to a retired person or persons.

a. Intrinsic value
b. Annuity
c. AT'T Inc.
d. Amortization

83. A _________ is the price of a single share of a no. of saleable stocks of the company. Once the stock is purchased, the owner becomes a shareholder of the company that issued the share.

a. Trading curb
b. Whisper numbers
c. Stock split
d. Share price

84. In finance, _________ refers to the way a corporation finances its assets through some combination of equity, debt, or hybrid securities. A firm's _________ is then the composition or 'structure' of its liabilities. For example, a firm that sells $20 billion in equity and $80 billion in debt is said to be 20% equity-financed and 80% debt-financed.

a. Market for corporate control
b. Rights issue
c. Book building
d. Capital structure

85. _________ are the earnings returned on the initial investment amount.

In the US, the Financial Accounting Standards Board (FASB) requires companies' income statements to report _________ for each of the major categories of the income statement: continuing operations, discontinued operations, extraordinary items, and net income.

The _________ formula does not include preferred dividends for categories outside of continued operations and net income.

a. Inventory turnover
b. Average accounting return
c. Assets turnover
d. Earnings per share

1. _________ is the planning process used to determine whether a firm's long term investments such as new machinery, replacement machinery, new plants, new products, and research development projects are worth pursuing. It is budget for major capital, or investment, expenditures.

Many formal methods are used in _________, including the techniques such as

- Net present value
- Profitability index
- Internal rate of return
- Modified Internal Rate of Return
- Equivalent annuity

These methods use the incremental cash flows from each potential investment, or project. Techniques based on accounting earnings and accounting rules are sometimes used - though economists consider this to be improper - such as the accounting rate of return, and 'return on investment.' Simplified and hybrid methods are used as well, such as payback period and discounted payback period.

a. Financial distress
b. Preferred stock
c. Shareholder value
d. Capital budgeting

2. In economics, business, and accounting, a _________ is the value of money that has been used up to produce something, and hence is not available for use anymore. In business, the _________ may be one of acquisition, in which case the amount of money expended to acquire it is counted as _________. In this case, money is the input that is gone in order to acquire the thing.

a. Sliding scale fees
b. Marginal cost
c. Fixed costs
d. Cost

3. In business, _________ is income that a company receives from its normal business activities, usually from the sale of goods and services to customers. Some companies also receive _________ from interest, dividends or royalties paid to them by other companies. _________ may refer to business income in general, or it may refer to the amount, in a monetary unit, received during a period of time, as in 'Last year, Company X had _________ of $32 million.'

In many countries, including the UK, _________ is referred to as turnover.

a. Bottom line
b. Matching principle
c. Furniture, Fixtures and Equipment
d. Revenue

4. _________ is the balance of the amounts of cash being received and paid by a business during a defined period of time, sometimes tied to a specific project. Measurement of _________ can be used

- to evaluate the state or performance of a business or project.
- to determine problems with liquidity. Being profitable does not necessarily mean being liquid. A company can fail because of a shortage of cash, even while profitable.
- to generate project rate of returns. The time of _________s into and out of projects are used as inputs to financial models such as internal rate of return, and net present value.
- to examine income or growth of a business when it is believed that accrual accounting concepts do not represent economic realities. Alternately, _________ can be used to 'validate' the net income generated by accrual accounting.

_________ as a generic term may be used differently depending on context, and certain _________ definitions may be adapted by analysts and users for their own uses. Common terms include operating _________ and free _________.

_________s can be classified into:

1. Operational _________s: Cash received or expended as a result of the company's core business activities.
2. Investment _________s: Cash received or expended through capital expenditure, investments or acquisitions.
3. Financing _________s: Cash received or expended as a result of financial activities, such as interests and dividends.

All three together - the net _________ - are necessary to reconcile the beginning cash balance to the ending cash balance. Loan draw downs or equity injections, that is just shifting of capital but no expenditure as such, are not considered in the net _________.

a. Real option
b. Corporate finance
c. Shareholder value
d. Cash flow

5. _________, in bookkeeping, refers to assets, liabilities, income, and expenses recorded on individual pages of the so called book of final entry or ledger. Changes in _________ value are made by chronologically posting debit (DR) and credit (CR) entries to its page. Examples of _________s are cash, _________s receivable, mortgages, loans, land and buildings, common stock, sales, services provided, wages, and payroll overhead.

a. Option
b. Alpha
c. Accretion
d. Account

6. _________ is a file or account that contains money that a person or company owes to suppliers, but hasn't paid yet (a form of debt.) When you receive an invoice you add it to the file, and then you remove it when you pay. Thus, the A/P is a form of credit that suppliers offer to their purchasers by allowing them to pay for a product or service after it has already been received.

a. Accounts payable
b. Accrual
c. Outstanding balance
d. Earnings before interest, taxes, depreciation and amortization

7. A _________ is an expenditure creating future benefits. A _________ is incurred when a business spends money either to buy fixed assets or to add to the value of an existing fixed asset with a useful life that extends beyond the taxable year. Capex are used by a company to acquire or upgrade physical assets such as equipment, property, or industrial buildings.

a. Capital expenditure
b. Weighted average cost of capital
c. Cost of capital
d. 4-4-5 Calendar

8. _________ plant, and equipment, is a term used in accountancy for assets and property which cannot easily be converted into cash. This can be compared with current assets such as cash or bank accounts, which are described as liquid assets. In most cases, only tangible assets are referred to as fixed.

a. Remittance advice
b. Percentage of Completion
c. Petty cash
d. Fixed asset

9. In business and accounting, _________s are everything of value that is owned by a person or company. The balance sheet of a firm records the monetary value of the _________s owned by the firm. The two major _________ classes are tangible _________s and intangible _________s.

a. EBITDA
b. Accounts payable
c. Income
d. Asset

10. A '_________' is a 'Charge' that is paid to obtain the right to delay a payment. Essentially, the payer purchases the right to make a given payment in the future instead of in the Present. The '_________', or 'Charge' that must be paid to delay the payment, is simply the difference between what the payment amount would be if it were paid in the present and what the payment amount would be paid if it were paid in the future.

a. Risk modeling
b. Risk aversion
c. Value at risk
d. Discount

11. In financial accounting, a _________ or statement of cash flows is a financial statement that shows a company's flow of cash. The money coming into the business is called cash inflow, and money going out from the business is called cash outflow. The statement shows how changes in balance sheet and income accounts affect cash and cash equivalents, and breaks the analysis down to operating, investing, and financing activities.

a. Cash flow statement
b. 7-Eleven
c. 4-4-5 Calendar
d. 529 plan

12. _________ is a life of security. It may also refer to the final payment date of a loan or other financial instrument, at which point all remaining interest and principal is due to be paid.

1, 3, 6 months _________ band can be calculated by using 30-day per month periods.

a. Replacement cost
b. False billing
c. Primary market
d. Maturity

13. _________ is the provision of resources (such as granting a loan) by one party to another party where that second party does not reimburse the first party immediately, thereby generating a debt, and instead arranges either to repay or return those resources (or material(s) of equal value) at a later date. The first party is called a creditor, also known as a lender, while the second party is called a debtor, also known as a borrower.

Movements of financial capital are normally dependent on either _________ or equity transfers.

a. Credit
b. Warrant
c. Comparable
d. Clearing house

14. _________ or economic opportunity loss is the value of the next best alternative foregone as the result of making a decision. _________ analysis is an important part of a company's decision-making processes but is not treated as an actual cost in any financial statement. The next best thing that a person can engage in is referred to as the _________ of doing the best thing and ignoring the next best thing to be done.

a. A Random Walk Down Wall Street
b. ABN Amro
c. AAB
d. Opportunity cost

15. In economics and business decision-making, _________ are costs that cannot be recovered once they have been incurred. _________ are sometimes contrasted with variable costs, which are the costs that will change due to the proposed course of action, and prospective costs which are costs that will be incurred if an action is taken. In microeconomic theory, only variable costs are relevant to a decision.

a. Hindsight bias
b. Sunk costs
c. 4-4-5 Calendar
d. Hyperbolic discounting

16. _________ is the task of determining how a business will afford to achieve its strategic goals and objectives. Usually, a company creates a Financial Plan immediately after the vision and objectives have been set. The Financial Plan describes each of the activities, resources, equipment and materials that are needed to achieve these objectives, as well as the timeframes involved.

a. Management by exception
b. Financial planning
c. Corporate Transparency
d. Performance measurement

17. In economic models, the _________ time frame assumes no fixed factors of production. Firms can enter or leave the marketplace, and the cost (and availability) of land, labor, raw materials, and capital goods can be assumed to vary. In contrast, in the short-run time frame, certain factors are assumed to be fixed, because there is not sufficient time for them to change.

a. Short-run
b. 529 plan
c. 4-4-5 Calendar
d. Long-run

18. _________ are securities that can be easily converted into cash. Such securities will generally have highly liquid markets allowing the security to be sold at a reasonable price very quickly.This is a usual feature in real estate .

a. Book entry
b. Tracking stock
c. Securities lending
d. Marketable

19. A _________ is a fungible, negotiable instrument representing financial value. They are broadly categorized into debt securities (such as banknotes, bonds and debentures), and equity securities; e.g., common stocks. The company or other entity issuing the _________ is called the issuer.

a. Book entry
b. Securities lending
c. Security
d. Tracking stock

20. _________ is a form of risk that arises from the change in price of one currency against another. Whenever investors or companies have assets or business operations across national borders, they face _________ if their positions are not hedged.

- Transaction risk is the risk that exchange rates will change unfavourably over time. It can be hedged against using forward currency contracts;
- Translation risk is an accounting risk, proportional to the amount of assets held in foreign currencies. Changes in the exchange rate over time will render a report inaccurate, and so assets are usually balanced by borrowings in that currency.

The exchange risk associated with a foreign denominated instrument is a key element in foreign investment. This risk flows from differential monetary policy and growth in real productivity, which results in differential inflation rates.

a. Credit risk
b. Market risk
c. Tracking error
d. Currency risk

21. _________ in its classic form is defined as a company from one country making a physical investment into building a factory in another country. It is the establishment of an enterprise by a foreigner. Its definition can be extended to include investments made to acquire lasting interest in enterprises operating outside of the economy of the investor.

a. Public company
b. Dow Jones ' Company
c. MicroPlace
d. Foreign direct investment

22. _________ is a type of risk faced by investors, corporations, and governments. It is a risk that can be understood and managed with proper aforethought and investment.

Broadly, _________ refers to the complications businesses and governments may face as a result of what are commonly referred to as political decisions--or 'any political change that alters the expected outcome and value of a given economic action by changing the probability of achieving business objectives.' .

a. Political risk
b. Capital asset
c. Mid price
d. Single-index model

23. In accounting, _________ or *Carrying value* is the value of an asset according to its balance sheet account balance. For assets, the value is based on the original cost of the asset less any depreciation, amortization or impairment costs made against the asset. A company's _________ is its total assets minus intangible assets and liabilities.

a. Retained earnings
b. Current liabilities
c. Pro forma
d. Book value

24. The phrase _________ refers to the aspect of corporate strategy, corporate finance and management dealing with the buying, selling and combining of different companies that can aid, finance, or help a growing company in a given industry grow rapidly without having to create another business entity.

An acquisition, also known as a takeover, is the buying of one company (the 'target') by another. An acquisition may be friendly or hostile.

a. 4-4-5 Calendar
b. Mergers and acquisitions
c. 7-Eleven
d. 529 plan

25. In probability theory and statistics, _________ indicates the strength and direction of a linear relationship between two random variables. That is in contrast with the usage of the term in colloquial speech, which denotes any relationship, not necessarily linear. In general statistical usage, _________ or co-relation refers to the departure of two random variables from independence.

a. Probability distribution
b. Variance
c. Geometric mean
d. Correlation

26. _________ is a term used in accounting, economics and finance to spread the cost of an asset over the span of several years.

In simple words we can say that _________ is the reduction in the value of an asset due to usage, passage of time, wear and tear, technological outdating or obsolescence, depletion or other such factors.

In accounting, _________ is a term used to describe any method of attributing the historical or purchase cost of an asset across its useful life, roughly corresponding to normal wear and tear.

a. Bottom line
b. Matching principle
c. Deferred financing costs
d. Depreciation

27. _________ is a financial metric which represents operating liquidity available to a business. Along with fixed assets such as plant and equipment, _________ is considered a part of operating capital. It is calculated as current assets minus current liabilities.

a. 529 plan
b. Working capital
c. Working capital management
d. 4-4-5 Calendar

28. A _________ is a profit that results from investments into a capital asset, such as stocks, bonds or real estate, which exceeds the purchase price. It is the difference between a higher selling price and a lower purchase price, resulting in a financial gain for the seller. Conversely, a capital loss arises if the proceeds from the sale of a capital asset are less than the purchase price.

a. Tax brackets
b. Capital gain
c. Payroll tax
d. Capital gains tax

29. Straight-line depreciation is the simplest and most-often-used technique, in which the company estimates the _________ of the asset at the end of the period during which it will be used to generate revenues (useful life) and will expense a portion of original cost in equal increments over that period. The _________ is an estimate of the value of the asset at the time it will be sold or disposed of; it may be zero or even negative. _________ is scrap value, by another name.

a. Depreciation
b. Salvage value
c. Net profit
d. Fixed investment

1. _________ is the planning process used to determine whether a firm's long term investments such as new machinery, replacement machinery, new plants, new products, and research development projects are worth pursuing. It is budget for major capital, or investment, expenditures.

Many formal methods are used in _________, including the techniques such as

- Net present value
- Profitability index
- Internal rate of return
- Modified Internal Rate of Return
- Equivalent annuity

These methods use the incremental cash flows from each potential investment, or project. Techniques based on accounting earnings and accounting rules are sometimes used - though economists consider this to be improper - such as the accounting rate of return, and 'return on investment.' Simplified and hybrid methods are used as well, such as payback period and discounted payback period.

a. Shareholder value
b. Preferred stock
c. Capital budgeting
d. Financial distress

2. _________ or net present worth (NPW) is defined as the total present value (PV) of a time series of cash flows. It is a standard method for using the time value of money to appraise long-term projects. Used for capital budgeting, and widely throughout economics, it measures the excess or shortfall of cash flows, in present value terms, once financing charges are met.

a. Tax shield
b. Negative gearing
c. Present value of costs
d. Net present value

3. _________ is the value on a given date of a future payment or series of future payments, discounted to reflect the time value of money and other factors such as investment risk. _________ calculations are widely used in business and economics to provide a means to compare cash flows at different times on a meaningful 'like to like' basis.

The most commonly applied model of the time value of money is compound interest.

a. Net present value
b. Present value
c. Present value of benefits
d. Negative gearing

4. _________ is the balance of the amounts of cash being received and paid by a business during a defined period of time, sometimes tied to a specific project. Measurement of _________ can be used

- to evaluate the state or performance of a business or project.
- to determine problems with liquidity. Being profitable does not necessarily mean being liquid. A company can fail because of a shortage of cash, even while profitable.
- to generate project rate of returns. The time of _________s into and out of projects are used as inputs to financial models such as internal rate of return, and net present value.
- to examine income or growth of a business when it is believed that accrual accounting concepts do not represent economic realities. Alternately, _________ can be used to 'validate' the net income generated by accrual accounting.

_________ as a generic term may be used differently depending on context, and certain _________ definitions may be adapted by analysts and users for their own uses. Common terms include operating _________ and free _________.

_________s can be classified into:

1. Operational _________s: Cash received or expended as a result of the company's core business activities.
2. Investment _________s: Cash received or expended through capital expenditure, investments or acquisitions.
3. Financing _________s: Cash received or expended as a result of financial activities, such as interests and dividends.

All three together - the net _________ - are necessary to reconcile the beginning cash balance to the ending cash balance. Loan draw downs or equity injections, that is just shifting of capital but no expenditure as such, are not considered in the net _________.

a. Shareholder value
b. Real option
c. Corporate finance
d. Cash flow

5. _________ in business and economics refers to the period of time required for the return on an investment to 'repay' the sum of the original investment. For example, a $1000 investment which returned $500 per year would have a two year _________. It intuitively measures how long something takes to 'pay for itself.' _________ is widely used due to its ease of use despite recognized limitations.

a. Seasoned equity offering
b. Consignment stock
c. Financial Gerontology
d. Payback period

6. In economics, business, and accounting, a _________ is the value of money that has been used up to produce something, and hence is not available for use anymore. In business, the _________ may be one of acquisition, in which case the amount of money expended to acquire it is counted as _________. In this case, money is the input that is gone in order to acquire the thing.

a. Marginal cost
b. Fixed costs
c. Sliding scale fees
d. Cost

7. The _________ is an expected return that the provider of capital plans to earn on their investment.

Capital (money) used for funding a business should earn returns for the capital providers who risk their capital. For an investment to be worthwhile, the expected return on capital must be greater than the _________.

a. Cost of capital
b. Weighted average cost of capital
c. 4-4-5 Calendar
d. Capital intensity

8. A '_________' is a 'Charge' that is paid to obtain the right to delay a payment. Essentially, the payer purchases the right to make a given payment in the future instead of in the Present. The '_________', or 'Charge' that must be paid to delay the payment, is simply the difference between what the payment amount would be if it were paid in the present and what the payment amount would be paid if it were paid in the future.

a. Risk modeling
b. Discount
c. Value at risk
d. Risk aversion

9. The _________ is an interest rate a central bank charges depository institutions that borrow reserves from it.

The term _________ has two meanings:

- the same as interest rate; the term 'discount' does not refer to the meaning of the word, but to the purpose of using the quantity, such as computations of present value, e.g. net present value / discounted cash flow

- the annual effective _________, which is the annual interest divided by the capital including that interest; this rate is lower than the interest rate; it corresponds to using the value after a year as the nominal value, and seeing the initial value as the nominal value minus a discount; it is used for Treasury Bills and similar financial instruments

The annual effective _________ is the annual interest divided by the capital including that interest, which is the interest rate divided by 100% plus the interest rate. It is the annual discount factor to be applied to the future cash flow, to find the discount, subtracted from a future value to find the value one year earlier.

For example, suppose there is a government bond that sells for $95 and pays $100 in a year's time.

a. Discount rate
b. Fisher equation
c. Black-Scholes
d. Stochastic volatility

10. _________ or economic opportunity loss is the value of the next best alternative foregone as the result of making a decision. _________ analysis is an important part of a company's decision-making processes but is not treated as an actual cost in any financial statement. The next best thing that a person can engage in is referred to as the _________ of doing the best thing and ignoring the next best thing to be done.

a. ABN Amro
b. A Random Walk Down Wall Street
c. AAB
d. Opportunity cost

11. The _________ is a capital budgeting metric used by firms to decide whether they should make investments. It is an indicator of the efficiency or quality of an investment, as opposed to net present value (NPV), which indicates value or magnitude.

The IRR is the annualized effective compounded return rate which can be earned on the invested capital, i.e., the yield on the investment.

a. AAB
b. A Random Walk Down Wall Street
c. ABN Amro
d. Internal rate of return

12. In finance, _________, also known as return on investment is the ratio of money gained or lost on an investment relative to the amount of money invested. The amount of money gained or lost may be referred to as interest, profit/loss, gain/loss, or net income/loss. The money invested may be referred to as the asset, capital, principal, or the cost basis of the investment.

a. Stock or scrip dividends
b. Doctrine of the Proper Law
c. Composiition of Creditors
d. Rate of return

13. In corporate finance, _________ is an estimate of true economic profit after making corrective adjustments to GAAP accounting, including deducting the opportunity cost of equity capital. GAAP is estimated to ignore US$300 billion in shareholder opportunity costs. _________ can be measured as Net Operating Profit After Taxes(or NOPAT) less the money cost of capital.

a. ABN Amro
b. A Random Walk Down Wall Street
c. Economic value added
d. AAB

14. _________ is the price at which an asset would trade in a competitive Walrasian auction setting. _________ is often used interchangeably with open _________, fair value or fair _________, although these terms have distinct definitions in different standards, and may differ in some circumstances.

International Valuation Standards defines _________ as 'the estimated amount for which a property should exchange on the date of valuation between a willing buyer and a willing seller in an arm'e;s-length transaction after proper marketing wherein the parties had each acted knowledgeably, prudently, and without compulsion.'

_________ is a concept distinct from market price, which is 'e;the price at which one can transact'e;, while _________ is 'e;the true underlying value'e; according to theoretical standards.

a. Wrap account
b. T-Model
c. Debt restructuring
d. Market value

15. _________ is the difference between the current market value of a firm and the capital contributed by investors. If _________ is positive, the firm has added value. If it is negative, the firm has destroyed value.

a. Wrap account
b. Monetary system
c. Decision process tool
d. Market value added

16. _________ refers to the additional value of a commodity over the cost of commodities used to produce it from the previous stage of production. An example is the price of gasoline at the pump over the price of the oil in it. In national accounts used in macroeconomics, it refers to the contribution of the factors of production, i.e., land, labor, and capital goods, to raising the value of a product and corresponds to the incomes received by the owners of these factors.

a. Supply shock
b. Value added
c. Deregulation
d. Demand shock

17. _________ is a financial measure used to determine the attractiveness of an investment. It is generally used as part of a capital budgeting process to rank various alternative choices. It is a modification of the Internal Rate of Return (IRR).

_________ ranks project efficiency consistently with the present worth ratio (variant of NPV/Discounted Negative Cash Flow), considered the gold standard in many finance textbooks.

MIRR is calculated as follows:

width=747 border=0>

where n is the number of (equal) periods in which the cash flows occur.

a. Binomial options pricing model
b. Black-Scholes
c. Modified internal rate of return
d. Current yield

18. In financial accounting, a _________ or statement of cash flows is a financial statement that shows a company's flow of cash. The money coming into the business is called cash inflow, and money going out from the business is called cash outflow. The statement shows how changes in balance sheet and income accounts affect cash and cash equivalents, and breaks the analysis down to operating, investing, and financing activities.

a. 4-4-5 Calendar
b. Cash flow statement
c. 529 plan
d. 7-Eleven

19. A _________ is a payment made by a corporation to its shareholder members. When a corporation earns a profit or surplus, that money can be put to two uses: it can either be re-invested in the business (called retained earnings), or it can be paid to the shareholders as a _________. Many corporations retain a portion of their earnings and pay the remainder as a _________.

a. Special dividend
b. Dividend puzzle
c. Dividend yield
d. Dividend

20. _________ is a life of security. It may also refer to the final payment date of a loan or other financial instrument, at which point all remaining interest and principal is due to be paid.

1, 3, 6 months _________ band can be calculated by using 30-day per month periods.

a. Replacement cost
b. Primary market
c. False billing
d. Maturity

1. The term _________ has three unrelated technical definitions, and is also used in a variety of non-technical ways.

- In financial economics, it refers to any asset used to make money, as opposed to assets used for personal enjoyment or consumption. This is an important distinction because two people can disagree sharply about the value of personal assets, one person might think a sports car is more valuable than a pickup truck, another person might have the opposite taste. But if an asset is held for the purpose of making money, taste has nothing to do with it, only differences of opinion about how much money the asset will produce. With the further assumption that people agree on the probability distribution of future cash flows, it is possible to have an objective _________ pricing model. Even without the assumption of agreement, it is possible to set rational limits on _________ value.
- In governmental accounting, it is defined as any asset used in operations with an initial useful life extending beyond one reporting period. Generally, government managers have a 'stewardship' duty to maintain _________s under their control. See International Public Sector Accounting Standards for details.
- In US tax accounting, it is defined as any property other than a list of exceptions. The main exceptions are anything held for sale, and any real estate or depreciable property used in business. Almost everything you own and use for personal purposes, pleasure or investment is a _________. If something is a _________ for tax purposes, gains or losses on sale or disposition are capital gains or capital losses. For individuals, however, capital losses on property held for personal use are generally not deductible. See the IRS publication Tax Facts about Capital Gains and Losses for details.

A well-known financial accounting textbook advises that the term be avoided except in tax accounting because it is used in so many different senses, not all of them well-defined. For example it is often used as a synonym for fixed assets or for investments in securities.

A common non-technical usage occurs when people ask that employees or the environment or something else be treated as a _________.

a. Solvency
b. Capital asset
c. Political risk
d. Settlement date

2. In finance, the _________ is used to determine a theoretically appropriate required rate of return of an asset, if that asset is to be added to an already well-diversified portfolio, given that asset's non-diversifiable risk. The model takes into account the asset's sensitivity to non-diversifiable risk (also known as systemic risk or market risk), often represented by the quantity beta (β) in the financial industry, as well as the expected return of the market and the expected return of a theoretical risk-free asset.

The model was introduced by Jack Treynor (1961, 1962), William Sharpe (1964), John Lintner (1965a,b) and Jan Mossin (1966) independently, building on the earlier work of Harry Markowitz on diversification and modern portfolio theory.

a. Random walk hypothesis
b. Hull-White model
c. Capital asset pricing model
d. Cox-Ingersoll-Ross model

3. _________ is the planning process used to determine whether a firm's long term investments such as new machinery, replacement machinery, new plants, new products, and research development projects are worth pursuing. It is budget for major capital, or investment, expenditures.

Many formal methods are used in _________, including the techniques such as

- Net present value
- Profitability index
- Internal rate of return
- Modified Internal Rate of Return
- Equivalent annuity

These methods use the incremental cash flows from each potential investment, or project. Techniques based on accounting earnings and accounting rules are sometimes used - though economists consider this to be improper - such as the accounting rate of return, and 'return on investment.' Simplified and hybrid methods are used as well, such as payback period and discounted payback period.

a. Preferred stock
b. Financial distress
c. Shareholder value
d. Capital budgeting

4. _________ is the balance of the amounts of cash being received and paid by a business during a defined period of time, sometimes tied to a specific project. Measurement of _________ can be used

- to evaluate the state or performance of a business or project.
- to determine problems with liquidity. Being profitable does not necessarily mean being liquid. A company can fail because of a shortage of cash, even while profitable.
- to generate project rate of returns. The time of _________s into and out of projects are used as inputs to financial models such as internal rate of return, and net present value.
- to examine income or growth of a business when it is believed that accrual accounting concepts do not represent economic realities. Alternately, _________ can be used to 'validate' the net income generated by accrual accounting.

_________ as a generic term may be used differently depending on context, and certain _________ definitions may be adapted by analysts and users for their own uses. Common terms include operating _________ and free _________.

_________s can be classified into:

1. Operational _________s: Cash received or expended as a result of the company's core business activities.
2. Investment _________s: Cash received or expended through capital expenditure, investments or acquisitions.
3. Financing _________s: Cash received or expended as a result of financial activities, such as interests and dividends.

All three together - the net _________ - are necessary to reconcile the beginning cash balance to the ending cash balance. Loan draw downs or equity injections, that is just shifting of capital but no expenditure as such, are not considered in the net _________.

a. Shareholder value
b. Real option
c. Corporate finance
d. Cash flow

5. In finance, _________ occurs when a debtor has not met its legal obligations according to the debt contract, e.g. it has not made a scheduled payment, or has violated a loan covenant (condition) of the debt contract. _________ may occur if the debtor is either unwilling or unable to pay their debt. This can occur with all debt obligations including bonds, mortgages, loans, and promissory notes.

a. Vendor finance
b. Credit crunch
c. Debt validation
d. Default

6. _________ is the risk of loss due to a debtor's non-payment of a loan or other line of credit (either the principal or interest (coupon) or both)

Most lenders employ their own models (credit scorecards) to rank potential and existing customers according to risk, and then apply appropriate strategies. With products such as unsecured personal loans or mortgages, lenders charge a higher price for higher risk customers and vice versa. With revolving products such as credit cards and overdrafts, risk is controlled through careful setting of credit limits.

a. Liquidity risk
b. Market risk
c. Transaction risk
d. Credit risk

7. A '_________' is a 'Charge' that is paid to obtain the right to delay a payment. Essentially, the payer purchases the right to make a given payment in the future instead of in the Present. The '_________', or 'Charge' that must be paid to delay the payment, is simply the difference between what the payment amount would be if it were paid in the present and what the payment amount would be paid if it were paid in the future.

a. Risk aversion
b. Value at risk
c. Risk modeling
d. Discount

8. In finance, the _________ between two currencies specifies how much one currency is worth in terms of the other. For example an _________ of 102 Japanese yen to the United States dollar means that JPY 102 is worth the same as USD 1. The foreign exchange market is one of the largest markets in the world.

a. AAB
b. A Random Walk Down Wall Street
c. Exchange rate
d. ABN Amro

9. _________ is a form of risk that arises from the change in price of one currency against another. Whenever investors or companies have assets or business operations across national borders, they face _________ if their positions are not hedged.

- Transaction risk is the risk that exchange rates will change unfavourably over time. It can be hedged against using forward currency contracts;
- Translation risk is an accounting risk, proportional to the amount of assets held in foreign currencies. Changes in the exchange rate over time will render a report inaccurate, and so assets are usually balanced by borrowings in that currency.

The exchange risk associated with a foreign denominated instrument is a key element in foreign investment. This risk flows from differential monetary policy and growth in real productivity, which results in differential inflation rates.

a. Market risk
b. Tracking error
c. Credit risk
d. Currency risk

10. _________ is a type of risk faced by investors, corporations, and governments. It is a risk that can be understood and managed with proper aforethought and investment.

Broadly, _________ refers to the complications businesses and governments may face as a result of what are commonly referred to as political decisions--or 'any political change that alters the expected outcome and value of a given economic action by changing the probability of achieving business objectives.' .

a. Capital asset
b. Mid price
c. Single-index model
d. Political risk

11. In financial accounting, a _________ or statement of cash flows is a financial statement that shows a company's flow of cash. The money coming into the business is called cash inflow, and money going out from the business is called cash outflow. The statement shows how changes in balance sheet and income accounts affect cash and cash equivalents, and breaks the analysis down to operating, investing, and financing activities.

a. 7-Eleven
b. 4-4-5 Calendar
c. 529 plan
d. Cash flow statement

12. In business and accounting, _________s are everything of value that is owned by a person or company. The balance sheet of a firm records the monetary value of the _________s owned by the firm. The two major _________ classes are tangible _________s and intangible _________s.

a. Income
b. Accounts payable
c. EBITDA
d. Asset

13. In finance, _________ is the process of estimating the potential market value of a financial asset or liability. they can be done on assets (for example, investments in marketable securities such as stocks, options, business enterprises, or intangible assets such as patents and trademarks) or on liabilities (e.g., Bonds issued by a company.) _________s are required in many contexts including investment analysis, capital budgeting, merger and acquisition transactions, financial reporting, taxable events to determine the proper tax liability, and in litigation.

a. Margin
b. Procter ' Gamble
c. Share
d. Valuation

14. In economics, business, and accounting, a _________ is the value of money that has been used up to produce something, and hence is not available for use anymore. In business, the _________ may be one of acquisition, in which case the amount of money expended to acquire it is counted as _________. In this case, money is the input that is gone in order to acquire the thing.

a. Sliding scale fees
b. Fixed costs
c. Marginal cost
d. Cost

15. _________ is a life of security. It may also refer to the final payment date of a loan or other financial instrument, at which point all remaining interest and principal is due to be paid.

1, 3, 6 months _________ band can be calculated by using 30-day per month periods.

a. False billing
b. Replacement cost
c. Primary market
d. Maturity

16. _________ or net present worth (NPW) is defined as the total present value (PV) of a time series of cash flows. It is a standard method for using the time value of money to appraise long-term projects. Used for capital budgeting, and widely throughout economics, it measures the excess or shortfall of cash flows, in present value terms, once financing charges are met.

a. Present value of costs
b. Net present value
c. Tax shield
d. Negative gearing

17. _________ is the value on a given date of a future payment or series of future payments, discounted to reflect the time value of money and other factors such as investment risk. _________ calculations are widely used in business and economics to provide a means to compare cash flows at different times on a meaningful 'like to like' basis.

The most commonly applied model of the time value of money is compound interest.

a. Present value of benefits
b. Negative gearing
c. Present value
d. Net present value

18. In corporate finance, _________ is an estimate of true economic profit after making corrective adjustments to GAAP accounting, including deducting the opportunity cost of equity capital. GAAP is estimated to ignore US$300 billion in shareholder opportunity costs. _________ can be measured as Net Operating Profit After Taxes(or NOPAT) less the money cost of capital.

a. Economic value added
b. ABN Amro
c. AAB
d. A Random Walk Down Wall Street

19. _________ refers to the additional value of a commodity over the cost of commodities used to produce it from the previous stage of production. An example is the price of gasoline at the pump over the price of the oil in it. In national accounts used in macroeconomics, it refers to the contribution of the factors of production, i.e., land, labor, and capital goods, to raising the value of a product and corresponds to the incomes received by the owners of these factors.

a. Supply shock
b. Deregulation
c. Value added
d. Demand shock

20. _________ is a process of analyzing possible future events by considering alternative possible outcomes (scenarios.) The analysis is designed to allow improved decision-making by allowing consideration of outcomes and their implications.

For example, in economics and finance, a financial institution might attempt to forecast several possible scenarios for the economy (e.g. rapid growth, moderate growth, slow growth) and it might also attempt to forecast financial market returns (for bonds, stocks and cash) in each of those scenarios.

a. Scenario analysis
b. 529 plan
c. Detection Risk
d. 4-4-5 Calendar

21. _________ is the study of how the variation (uncertainty) in the output of a mathematical model can be apportioned, qualitatively or quantitatively, to different sources of variation in the input of a model .

In more general terms uncertainty and sensitivity analyses investigate the robustness of a study when the study includes some form of mathematical modelling. While uncertainty analysis studies the overall uncertainty in the conclusions of the study, _________ tries to identify what source of uncertainty weights more on the study's conclusions.

a. Synthetic CDO
b. Golden parachute
c. Sensitivity analysis
d. Proxy fight

22. An _________ is a company whose main business is holding securities of other companies purely for investment purposes. The _________ invests money on behalf of its shareholders who in turn share in the profits and losses.
a. A Random Walk Down Wall Street
b. AAB
c. Unit investment trust
d. Investment company

23. _________ measures the rate of return on the ownership interest (shareholders' equity) of the common stock owners. _________ is viewed as one of the most important financial ratios. It measures a firm's efficiency at generating profits from every dollar of shareholders' equity (also known as net assets or assets minus liabilities.)
a. Return on equity
b. Return on sales
c. Return of capital
d. Diluted Earnings Per Share

24. _________ refers to the pricing of contributions (assets, tangible and intangible, services, and funds) transferred within an organization. For example, goods from the production division may be sold to the marketing division, or goods from a parent company may be sold to a foreign subsidiary. Since the prices are set within an organization (i.e. controlled), the typical market mechanisms that establish prices for such transactions between third parties may not apply.
a. Transfer pricing
b. Price discrimination
c. Discounts and allowances
d. Price index

25. The _________ is an interest rate a central bank charges depository institutions that borrow reserves from it.

The term _________ has two meanings:

- the same as interest rate; the term 'discount' does not refer to the meaning of the word, but to the purpose of using the quantity, such as computations of present value, e.g. net present value / discounted cash flow

- the annual effective _________, which is the annual interest divided by the capital including that interest; this rate is lower than the interest rate; it corresponds to using the value after a year as the nominal value, and seeing the initial value as the nominal value minus a discount; it is used for Treasury Bills and similar financial instruments

The annual effective _________ is the annual interest divided by the capital including that interest, which is the interest rate divided by 100% plus the interest rate. It is the annual discount factor to be applied to the future cash flow, to find the discount, subtracted from a future value to find the value one year earlier.

For example, suppose there is a government bond that sells for $95 and pays $100 in a year's time.

a. Fisher equation
b. Stochastic volatility
c. Black-Scholes
d. Discount rate

26. A _________ is a fungible, negotiable instrument representing financial value. They are broadly categorized into debt securities (such as banknotes, bonds and debentures), and equity securities; e.g., common stocks. The company or other entity issuing the _________ is called the issuer.

a. Tracking stock
b. Book entry
c. Security
d. Securities lending

27. In Modern Portfolio Theory, the _________ is the graphical representation of the Capital Asset Pricing Model. It displays the expected rate of return for an overall market as a function of systematic (non-diversifiable) risk (beta.)

The Y-Intercept (beta=0) of the _________ is equal to the risk-free interest rate.

a. Certificate in Investment Performance Measurement
b. Security market line
c. Rebalancing
d. Divestment

28. _________ in finance is a risk management technique, related to hedging, that mixes a wide variety of investments within a portfolio. Because the fluctuations of a single security have less impact on a diverse portfolio, _________ minimizes the risk from any one investment.

A simple example of _________ is the following: On a particular island the entire economy consists of two companies: one that sells umbrellas and another that sells sunscreen.

a. 529 plan
b. Diversification
c. 4-4-5 Calendar
d. 7-Eleven

29. In finance, _________, also known as return on investment is the ratio of money gained or lost on an investment relative to the amount of money invested. The amount of money gained or lost may be referred to as interest, profit/loss, gain/loss, or net income/loss. The money invested may be referred to as the asset, capital, principal, or the cost basis of the investment.

a. Rate of return
b. Composiition of Creditors
c. Stock or scrip dividends
d. Doctrine of the Proper Law

30. In corporate finance, _________ analysis applies put option and call option valuation techniques to capital budgeting decisions. A _________ itself, is the right--but not the obligation--to undertake some business decision; typically the option to make, or abandon, a capital investment. For example, the opportunity to invest in the expansion of a firm's factory, or alternatively to sell the factory, is a _________.

a. Real option
b. Cash flow
c. Book building
d. Capital budgeting

31. An _________ is a contract written by a seller that conveys to the buyer the right -- but not the obligation -- to buy (in the case of a call _________) or to sell (in the case of a put _________) a particular asset, such as a piece of property such as, among others, a futures contract. In return for granting the _________, the seller collects a payment (the premium) from the buyer.

For example, buying a call _________ provides the right to buy a specified quantity of a security at a set strike price at some time on or before expiration, while buying a put _________ provides the right to sell.

a. Amortization
b. Annuity
c. Option
d. AT'T Mobility LLC

32. _________ or financing is to provide capital (funds), which means money for a project, a person, a business or any other private or public institutions.

Those funds can be allocated for either short term or long term purposes. The health fund is a new way of _________ private healthcare centers.

a. Proxy fight
b. Product life cycle
c. Synthetic CDO
d. Funding

33. The _________ is a capital budgeting metric used by firms to decide whether they should make investments. It is an indicator of the efficiency or quality of an investment, as opposed to net present value (NPV), which indicates value or magnitude.

The IRR is the annualized effective compounded return rate which can be earned on the invested capital, i.e., the yield on the investment.

a. A Random Walk Down Wall Street
b. AAB
c. ABN Amro
d. Internal rate of return

34. The institution most often referenced by the word '_________' is a public or publicly traded _________, the shares of which are traded on a public stock exchange (e.g., the New York Stock Exchange or Nasdaq in the United States) where shares of stock of _________s are bought and sold by and to the general public. Most of the largest businesses in the world are publicly traded _________s. However, the majority of _________s are said to be closely held, privately held or close _________s, meaning that no ready market exists for the trading of shares.

a. Depository Trust Company
b. Federal Home Loan Mortgage Corporation
c. Protect
d. Corporation

35. A _________ is the price of a single share of a no. of saleable stocks of the company. Once the stock is purchased, the owner becomes a shareholder of the company that issued the share.

a. Stock split
b. Share price
c. Trading curb
d. Whisper numbers

36. In finance, _________ refers to the way a corporation finances its assets through some combination of equity, debt, or hybrid securities. A firm's _________ is then the composition or 'structure' of its liabilities. For example, a firm that sells $20 billion in equity and $80 billion in debt is said to be 20% equity-financed and 80% debt-financed.

a. Book building
b. Capital structure
c. Rights issue
d. Market for corporate control

1. In economics, business, and accounting, a _________ is the value of money that has been used up to produce something, and hence is not available for use anymore. In business, the _________ may be one of acquisition, in which case the amount of money expended to acquire it is counted as _________. In this case, money is the input that is gone in order to acquire the thing.

a. Fixed costs
b. Marginal cost
c. Cost
d. Sliding scale fees

2. The _________ is an expected return that the provider of capital plans to earn on their investment.

Capital (money) used for funding a business should earn returns for the capital providers who risk their capital. For an investment to be worthwhile, the expected return on capital must be greater than the _________.

a. 4-4-5 Calendar
b. Weighted average cost of capital
c. Capital intensity
d. Cost of capital

3. _________ is a measurement of corporate or economic size equal to the share price times the number of shares outstanding of a public company. As owning stock represents owning the company, including all its equity, capitalization could represent the public opinion of a company's net worth and is a determining factor in stock valuation. Likewise, the capitalization of stock markets or economic regions may be compared to other economic indicators.

a. Market capitalization
b. Just-in-time
c. Synthetic CDO
d. Proxy fight

4. _________ is a type of private equity capital typically provided to early-stage, high-potential, growth companies in the interest of generating a return through an eventual realization event such as an IPO or trade sale of the company. _________ investments are generally made as cash in exchange for shares in the invested company. It is typical for _________ investors to identify and back companies in high technology industries such as biotechnology and ICT.

a. Venture capital
b. Tail risk
c. Treasury Inflation-Protected Securities
d. Probability distribution

5. The _________ is the rate that a company is expected to pay to finance its assets. WACC is the minimum return that a company must earn on existing asset base to satisfy its creditors, owners, and other providers of capital.

Companies raise money from a number of sources: common equity, preferred equity, straight debt, convertible debt, exchangeable debt, warrants, options, pension liabilities, executive stock options, governmental subsidies, and so on.

a. Capital intensity
b. Cost of capital
c. Weighted average cost of capital
d. 4-4-5 Calendar

6. _________ are costs incurred on the purchase of land, buildings, construction and equipment to be used in the production of goods or the rendering of services. In other words, the total cost needed to bring a project to a commercially operable status. However, _________ are not limited to the initial construction of a factory or other business.

a. Capital outflow
b. Trade-off
c. Defined contribution plan
d. Capital costs

7. In economics and finance, _________ is the change in total cost that arises when the quantity produced changes by one unit. It is the cost of producing one more unit of a good. Mathematically, the _________ function is expressed as the first derivative of the total cost (TC) function with respect to quantity (Q). Note that the _________ may change with volume, and so at each level of production, the _________ is the cost of the next unit produced.

A typical _________ Curve

>

a. Sliding scale fees
b. Marginal cost
c. Cost accounting
d. Fixed costs

8. _________ or financing is to provide capital (funds), which means money for a project, a person, a business or any other private or public institutions.

Those funds can be allocated for either short term or long term purposes. The health fund is a new way of _________ private healthcare centers.

a. Product life cycle
b. Proxy fight
c. Funding
d. Synthetic CDO

9. _________ is normally any risk associated with any form of financing.

Depending on the nature of the investment, the type of 'investment' risk will vary. High risk investments have greater potential rewards, but you may lose your money instead by taking the risk for more money.

a. Financial risk
b. Stock market index option
c. Revaluation
d. Liquidating dividend

10. In finance, _________ refers to the way a corporation finances its assets through some combination of equity, debt, or hybrid securities. A firm's _________ is then the composition or 'structure' of its liabilities. For example, a firm that sells $20 billion in equity and $80 billion in debt is said to be 20% equity-financed and 80% debt-financed.

a. Rights issue
b. Capital structure
c. Market for corporate control
d. Book building

11. In the United States, _________ are overnight borrowings by banks to maintain their bank reserves at the Federal Reserve. Banks keep reserves at Federal Reserve Banks to meet their reserve requirements and to clear financial transactions. Transactions in the _________ market enable depository institutions with reserve balances in excess of reserve requirements to lend reserves to institutions with reserve deficiencies.

a. Federal funds
b. 4-4-5 Calendar
c. Federal funds rate
d. Regulation T

12. In economic models, the _________ time frame assumes no fixed factors of production. Firms can enter or leave the marketplace, and the cost (and availability) of land, labor, raw materials, and capital goods can be assumed to vary. In contrast, in the short-run time frame, certain factors are assumed to be fixed, because there is not sufficient time for them to change.

a. 529 plan
b. 4-4-5 Calendar
c. Short-run
d. Long-run

13. _________ in technical analysis is typical price multiplied by volume, a kind of approximation to the dollar value of a day's trading.

_________ index (Money flowl) is an oscillator calculated over an N-day period, ranging from 0 to 100, showing _________ on up days as a percentage of the total of up and down days.

The calculations are as follows. The typical price for each day is the average of high, low and close,

>

_________ is the product of typical price and the volume on that day.

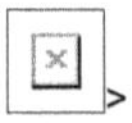
>

a. Money flow
b. Technical analysis
c. Dow theory
d. Support and resistance

14. _________ is the planning process used to determine whether a firm's long term investments such as new machinery, replacement machinery, new plants, new products, and research development projects are worth pursuing. It is budget for major capital, or investment, expenditures.

Many formal methods are used in _________, including the techniques such as

- Net present value
- Profitability index
- Internal rate of return
- Modified Internal Rate of Return
- Equivalent annuity

These methods use the incremental cash flows from each potential investment, or project. Techniques based on accounting earnings and accounting rules are sometimes used - though economists consider this to be improper - such as the accounting rate of return, and 'return on investment.' Simplified and hybrid methods are used as well, such as payback period and discounted payback period.

a. Capital budgeting
b. Shareholder value
c. Financial distress
d. Preferred stock

15. _________ is the balance of the amounts of cash being received and paid by a business during a defined period of time, sometimes tied to a specific project. Measurement of _________ can be used

- to evaluate the state or performance of a business or project.
- to determine problems with liquidity. Being profitable does not necessarily mean being liquid. A company can fail because of a shortage of cash, even while profitable.
- to generate project rate of returns. The time of _________s into and out of projects are used as inputs to financial models such as internal rate of return, and net present value.
- to examine income or growth of a business when it is believed that accrual accounting concepts do not represent economic realities. Alternately, _________ can be used to 'validate' the net income generated by accrual accounting.

_________ as a generic term may be used differently depending on context, and certain _________ definitions may be adapted by analysts and users for their own uses. Common terms include operating _________ and free _________.

_________s can be classified into:

1. Operational _________s: Cash received or expended as a result of the company's core business activities.
2. Investment _________s: Cash received or expended through capital expenditure, investments or acquisitions.
3. Financing _________s: Cash received or expended as a result of financial activities, such as interests and dividends.

All three together - the net _________ - are necessary to reconcile the beginning cash balance to the ending cash balance. Loan draw downs or equity injections, that is just shifting of capital but no expenditure as such, are not considered in the net _________.

a. Shareholder value
b. Corporate finance
c. Real option
d. Cash flow

16. A '_________' is a 'Charge' that is paid to obtain the right to delay a payment. Essentially, the payer purchases the right to make a given payment in the future instead of in the Present. The '_________', or 'Charge' that must be paid to delay the payment, is simply the difference between what the payment amount would be if it were paid in the present and what the payment amount would be paid if it were paid in the future.

a. Risk modeling
b. Value at risk
c. Discount
d. Risk aversion

17. _________, is when a company issues common stock or shares to the public for the first time. They are often issued by smaller, younger companies seeking capital to expand, but can also be done by large privately-owned companies looking to become publicly traded.

In an _________ the issuer may obtain the assistance of an underwriting firm, which helps it determine what type of security to issue (common or preferred), best offering price and time to bring it to market.

a. Initial public offering
b. Asian Financial Crisis
c. Interest
d. Insolvency

18. The _________ is a capital budgeting metric used by firms to decide whether they should make investments. It is an indicator of the efficiency or quality of an investment, as opposed to net present value (NPV), which indicates value or magnitude.

The IRR is the annualized effective compounded return rate which can be earned on the invested capital, i.e., the yield on the investment.

a. ABN Amro
b. AAB
c. Internal rate of return
d. A Random Walk Down Wall Street

19. In financial accounting, a _________ or statement of cash flows is a financial statement that shows a company's flow of cash. The money coming into the business is called cash inflow, and money going out from the business is called cash outflow. The statement shows how changes in balance sheet and income accounts affect cash and cash equivalents, and breaks the analysis down to operating, investing, and financing activities.

a. 4-4-5 Calendar
b. 529 plan
c. 7-Eleven
d. Cash flow statement

20. In finance, the term _________ describes the amount in cash that returns to the owners of a security. Normally it does not include the price variations, at the difference of the total return. _________ applies to various stated rates of return on stocks (common and preferred, and convertible), fixed income instruments (bonds, notes, bills, strips, zero coupon), and some other investment type insurance products (e.g. annuities.)

a. Yield to maturity
b. 4-4-5 Calendar
c. Yield
d. Macaulay duration

21. The _________ or redemption yield is the yield promised to the bondholder on the assumption that the bond or other fixed-interest security such as gilts will be held to maturity, that all coupon and principal payments will be made and coupon payments are reinvested at the bond's promised yield at the same rate as invested. It is a measure of the return of the bond. This technique in theory allows investors to calculate the fair value of different financial instruments.

a. Yield
b. Macaulay duration
c. Yield to maturity
d. 4-4-5 Calendar

22. In accounting and finance, _________ is the portion of receivables that can no longer be collected, typically from accounts receivable or loans. _________ in accounting is considered an expense.

There are two methods to account for _________:

1. Direct write off method (Non - GAAP)

A receivable which is not considered collectible is charged directly to the income statement.

1. Allowance method (GAAP)

An estimate is made at the end of each fiscal year of the amount of _________. This is then accumulated in a provision which is then used to reduce specific receivable accounts as and when necessary.

a. 529 plan
b. Tax expense
c. 4-4-5 Calendar
d. Bad debt

23. _________ is that which is owed; usually referencing assets owed, but the term can cover other obligations. In the case of assets, _________ is a means of using future purchasing power in the present before a summation has been earned. Some companies and corporations use _________ as a part of their overall corporate finance strategy.

a. Credit cycle
b. Partial Payment
c. Debt
d. Cross-collateralization

24. _________ is a fee paid on borrowed assets. It is the price paid for the use of borrowed money , or, money earned by deposited funds . Assets that are sometimes lent with _________ include money, shares, consumer goods through hire purchase, major assets such as aircraft, and even entire factories in finance lease arrangements.

a. A Random Walk Down Wall Street
b. Insolvency
c. AAB
d. Interest

25. _________ is a life of security. It may also refer to the final payment date of a loan or other financial instrument, at which point all remaining interest and principal is due to be paid.

1, 3, 6 months _________ band can be calculated by using 30-day per month periods.

a. Maturity
b. Replacement cost
c. False billing
d. Primary market

26. In financial accounting, _________s are precautions for which the amount or probability of occurrence are not known. Typical examples are _________s for warranty costs and _________ for taxes the term reserve is used instead of term _________; such a use, however, is inconsistent with the terminology suggested by International Accounting Standards Board.

a. Momentum Accounting and Triple-Entry Bookkeeping
b. Provision
c. Petty cash
d. Money measurement concept

27. In finance, _________, also known as return on investment is the ratio of money gained or lost on an investment relative to the amount of money invested. The amount of money gained or lost may be referred to as interest, profit/loss, gain/loss, or net income/loss. The money invested may be referred to as the asset, capital, principal, or the cost basis of the investment.

a. Stock or scrip dividends
b. Composiition of Creditors
c. Doctrine of the Proper Law
d. Rate of return

28. In finance, a _________ is a debt security, in which the authorized issuer owes the holders a debt and, depending on the terms of the _________, is obliged to pay interest (the coupon) and/or to repay the principal at a later date, termed maturity.

Thus a _________ is a loan: the issuer is the borrower, the _________ holder is the lender, and the coupon is the interest. _________s provide the borrower with external funds to finance long-term investments, or, in the case of government _________s, to finance current expenditure.

a. Catastrophe bonds
b. Convertible bond
c. Puttable bond
d. Bond

29. _________ is the provision of resources (such as granting a loan) by one party to another party where that second party does not reimburse the first party immediately, thereby generating a debt, and instead arranges either to repay or return those resources (or material(s) of equal value) at a later date. The first party is called a creditor, also known as a lender, while the second party is called a debtor, also known as a borrower.

Movements of financial capital are normally dependent on either _________ or equity transfers.

a. Warrant
b. Credit
c. Comparable
d. Clearing house

30. The _________ (NYSE: FRE) is an insolvent government sponsored enterprise (GSE) of the United States federal government.

The _________ was created in 1970 to expand the secondary market for mortgages in the US. Along with other GSEs, Freddie Mac buys mortgages on the secondary market, pools them, and sells them as mortgage-backed securities to investors on the open market.

a. The Depository Trust ' Clearing Corporation
b. Public company
c. Governmental Accounting Standards Board
d. Federal Home Loan Mortgage Corporation

31. The terms _________ , nominal _________, and effective _________ describe the interest rate for a whole year (annualized), rather than just a monthly fee/rate, as applied on a loan, mortgage, credit card, etc. Those terms have formal, legal definitions in some countries or legal jurisdictions, but in general:

- The nominal _________ is the simple-interest rate (for a year.)
- The effective _________ is the fee+compound interest rate (calculated across a year.)

The nominal _________ is calculated as: the rate, for a payment period, multiplied by the number of payment periods in a year. However, the exact legal definition of 'effective _________' can vary greatly in each jurisdiction, depending on the type of fees included, such as participation fees, loan origination fees, monthly service charges, or late fees. The effective _________ has been called the 'mathematically-true' interest rate for each year. The computation for the effective _________, as the fee+compound interest rate, can also vary depending on whether the up-front fees, such as origination or participation fees, are added to the entire amount, or treated as a short-term loan due in the first payment.

a. A Random Walk Down Wall Street
b. ABN Amro
c. Annual percentage rate
d. AAB

32. A _________ is a payment made by a corporation to its shareholder members. When a corporation earns a profit or surplus, that money can be put to two uses: it can either be re-invested in the business (called retained earnings), or it can be paid to the shareholders as a _________. Many corporations retain a portion of their earnings and pay the remainder as a _________.

a. Dividend
b. Dividend yield
c. Special dividend
d. Dividend puzzle

33. _________ is typically a higher ranking stock than voting shares, and its terms are negotiated between the corporation and the investor.

_________ usually carry no voting rights, but may carry superior priority over common stock in the payment of dividends and upon liquidation. _________ may carry a dividend that is paid out prior to any dividends to common stock holders.

a. Second lien loan
b. Follow-on offering
c. Trade-off theory
d. Preferred stock

34. _________ are those dividends paid out in form of additional stock shares of the issuing corporation or other corporation They are usually issued in proportion to shares owned (for example for every 100 shares of stock owned, 5% stock dividend will yield 5 extra shares). If this payment involves the issue of new shares, this is very similar to a stock split in that it increases the total number of shares while lowering the price of each share and does not change the market capitalization or the total value of the shares held

a. The Hong Kong Securities Institute
b. Stock or scrip dividends
c. Database auditing
d. Time-based currency

35. _________ is a form of corporation equity ownership represented in the securities. It is dangerous in comparison to preferred shares and some other investment options, in that in the event of bankruptcy, _________ investors receive their funds after preferred stockholders, bondholders, creditors, etc. On the other hand, common shares on average perform better than preferred shares or bonds over time.

a. Stock split
b. Common stock
c. Stock market bubble
d. Stop-limit order

36. _________ is a variant of the Discounted cash flow model, a method for valuing a stock or business. Often used to provide difficult-to-resolve valuation issues for litigation, tax planning, and business transactions that are currently off market.

It assumes that the company issues a dividend that has a current value of D that grows at a constant rate g. It also assumes that the required rate of return for the stock remains constant at k which is equal to the cost of equity for that company. It involves summing the infinite series which gives the value of price current P.

a. Special journals
b. Securitization
c. Stock or scrip dividends
d. Gordon growth model

37. In finance, _________ is the process of estimating the potential market value of a financial asset or liability. they can be done on assets (for example, investments in marketable securities such as stocks, options, business enterprises, or intangible assets such as patents and trademarks) or on liabilities (e.g., Bonds issued by a company.) _________s are required in many contexts including investment analysis, capital budgeting, merger and acquisition transactions, financial reporting, taxable events to determine the proper tax liability, and in litigation.

a. Procter ' Gamble
b. Margin
c. Valuation
d. Share

38. The term _________ has three unrelated technical definitions, and is also used in a variety of non-technical ways.

- In financial economics, it refers to any asset used to make money, as opposed to assets used for personal enjoyment or consumption. This is an important distinction because two people can disagree sharply about the value of personal assets, one person might think a sports car is more valuable than a pickup truck, another person might have the opposite taste. But if an asset is held for the purpose of making money, taste has nothing to do with it, only differences of opinion about how much money the asset will produce. With the further assumption that people agree on the probability distribution of future cash flows, it is possible to have an objective _________ pricing model. Even without the assumption of agreement, it is possible to set rational limits on _________ value.
- In governmental accounting, it is defined as any asset used in operations with an initial useful life extending beyond one reporting period. Generally, government managers have a 'stewardship' duty to maintain _________s under their control. See International Public Sector Accounting Standards for details.
- In US tax accounting, it is defined as any property other than a list of exceptions. The main exceptions are anything held for sale, and any real estate or depreciable property used in business. Almost everything you own and use for personal purposes, pleasure or investment is a _________. If something is a _________ for tax purposes, gains or losses on sale or disposition are capital gains or capital losses. For individuals, however, capital losses on property held for personal use are generally not deductible. See the IRS publication Tax Facts about Capital Gains and Losses for details.

A well-known financial accounting textbook advises that the term be avoided except in tax accounting because it is used in so many different senses, not all of them well-defined. For example it is often used as a synonym for fixed assets or for investments in securities.

A common non-technical usage occurs when people ask that employees or the environment or something else be treated as a _________.

a. Solvency
b. Capital asset
c. Settlement date
d. Political risk

39. In finance, the _________ is used to determine a theoretically appropriate required rate of return of an asset, if that asset is to be added to an already well-diversified portfolio, given that asset's non-diversifiable risk. The model takes into account the asset's sensitivity to non-diversifiable risk (also known as systemic risk or market risk), often represented by the quantity beta (β) in the financial industry, as well as the expected return of the market and the expected return of a theoretical risk-free asset.

The model was introduced by Jack Treynor (1961, 1962), William Sharpe (1964), John Lintner (1965a,b) and Jan Mossin (1966) independently, building on the earlier work of Harry Markowitz on diversification and modern portfolio theory.

a. Hull-White model
b. Cox-Ingersoll-Ross model
c. Capital asset pricing model
d. Random walk hypothesis

40. A _________ is a fungible, negotiable instrument representing financial value. They are broadly categorized into debt securities (such as banknotes, bonds and debentures), and equity securities; e.g., common stocks. The company or other entity issuing the _________ is called the issuer.
a. Tracking stock
b. Securities lending
c. Book entry
d. Security

41. In Modern Portfolio Theory, the _________ is the graphical representation of the Capital Asset Pricing Model. It displays the expected rate of return for an overall market as a function of systematic (non-diversifiable) risk (beta.)

The Y-Intercept (beta=0) of the _________ is equal to the risk-free interest rate.

a. Certificate in Investment Performance Measurement
b. Divestment
c. Rebalancing
d. Security market line

42. In business and accounting, _________s are everything of value that is owned by a person or company. The balance sheet of a firm records the monetary value of the _________s owned by the firm. The two major _________ classes are tangible _________s and intangible _________s.
a. Asset
b. Income
c. Accounts payable
d. EBITDA

43. In accounting, _________ refers to the portion of net income which is retained by the corporation rather than distributed to its owners as dividends. Similarly, if the corporation makes a loss, then that loss is retained and called variously retained losses, accumulated losses or accumulated deficit. _________ and losses are cumulative from year to year with losses offsetting earnings.
a. Historical cost
b. Retained earnings
c. Matching principle
d. Generally Accepted Accounting Principles

44. In accounting, _________ or *Carrying value* is the value of an asset according to its balance sheet account balance. For assets, the value is based on the original cost of the asset less any depreciation, amortization or impairment costs made against the asset. A company's _________ is its total assets minus intangible assets and liabilities.
a. Retained earnings
b. Pro forma
c. Current liabilities
d. Book value

45. _________ is the price at which an asset would trade in a competitive Walrasian auction setting. _________ is often used interchangeably with open _________, fair value or fair _________, although these terms have distinct definitions in different standards, and may differ in some circumstances.

International Valuation Standards defines _________ as 'the estimated amount for which a property should exchange on the date of valuation between a willing buyer and a willing seller in an arm'e;s-length transaction after proper marketing wherein the parties had each acted knowledgeably, prudently, and without compulsion.'

_________ is a concept distinct from market price, which is 'e;the price at which one can transact'e;, while _________ is 'e;the true underlying value'e; according to theoretical standards.

a. T-Model
b. Debt restructuring
c. Wrap account
d. Market value

46. _________ are made by investors and investment managers.

Investors commonly perform investment analysis by making use of fundamental analysis, technical analysis and gut feel.

_________ are often supported by decision tools.

a. Investment performance
b. Asset allocation
c. Investing online
d. Investment decisions

47. The institution most often referenced by the word '_________' is a public or publicly traded _________, the shares of which are traded on a public stock exchange (e.g., the New York Stock Exchange or Nasdaq in the United States) where shares of stock of _________s are bought and sold by and to the general public. Most of the largest businesses in the world are publicly traded _________s. However, the majority of _________s are said to be closely held, privately held or close _________s, meaning that no ready market exists for the trading of shares.

a. Protect
b. Depository Trust Company
c. Corporation
d. Federal Home Loan Mortgage Corporation

48. _________ is a concept whereby a person's financial liability is limited to a fixed sum, most commonly the value of a person's investment in a company or partnership with _________. A shareholder in a limited company is not personally liable for any of the debts of the company, other than for the value of his investment in that company. The same is true for the members of a _________ partnership and the limited partners in a limited partnership.

a. Personal property
b. Sarbanes-Oxley Act
c. Beneficial owner
d. Limited liability

49. A _________ in the law of the vast majority of United States jurisdictions is a legal form of business company that provides limited liability to its owners. It is a hybrid business entity having certain characteristics of both a corporation and a partnership or sole proprietorship (depending on how many owners there are.) The primary characteristic an _________ shares with a corporation is limited liability, and the primary characteristic it shares with a partnership is the availability of pass-through income taxation.

a. Financial endowment
b. Fund of funds
c. Pension fund
d. Limited liability company

50. An _________ is a corporation that makes a valid election to be taxed under Subchapter S of Chapter 1 of the Internal Revenue Code.

In general, _________s do not pay any income taxes. Instead, the corporation's income or losses are divided among and passed through to its shareholders.

a. 4-4-5 Calendar
b. 7-Eleven
c. 529 plan
d. S corporation

51. In the most general sense, a _________ is anything that is a hindrance, or puts individuals at a disadvantage.

Before we discuss the financial terms, we should note that a _________ can also have a much more important slang meaning.

This is best described in an example.

a. Covenant
b. Liability
c. Limited liability
d. McFadden Act

52. _________ or net present worth (NPW) is defined as the total present value (PV) of a time series of cash flows. It is a standard method for using the time value of money to appraise long-term projects. Used for capital budgeting, and widely throughout economics, it measures the excess or shortfall of cash flows, in present value terms, once financing charges are met.

a. Negative gearing
b. Net present value
c. Tax shield
d. Present value of costs

53. _________ is the value on a given date of a future payment or series of future payments, discounted to reflect the time value of money and other factors such as investment risk. _________ calculations are widely used in business and economics to provide a means to compare cash flows at different times on a meaningful 'like to like' basis.

The most commonly applied model of the time value of money is compound interest.

a. Net present value
b. Present value of benefits
c. Present value
d. Negative gearing

1. In finance, _________ refers to the way a corporation finances its assets through some combination of equity, debt, or hybrid securities. A firm's _________ is then the composition or 'structure' of its liabilities. For example, a firm that sells $20 billion in equity and $80 billion in debt is said to be 20% equity-financed and 80% debt-financed.

a. Capital structure
b. Rights issue
c. Market for corporate control
d. Book building

2. In finance, _________ (or gearing) is borrowing money to supplement existing funds for investment in such a way that the potential positive or negative outcome is magnified and/or enhanced. It generally refers to using borrowed funds, or debt, so as to attempt to increase the returns to equity. Deleveraging is the action of reducing borrowings.

a. Pension fund
b. Leverage
c. Financial endowment
d. Limited partnership

3. In economics, business, and accounting, a _________ is the value of money that has been used up to produce something, and hence is not available for use anymore. In business, the _________ may be one of acquisition, in which case the amount of money expended to acquire it is counted as _________. In this case, money is the input that is gone in order to acquire the thing.

a. Cost
b. Fixed costs
c. Sliding scale fees
d. Marginal cost

4. The term _________ has three unrelated technical definitions, and is also used in a variety of non-technical ways.

- In financial economics, it refers to any asset used to make money, as opposed to assets used for personal enjoyment or consumption. This is an important distinction because two people can disagree sharply about the value of personal assets, one person might think a sports car is more valuable than a pickup truck, another person might have the opposite taste. But if an asset is held for the purpose of making money, taste has nothing to do with it, only differences of opinion about how much money the asset will produce. With the further assumption that people agree on the probability distribution of future cash flows, it is possible to have an objective _________ pricing model. Even without the assumption of agreement, it is possible to set rational limits on _________ value.
- In governmental accounting, it is defined as any asset used in operations with an initial useful life extending beyond one reporting period. Generally, government managers have a 'stewardship' duty to maintain _________s under their control. See International Public Sector Accounting Standards for details.
- In US tax accounting, it is defined as any property other than a list of exceptions. The main exceptions are anything held for sale, and any real estate or depreciable property used in business. Almost everything you own and use for personal purposes, pleasure or investment is a _________. If something is a _________ for tax purposes, gains or losses on sale or disposition are capital gains or capital losses. For individuals, however, capital losses on property held for personal use are generally not deductible. See the IRS publication Tax Facts about Capital Gains and Losses for details.

A well-known financial accounting textbook advises that the term be avoided except in tax accounting because it is used in so many different senses, not all of them well-defined. For example it is often used as a synonym for fixed assets or for investments in securities.

A common non-technical usage occurs when people ask that employees or the environment or something else be treated as a _________.

a. Settlement date
b. Solvency
c. Political risk
d. Capital asset

5. In finance, the _________ is used to determine a theoretically appropriate required rate of return of an asset, if that asset is to be added to an already well-diversified portfolio, given that asset's non-diversifiable risk. The model takes into account the asset's sensitivity to non-diversifiable risk (also known as systemic risk or market risk), often represented by the quantity beta (β) in the financial industry, as well as the expected return of the market and the expected return of a theoretical risk-free asset.

The model was introduced by Jack Treynor (1961, 1962), William Sharpe (1964), John Lintner (1965a,b) and Jan Mossin (1966) independently, building on the earlier work of Harry Markowitz on diversification and modern portfolio theory.

a. Hull-White model
b. Capital asset pricing model
c. Cox-Ingersoll-Ross model
d. Random walk hypothesis

6. In finance, _________ occurs when a debtor has not met its legal obligations according to the debt contract, e.g. it has not made a scheduled payment, or has violated a loan covenant (condition) of the debt contract. _________ may occur if the debtor is either unwilling or unable to pay their debt. This can occur with all debt obligations including bonds, mortgages, loans, and promissory notes.

a. Credit crunch
b. Debt validation
c. Vendor finance
d. Default

7. _________ is the risk of loss due to a debtor's non-payment of a loan or other line of credit (either the principal or interest (coupon) or both)

Most lenders employ their own models (credit scorecards) to rank potential and existing customers according to risk, and then apply appropriate strategies. With products such as unsecured personal loans or mortgages, lenders charge a higher price for higher risk customers and vice versa. With revolving products such as credit cards and overdrafts, risk is controlled through careful setting of credit limits.

a. Market risk
b. Liquidity risk
c. Transaction risk
d. Credit risk

8. In finance, the _________ between two currencies specifies how much one currency is worth in terms of the other. For example an _________ of 102 Japanese yen to the United States dollar means that JPY 102 is worth the same as USD 1. The foreign exchange market is one of the largest markets in the world.

a. Exchange rate
b. ABN Amro
c. A Random Walk Down Wall Street
d. AAB

9. _________ is a form of risk that arises from the change in price of one currency against another. Whenever investors or companies have assets or business operations across national borders, they face _________ if their positions are not hedged.

- Transaction risk is the risk that exchange rates will change unfavourably over time. It can be hedged against using forward currency contracts;
- Translation risk is an accounting risk, proportional to the amount of assets held in foreign currencies. Changes in the exchange rate over time will render a report inaccurate, and so assets are usually balanced by borrowings in that currency.

The exchange risk associated with a foreign denominated instrument is a key element in foreign investment. This risk flows from differential monetary policy and growth in real productivity, which results in differential inflation rates.

a. Tracking error
b. Market risk
c. Credit risk
d. Currency risk

10. _________ is a type of risk faced by investors, corporations, and governments. It is a risk that can be understood and managed with proper aforethought and investment.

Broadly, _________ refers to the complications businesses and governments may face as a result of what are commonly referred to as political decisions--or 'any political change that alters the expected outcome and value of a given economic action by changing the probability of achieving business objectives.' .

a. Political risk
b. Mid price
c. Single-index model
d. Capital asset

11. In business and accounting, _________s are everything of value that is owned by a person or company. The balance sheet of a firm records the monetary value of the _________s owned by the firm. The two major _________ classes are tangible _________s and intangible _________s.

a. Income
b. Accounts payable
c. EBITDA
d. Asset

12. In finance, _________ is the process of estimating the potential market value of a financial asset or liability. they can be done on assets (for example, investments in marketable securities such as stocks, options, business enterprises, or intangible assets such as patents and trademarks) or on liabilities (e.g., Bonds issued by a company.) _________s are required in many contexts including investment analysis, capital budgeting, merger and acquisition transactions, financial reporting, taxable events to determine the proper tax liability, and in litigation.

a. Share
b. Margin
c. Valuation
d. Procter ' Gamble

13. In accounting and finance, _________ is the portion of receivables that can no longer be collected, typically from accounts receivable or loans. _________ in accounting is considered an expense.

There are two methods to account for _________:

1. Direct write off method (Non - GAAP)

A receivable which is not considered collectible is charged directly to the income statement.

1. Allowance method (GAAP)

An estimate is made at the end of each fiscal year of the amount of _________. This is then accumulated in a provision which is then used to reduce specific receivable accounts as and when necessary.

a. Bad debt
b. 4-4-5 Calendar
c. 529 plan
d. Tax expense

14. _________ is the planning process used to determine whether a firm's long term investments such as new machinery, replacement machinery, new plants, new products, and research development projects are worth pursuing. It is budget for major capital, or investment, expenditures.

Many formal methods are used in _________, including the techniques such as

- Net present value
- Profitability index
- Internal rate of return
- Modified Internal Rate of Return
- Equivalent annuity

These methods use the incremental cash flows from each potential investment, or project. Techniques based on accounting earnings and accounting rules are sometimes used - though economists consider this to be improper - such as the accounting rate of return, and 'return on investment.' Simplified and hybrid methods are used as well, such as payback period and discounted payback period.

a. Financial distress
b. Preferred stock
c. Shareholder value
d. Capital budgeting

15. _________ is that which is owed; usually referencing assets owed, but the term can cover other obligations. In the case of assets, _________ is a means of using future purchasing power in the present before a summation has been earned. Some companies and corporations use _________ as a part of their overall corporate finance strategy.

a. Partial Payment
b. Cross-collateralization
c. Credit cycle
d. Debt

16. In financial accounting, _________s are precautions for which the amount or probability of occurrence are not known. Typical examples are _________s for warranty costs and _________ for taxes the term reserve is used instead of term _________; such a use, however, is inconsistent with the terminology suggested by International Accounting Standards Board.

a. Momentum Accounting and Triple-Entry Bookkeeping
b. Money measurement concept
c. Provision
d. Petty cash

17. In financial and business accounting, _________ is a measure of a firm's profitability that excludes interest and income tax expenses.

EBIT = Operating Revenue - Operating Expenses (OPEX) + Non-operating Income

Operating Income = Operating Revenue - Operating Expenses

Operating income is the difference between operating revenues and operating expenses, but it is also sometimes used as a synonym for EBIT and operating profit. This is true if the firm has no non-operating income.

a. ABN Amro
b. AAB
c. A Random Walk Down Wall Street
d. Earnings before interest and taxes

18. The _________ is a measure of how revenue growth translates into growth in operating income. It is a measure of leverage, and of how risky (volatile) a company's operating income is.

There are various measures of _________, which can be interpreted analogously to financial leverage.

a. Asset turnover
b. Average accounting return
c. Invested capital
d. Operating leverage

19. _________ is a measure of a company's earning power from ongoing operations, equal to earnings before the deduction of interest payments and income taxes.

To accountants, economic profit, or EP, is a single-period metric to determine the value created by a company in one period - usually a year. It is the net profit after tax less the equity charge, a risk-weighted cost of capital.

a. A Random Walk Down Wall Street
b. Operating profit
c. Economic profit
d. AAB

20. _________ is a fee paid on borrowed assets. It is the price paid for the use of borrowed money , or, money earned by deposited funds . Assets that are sometimes lent with _________ include money, shares, consumer goods through hire purchase, major assets such as aircraft, and even entire factories in finance lease arrangements.

a. A Random Walk Down Wall Street
b. Interest
c. Insolvency
d. AAB

21. _________ is the difference between price and the costs of bringing to market whatever it is that is accounted as an enterprise (whether by harvest, extraction, manufacture, or purchase) in terms of the component costs of delivered goods and/or services and any operating or other expenses.

A key difficulty in measuring profit is in defining costs. Pure economic monetary profits can be zero or negative even in competitive equilibrium when accounted monetized costs exceed monetized price.

a. Economic profit
b. Accounting profit
c. AAB
d. A Random Walk Down Wall Street

22. _________ are business expenses that are not dependent on the level of production or sales. They tend to be time-related, such as salaries or rents being paid per month. This is in contrast to Variable costs, which are volume-related (and are paid per quantity.)

a. Marginal cost
b. Sliding scale fees
c. Transaction cost
d. Fixed costs

23. _________ are expenses that change in proportion to the activity of a business. In other words, _________ are the sum of marginal costs. It can also be considered normal costs. Along with fixed costs, _________ make up the two components of total cost. Direct Costs, however, are costs that can be associated with a particular cost object.

a. Fixed costs
b. Cost accounting
c. Transaction cost
d. Variable costs

24. The institution most often referenced by the word '_________' is a public or publicly traded _________, the shares of which are traded on a public stock exchange (e.g., the New York Stock Exchange or Nasdaq in the United States) where shares of stock of _________s are bought and sold by and to the general public. Most of the largest businesses in the world are publicly traded _________s. However, the majority of _________s are said to be closely held, privately held or close _________s, meaning that no ready market exists for the trading of shares.

a. Protect
b. Corporation
c. Depository Trust Company
d. Federal Home Loan Mortgage Corporation

25. _________ is the capital that a business raises by taking out a loan. It is a loan made to a company that is normally repaid at some future date. _________ differs from equity or share capital because subscribers to _________ do not become part owners of the business, but are merely creditors, and the suppliers of _________ usually receive a contractually fixed annual percentage return on their loan, and this is known as the coupon rate.

a. Risk-return spectrum
b. Financial assistance
c. Floating charge
d. Debt capital

26. A _________ is a bond issued by a corporation. The term is usually applied to longer-term debt instruments, generally with a maturity date falling at least a year after their issue date. (The term 'commercial paper' is sometimes used for instruments with a shorter maturity.)

a. Serial bond
b. Brady bonds
c. Government bond
d. Corporate bond

27. _________ is a financial ratio that indicates the percentage of a company's assets are provided via debt. It is the ratio of total debt (the sum of current liabilities and long-term liabilities) and total assets (the sum of current assets, fixed assets, and other assets such as 'goodwill'.)

>

or alternatively:

For example, a company with $2 million in total assets and $500,000 in total liabilities would have a _________ of 25%

Like all financial ratios, a company's _________ should be compared with their industry average or other competing firms.

a. Capitalization rate
b. Debt ratio
c. Cash management
d. Cash concentration

28. _________ is a measurement of corporate or economic size equal to the share price times the number of shares outstanding of a public company. As owning stock represents owning the company, including all its equity, capitalization could represent the public opinion of a company's net worth and is a determining factor in stock valuation. Likewise, the capitalization of stock markets or economic regions may be compared to other economic indicators.

a. Market capitalization
b. Proxy fight
c. Synthetic CDO
d. Just-in-time

29. _________ or interest coverage ratio is a measure of a company's ability to honor its debt payments. It may be calculated as either EBIT or EBITDA divided by the total interest payable.

$$\text{Times-Interest-Earned} = \frac{\text{EBIT or EBITDA}}{\text{Interest Charges}}$$

- Financial ratio
- Financial leverage
- EBIT
- EBITDA
- Debt service coverage ratio

Interest Charges = Traditionally 'charges' refers to interest expense found on the income statement.

_________ or Interest Coverage is a great tool when measuring a company's ability to meet its debt obligations.

a. Times interest earned
b. Net assets
c. Return of capital
d. Cash conversion cycle

30. _________ is a type of private equity capital typically provided to early-stage, high-potential, growth companies in the interest of generating a return through an eventual realization event such as an IPO or trade sale of the company. _________ investments are generally made as cash in exchange for shares in the invested company. It is typical for _________ investors to identify and back companies in high technology industries such as biotechnology and ICT.

a. Probability distribution
b. Treasury Inflation-Protected Securities
c. Tail risk
d. Venture capital

31. The _________ is the rate that a company is expected to pay to finance its assets. WACC is the minimum return that a company must earn on existing asset base to satisfy its creditors, owners, and other providers of capital.

Companies raise money from a number of sources: common equity, preferred equity, straight debt, convertible debt, exchangeable debt, warrants, options, pension liabilities, executive stock options, governmental subsidies, and so on.

a. Cost of capital
b. Weighted average cost of capital
c. 4-4-5 Calendar
d. Capital intensity

32. In finance, a _________ is a debt security, in which the authorized issuer owes the holders a debt and, depending on the terms of the _________, is obliged to pay interest (the coupon) and/or to repay the principal at a later date, termed maturity.

Thus a _________ is a loan: the issuer is the borrower, the _________ holder is the lender, and the coupon is the interest. _________s provide the borrower with external funds to finance long-term investments, or, in the case of government _________s, to finance current expenditure.

a. Puttable bond
b. Catastrophe bonds
c. Bond
d. Convertible bond

33. _________ are costs incurred on the purchase of land, buildings, construction and equipment to be used in the production of goods or the rendering of services. In other words, the total cost needed to bring a project to a commercially operable status. However, _________ are not limited to the initial construction of a factory or other business.

a. Capital outflow
b. Trade-off
c. Capital costs
d. Defined contribution plan

34. The _________ is an expected return that the provider of capital plans to earn on their investment.

Capital (money) used for funding a business should earn returns for the capital providers who risk their capital. For an investment to be worthwhile, the expected return on capital must be greater than the _________.

a. Capital intensity
b. Cost of capital
c. Weighted average cost of capital
d. 4-4-5 Calendar

35. In economics and finance, _________ is the change in total cost that arises when the quantity produced changes by one unit. It is the cost of producing one more unit of a good. Mathematically, the _________ function is expressed as the first derivative of the total cost (TC) function with respect to quantity (Q). Note that the _________ may change with volume, and so at each level of production, the _________ is the cost of the next unit produced.

A typical _________ Curve

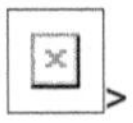>

a. Fixed costs
b. Cost accounting
c. Sliding scale fees
d. Marginal cost

36. An _________ is an economic concept that relates to the cost incurred by an entity (such as organizations) associated with problems such as divergent management-shareholder objectives and information asymmetry. The costs consist of two main sources:

1. The costs inherently associated with using an agent (e.g., the risk that agents will use organizational resource for their own benefit) and
2. The costs of techniques used to mitigate the problems associated with using an agent (e.g., the costs of producing financial statements or the use of stock options to align executive interests to shareholder interests.)

Though effects of _________ are present in any agency relationship, the term is most used in business contexts.

The information asymmetry that exists between shareholders and the Chief Executive Officer is generally considered to be a classic example of a principal-agent problem. The agent (the manager) is working on behalf of the principal (the shareholders), who does not observe the actions of the agent.

a. AAB
b. A Random Walk Down Wall Street
c. ABN Amro
d. Agency cost

37. _________ is a legally declared inability or impairment of ability of an individual or organization to pay their creditors. Creditors may file a _________ petition against a debtor ('involuntary _________') in an effort to recoup a portion of what they are owed or initiate a restructuring. In the majority of cases, however, _________ is initiated by the debtor (a 'voluntary _________' that is filed by the bankrupt individual or organization.)

a. Debt settlement
b. Bankruptcy
c. 529 plan
d. 4-4-5 Calendar

38. _________ or financing is to provide capital (funds), which means money for a project, a person, a business or any other private or public institutions.

Those funds can be allocated for either short term or long term purposes. The health fund is a new way of _________ private healthcare centers.

a. Synthetic CDO
b. Product life cycle
c. Proxy fight
d. Funding

39. _________ is normally any risk associated with any form of financing.

Depending on the nature of the investment, the type of 'investment' risk will vary. High risk investments have greater potential rewards, but you may lose your money instead by taking the risk for more money.

a. Financial risk
b. Stock market index option
c. Revaluation
d. Liquidating dividend

40. In business, _________ is income that a company receives from its normal business activities, usually from the sale of goods and services to customers. Some companies also receive _________ from interest, dividends or royalties paid to them by other companies. _________ may refer to business income in general, or it may refer to the amount, in a monetary unit, received during a period of time, as in 'Last year, Company X had _________ of $32 million.'

In many countries, including the UK, _________ is referred to as turnover.

a. Bottom line
b. Furniture, Fixtures and Equipment
c. Matching principle
d. Revenue

41. _________ are the earnings returned on the initial investment amount.

In the US, the Financial Accounting Standards Board (FASB) requires companies' income statements to report _________ for each of the major categories of the income statement: continuing operations, discontinued operations, extraordinary items, and net income.

The _________ formula does not include preferred dividends for categories outside of continued operations and net income.

a. Average accounting return
b. Inventory turnover
c. Assets turnover
d. Earnings per share

42. In business and finance, a _________ (also referred to as equity _________) of stock means a _________ of ownership in a corporation (company.) In the plural, stocks is often used as a synonym for _________s especially in the United States, but it is less commonly used that way outside of North America.

In the United Kingdom, South Africa, and Australia, stock can also refer to completely different financial instruments such as government bonds or, less commonly, to all kinds of marketable securities.

a. Bucket shop
b. Share
c. Procter ' Gamble
d. Margin

43. A _________ is a situation that involves losing one quality or aspect of something in return for gaining another quality or aspect. It implies a decision to be made with full comprehension of both the upside and downside of a particular choice.

In economics the term is expressed as opportunity cost, referring the most preferred alternative given up.

a. Total revenue
b. Capital outflow
c. Break-even point
d. Trade-off

44. In political science and economics, the _________ or agency dilemma treats the difficulties that arise under conditions of incomplete and asymmetric information when a principal hires an agent. Various mechanisms may be used to try to align the interests of the agent with those of the principal, such as piece rates/commissions, profit sharing, efficiency wages, performance measurement (including financial statements), the agent posting a bond, or fear of firing. The _________ is found in most employer/employee relationships, for example, when stockholders hire top executives of corporations.

a. Principal-agent problem
b. 7-Eleven
c. 4-4-5 Calendar
d. 529 plan

45. In economics and contract theory, _________ deals with the study of decisions in transactions where one party has more or better information than the other. This creates an imbalance of power in transactions which can sometimes cause the transactions to go awry. Examples of this problem are adverse selection and moral hazard.

a. A Random Walk Down Wall Street
b. AAB
c. Information asymmetry
d. ABN Amro

46. _________ is a form of corporation equity ownership represented in the securities. It is dangerous in comparison to preferred shares and some other investment options, in that in the event of bankruptcy, _________ investors receive their funds after preferred stockholders, bondholders, creditors, etc. On the other hand, common shares on average perform better than preferred shares or bonds over time.

a. Stock market bubble
b. Stock split
c. Stop-limit order
d. Common stock

47. _________ is typically a higher ranking stock than voting shares, and its terms are negotiated between the corporation and the investor.

_________ usually carry no voting rights, but may carry superior priority over common stock in the payment of dividends and upon liquidation. _________ may carry a dividend that is paid out prior to any dividends to common stock holders.

a. Second lien loan
b. Preferred stock
c. Trade-off theory
d. Follow-on offering

48. A mutual shareholder or _________ is an individual or company (including a corporation) that legally owns one or more shares of stock in a joint stock company. A company's shareholders collectively own that company. Thus, the typical goal of such companies is to enhance shareholder value.

a. Trading curb
b. Stockholder
c. Limit order
d. Stock market bubble

49. A _________ is the price of a single share of a no. of saleable stocks of the company. Once the stock is purchased, the owner becomes a shareholder of the company that issued the share.

a. Share price
b. Stock split
c. Whisper numbers
d. Trading curb

1. A _________ is a payment made by a corporation to its shareholder members. When a corporation earns a profit or surplus, that money can be put to two uses: it can either be re-invested in the business (called retained earnings), or it can be paid to the shareholders as a _________. Many corporations retain a portion of their earnings and pay the remainder as a _________.

a. Dividend yield
b. Special dividend
c. Dividend
d. Dividend puzzle

2. _________ is a measurement of corporate or economic size equal to the share price times the number of shares outstanding of a public company. As owning stock represents owning the company, including all its equity, capitalization could represent the public opinion of a company's net worth and is a determining factor in stock valuation. Likewise, the capitalization of stock markets or economic regions may be compared to other economic indicators.

a. Proxy fight
b. Just-in-time
c. Market capitalization
d. Synthetic CDO

3. In some countries, including the United States and the United Kingdom, corporations can buy back their own stock in a share repurchase, also known as a _________ or share buyback. There has been a meteoric rise in the use of share repurchases in the U.S. in the past twenty years, from $5b in 1980 to $349b in 2005. A share repurchase distributes cash to existing shareholders in exchange for a fraction of the firm's outstanding equity.

a. Trading curb
b. Common stock
c. Stockholder
d. Stock repurchase

4. A mutual shareholder or _________ is an individual or company (including a corporation) that legally owns one or more shares of stock in a joint stock company. A company's shareholders collectively own that company. Thus, the typical goal of such companies is to enhance shareholder value.

a. Stock market bubble
b. Trading curb
c. Limit order
d. Stockholder

5. In the theory of capital structure, _________ is the phrase used to describe funds that firms obtain from outside of the firm. It is contrasted to internal financing which consists mainly of profits retained by the firm for investment. There are many kinds of _________.

a. Adjustment
b. Asset-backed commercial paper
c. Ownership equity
d. External financing

6. In the theory of capital structure _________ is the name for a firm using its profits as a source of capital for new investment, rather than a) distributing them to firm's owners or other investors and b) obtaining capital elsewhere. It is to be contrasted with external financing which consists of new money from outside of the firm brought in for investment. _________ is generally thought to be less expensive for the firm than external financing because the firm does not have to incur transaction costs to obtain it, nor does it have to pay the taxes associated with paying dividends.

a. Operating ratio
b. Underwriting contract
c. Internal financing
d. Employee stock option

7. In accounting, _________ refers to the portion of net income which is retained by the corporation rather than distributed to its owners as dividends. Similarly, if the corporation makes a loss, then that loss is retained and called variously retained losses, accumulated losses or accumulated deficit. _________ and losses are cumulative from year to year with losses offsetting earnings.

a. Historical cost
b. Retained earnings
c. Generally Accepted Accounting Principles
d. Matching principle

8. _________ or financing is to provide capital (funds), which means money for a project, a person, a business or any other private or public institutions.

Those funds can be allocated for either short term or long term purposes. The health fund is a new way of _________ private healthcare centers.

a. Synthetic CDO
b. Proxy fight
c. Product life cycle
d. Funding

9. A _________ is an equity investment option offered directly from the underlying company. The investor does not receive quarterly dividends directly as cash; instead, the investor's dividends are directly reinvested in the underlying equity. It should be noted that the investor still must pay tax annually on his or her dividend income, whether it is received or reinvested.

a. Dividend puzzle
b. Dividend reinvestment plan
c. Dividend decision
d. Dividend payout ratio

10. _________ refers to a business or organization attempting to acquire goods or services to accomplish the goals of the enterprise. Though there are several organizations that attempt to set standards in the _________ process, processes can vary greatly between organizations. Typically the word '_________' is not used interchangeably with the word 'procurement', since procurement typically includes Expediting, Supplier Quality, and Traffic and Logistics (T'L) in addition to _________.

a. Purchasing
b. 4-4-5 Calendar
c. 529 plan
d. 7-Eleven

11. In economics, business, and accounting, a _________ is the value of money that has been used up to produce something, and hence is not available for use anymore. In business, the _________ may be one of acquisition, in which case the amount of money expended to acquire it is counted as _________. In this case, money is the input that is gone in order to acquire the thing.

a. Fixed costs
b. Marginal cost
c. Sliding scale fees
d. Cost

12. The _________ is an expected return that the provider of capital plans to earn on their investment.

Capital (money) used for funding a business should earn returns for the capital providers who risk their capital. For an investment to be worthwhile, the expected return on capital must be greater than the _________.

a. Cost of capital
b. 4-4-5 Calendar
c. Capital intensity
d. Weighted average cost of capital

13. In economics and finance, _________ is the change in total cost that arises when the quantity produced changes by one unit. It is the cost of producing one more unit of a good. Mathematically, the _________ function is expressed as the first derivative of the total cost (TC) function with respect to quantity (Q). Note that the _________ may change with volume, and so at each level of production, the _________ is the cost of the next unit produced.

A typical _________ Curve

>

a. Sliding scale fees
b. Fixed costs
c. Cost accounting
d. Marginal cost

14. _________ represents the impact on the stock price that investors would cause in reaction to a change in policy of a company.

a. Clientele effect
b. Bonus share
c. Trade date
d. Volatility clustering

15. In business, _________ is income that a company receives from its normal business activities, usually from the sale of goods and services to customers. Some companies also receive _________ from interest, dividends or royalties paid to them by other companies. _________ may refer to business income in general, or it may refer to the amount, in a monetary unit, received during a period of time, as in 'Last year, Company X had _________ of $32 million.'

In many countries, including the UK, _________ is referred to as turnover.

a. Matching principle
b. Bottom line
c. Furniture, Fixtures and Equipment
d. Revenue

16. _________ is the fraction of net income a firm pays to its stockholders in dividends:

>

The part of the earnings not paid to investors is left for investment to provide for future earnings growth. Investors seeking high current income and limited capital growth prefer companies with high _________. However investors seeking capital growth may prefer lower payout ratio because capital gains are taxed at a lower rate.

a. Dividend puzzle
b. Dividend payout ratio
c. Dividend yield
d. Dividend imputation

17. _________ is the difference between price and the costs of bringing to market whatever it is that is accounted as an enterprise (whether by harvest, extraction, manufacture, or purchase) in terms of the component costs of delivered goods and/or services and any operating or other expenses.

A key difficulty in measuring profit is in defining costs. Pure economic monetary profits can be zero or negative even in competitive equilibrium when accounted monetized costs exceed monetized price.

a. AAB
b. Economic profit
c. A Random Walk Down Wall Street
d. Accounting profit

18. _________ are those dividends paid out in form of additional stock shares of the issuing corporation or other corporation They are usually issued in proportion to shares owned (for example for every 100 shares of stock owned, 5% stock dividend will yield 5 extra shares). If this payment involves the issue of new shares, this is very similar to a stock split in that it increases the total number of shares while lowering the price of each share and does not change the market capitalization or the total value of the shares held

a. The Hong Kong Securities Institute
b. Time-based currency
c. Database auditing
d. Stock or scrip dividends

19. A _________ or stock divide increases or decreases the number of shares in a public company. The price is adjusted such that the before and after market capitalization of the company remains the same and dilution does not occur. Options and warrants are included.

a. Stop order
b. Contract for difference
c. Stop price
d. Stock split

20. On a stock exchange, a _________ is the opposite of a stock split, i.e. a stock merge - a reduction in the number of shares and an accompanying increase in the share price. The ratio is also reversed: 1-for-2, 1-for-3 and so on.

There is a stigma attached to doing this so it is not initiated without very good reason.

a. Trade date
b. Reverse stock split
c. Conglomerate merger
d. Correlation trading

21. A _________ is a fungible, negotiable instrument representing financial value. They are broadly categorized into debt securities (such as banknotes, bonds and debentures), and equity securities; e.g., common stocks. The company or other entity issuing the _________ is called the issuer.

a. Tracking stock
b. Book entry
c. Securities lending
d. Security

22. The U.S. _________ is an independent agency of the United States government which holds primary responsibility for enforcing the federal securities laws and regulating the securities industry, the nation's stock and options exchanges, and other electronic securities markets. The SEC was created by section 4 of the SEC of 1934 (now codified as 15 U.S.C. Â§ 78d and commonly referred to as the 1934 Act.)

a. 4-4-5 Calendar
b. 7-Eleven
c. Securities and Exchange Commission
d. 529 plan

23. _________ is a form of corporation equity ownership represented in the securities. It is dangerous in comparison to preferred shares and some other investment options, in that in the event of bankruptcy, _________ investors receive their funds after preferred stockholders, bondholders, creditors, etc. On the other hand, common shares on average perform better than preferred shares or bonds over time.

a. Stop-limit order
b. Stock split
c. Stock market bubble
d. Common stock

24. The _________ of a stock is a measure of the price paid for a share relative to the annual income or profit earned by the firm per share. It is a financial ratio used for valuation: a higher _________ means that investors are paying more for each unit of income, so the stock is more expensive compared to one with lower _________.

The _________ has units of years, which can be interpreted as 'number of years of earnings to pay back purchase price'.

a. Sustainable growth rate
b. Return of capital
c. Quick ratio
d. P/E ratio

25. _________ is a corporate finance term denoting a type of takeover bid. The _________ is a public, open offer or invitation (usually announced in a newspaper advertisement) by a prospective acquirer to all stockholders of a publicly traded corporation (the target corporation) to tender their stock for sale at a specified price during a specified time, subject to the tendering of a minimum and maximum number of shares. In a _________, the bidder contacts shareholders directly; the directors of the company may or may not have endorsed the _________ proposal.

a. Shareholder value
b. Cash is king
c. Follow-on offering
d. Tender offer

26. A _________ or reacquired stock is stock which is bought back by the issuing company, reducing the amount of outstanding stock on the open market ('open market' including insiders' holdings.)

Stock repurchases are often used as a tax-efficient method to put cash into shareholders' hands, rather than pay dividends. Sometimes, companies do this when they feel that their stock is undervalued on the open market.

a. Generally Accepted Accounting Principles
b. Current asset
c. Trial balance
d. Treasury stock

27. The institution most often referenced by the word '_________' is a public or publicly traded _________, the shares of which are traded on a public stock exchange (e.g., the New York Stock Exchange or Nasdaq in the United States) where shares of stock of _________s are bought and sold by and to the general public. Most of the largest businesses in the world are publicly traded _________s. However, the majority of _________s are said to be closely held, privately held or close _________s, meaning that no ready market exists for the trading of shares.

a. Federal Home Loan Mortgage Corporation
b. Depository Trust Company
c. Protect
d. Corporation

28. A _________ is the price of a single share of a no. of saleable stocks of the company. Once the stock is purchased, the owner becomes a shareholder of the company that issued the share.

a. Share price
b. Whisper numbers
c. Stock split
d. Trading curb

29. In finance, _________ refers to the way a corporation finances its assets through some combination of equity, debt, or hybrid securities. A firm's _________ is then the composition or 'structure' of its liabilities. For example, a firm that sells $20 billion in equity and $80 billion in debt is said to be 20% equity-financed and 80% debt-financed.

a. Rights issue
b. Book building
c. Capital structure
d. Market for corporate control

30. In business and finance, a _________ (also referred to as equity _________) of stock means a _________ of ownership in a corporation (company.) In the plural, stocks is often used as a synonym for _________s especially in the United States, but it is less commonly used that way outside of North America.

In the United Kingdom, South Africa, and Australia, stock can also refer to completely different financial instruments such as government bonds or, less commonly, to all kinds of marketable securities.

a. Procter ' Gamble
b. Margin
c. Bucket shop
d. Share

1. The _________ measures how long an investment with suppliers deprives a firm of cash -- it is (in the generic case of a retailer) the time between disbursement for inventory and collection on its sale. Thus, the _________ measures how risky it would be to increase this investment with suppliers in the course of expanding customer sales. However, shortening the _________ creates its own risks: while a firm could even achieve a negative _________ by collecting from customers before paying suppliers, a policy of strict collections and lax payments is not always sustainable.

a. Price/cash flow ratio
b. Return on capital employed
c. Return on sales
d. Cash conversion cycle

2. _________ is the provision of resources (such as granting a loan) by one party to another party where that second party does not reimburse the first party immediately, thereby generating a debt, and instead arranges either to repay or return those resources (or material(s) of equal value) at a later date. The first party is called a creditor, also known as a lender, while the second party is called a debtor, also known as a borrower.

Movements of financial capital are normally dependent on either _________ or equity transfers.

a. Comparable
b. Clearing house
c. Warrant
d. Credit

3. _________ is a list for goods and materials held available in stock by a business. It is also used for a list of the contents of a household and for a list for testamentary purposes of the possessions of someone who has died. In accounting _________ is considered an asset.

a. ABN Amro
b. AAB
c. A Random Walk Down Wall Street
d. Inventory

4. In economics, the concept of the _________ refers to the decision-making time frame of a firm in which at least one factor of production is fixed. Costs which are fixed in the _________ have no impact on a firms decisions. For example a firm can raise output by increasing the amount of labour through overtime.

a. 4-4-5 Calendar
b. Long-run
c. 529 plan
d. Short-run

5. A '_________' is a 'Charge' that is paid to obtain the right to delay a payment. Essentially, the payer purchases the right to make a given payment in the future instead of in the Present. The '_________', or 'Charge' that must be paid to delay the payment, is simply the difference between what the payment amount would be if it were paid in the present and what the payment amount would be paid if it were paid in the future.

a. Risk aversion
b. Value at risk
c. Risk modeling
d. Discount

6. In financial accounting, a _________ or statement of financial position is a summary of a person's or organization's balances. Assets, liabilities and ownership equity are listed as of a specific date, such as the end of its financial year. A _________ is often described as a snapshot of a company's financial condition.

a. Statement of retained earnings
b. Statement on Auditing Standards No. 70: Service Organizations
c. Financial statements
d. Balance sheet

7. _________ is an area of finance dealing with the financial decisions corporations make and the tools and analysis used to make these decisions. The primary goal of _________ is to maximize corporate value while managing the firm's financial risks. Although it is in principle different from managerial finance which studies the financial decisions of all firms, rather than corporations alone, the main concepts in the study of _________ are applicable to the financial problems of all kinds of firms.

a. Cash flow
b. Special purpose entity
c. Corporate finance
d. Gross profit

8. _________ are securities that can be easily converted into cash. Such securities will generally have highly liquid markets allowing the security to be sold at a reasonable price very quickly.This is a usual feature in real estate .

a. Book entry
b. Marketable
c. Tracking stock
d. Securities lending

9. _________ is a financial metric which represents operating liquidity available to a business. Along with fixed assets such as plant and equipment, _________ is considered a part of operating capital. It is calculated as current assets minus current liabilities.

a. Working capital management
b. 4-4-5 Calendar
c. Working capital
d. 529 plan

10. A _________ is a fungible, negotiable instrument representing financial value. They are broadly categorized into debt securities (such as banknotes, bonds and debentures), and equity securities; e.g., common stocks. The company or other entity issuing the _________ is called the issuer.

a. Security
b. Book entry
c. Securities lending
d. Tracking stock

11. The term _________ has three unrelated technical definitions, and is also used in a variety of non-technical ways.

- In financial economics, it refers to any asset used to make money, as opposed to assets used for personal enjoyment or consumption. This is an important distinction because two people can disagree sharply about the value of personal assets, one person might think a sports car is more valuable than a pickup truck, another person might have the opposite taste. But if an asset is held for the purpose of making money, taste has nothing to do with it, only differences of opinion about how much money the asset will produce. With the further assumption that people agree on the probability distribution of future cash flows, it is possible to have an objective _________ pricing model. Even without the assumption of agreement, it is possible to set rational limits on _________ value.
- In governmental accounting, it is defined as any asset used in operations with an initial useful life extending beyond one reporting period. Generally, government managers have a 'stewardship' duty to maintain _________s under their control. See International Public Sector Accounting Standards for details.
- In US tax accounting, it is defined as any property other than a list of exceptions. The main exceptions are anything held for sale, and any real estate or depreciable property used in business. Almost everything you own and use for personal purposes, pleasure or investment is a _________. If something is a _________ for tax purposes, gains or losses on sale or disposition are capital gains or capital losses. For individuals, however, capital losses on property held for personal use are generally not deductible. See the IRS publication Tax Facts about Capital Gains and Losses for details.

A well-known financial accounting textbook advises that the term be avoided except in tax accounting because it is used in so many different senses, not all of them well-defined. For example it is often used as a synonym for fixed assets or for investments in securities.

A common non-technical usage occurs when people ask that employees or the environment or something else be treated as a _________.

a. Settlement date
b. Solvency
c. Political risk
d. Capital asset

12. In finance, the _________ is used to determine a theoretically appropriate required rate of return of an asset, if that asset is to be added to an already well-diversified portfolio, given that asset's non-diversifiable risk. The model takes into account the asset's sensitivity to non-diversifiable risk (also known as systemic risk or market risk), often represented by the quantity beta (β) in the financial industry, as well as the expected return of the market and the expected return of a theoretical risk-free asset.

The model was introduced by Jack Treynor (1961, 1962), William Sharpe (1964), John Lintner (1965a,b) and Jan Mossin (1966) independently, building on the earlier work of Harry Markowitz on diversification and modern portfolio theory.

a. Cox-Ingersoll-Ross model
b. Capital asset pricing model
c. Random walk hypothesis
d. Hull-White model

13. In accounting, a _________ is an asset on the balance sheet which is expected to be sold or otherwise used up in the near future, usually within one year, or one business cycle - whichever is longer. Typical _________s include cash, cash equivalents, accounts receivable, inventory, the portion of prepaid accounts which will be used within a year, and short-term investments.

On the balance sheet, assets will typically be classified into _________s and long-term assets.

a. Write-off
b. Current asset
c. Historical cost
d. Long-term liabilities

14. In finance, _________ occurs when a debtor has not met its legal obligations according to the debt contract, e.g. it has not made a scheduled payment, or has violated a loan covenant (condition) of the debt contract. _________ may occur if the debtor is either unwilling or unable to pay their debt. This can occur with all debt obligations including bonds, mortgages, loans, and promissory notes.

a. Credit crunch
b. Default
c. Vendor finance
d. Debt validation

15. _________ is the risk of loss due to a debtor's non-payment of a loan or other line of credit (either the principal or interest (coupon) or both)

Most lenders employ their own models (credit scorecards) to rank potential and existing customers according to risk, and then apply appropriate strategies. With products such as unsecured personal loans or mortgages, lenders charge a higher price for higher risk customers and vice versa. With revolving products such as credit cards and overdrafts, risk is controlled through careful setting of credit limits.

a. Credit risk
b. Liquidity risk
c. Transaction risk
d. Market risk

16. In finance, the _________ between two currencies specifies how much one currency is worth in terms of the other. For example an _________ of 102 Japanese yen to the United States dollar means that JPY 102 is worth the same as USD 1. The foreign exchange market is one of the largest markets in the world.

a. Exchange rate
b. ABN Amro
c. AAB
d. A Random Walk Down Wall Street

17. _________ is a form of risk that arises from the change in price of one currency against another. Whenever investors or companies have assets or business operations across national borders, they face _________ if their positions are not hedged.

- Transaction risk is the risk that exchange rates will change unfavourably over time. It can be hedged against using forward currency contracts;
- Translation risk is an accounting risk, proportional to the amount of assets held in foreign currencies. Changes in the exchange rate over time will render a report inaccurate, and so assets are usually balanced by borrowings in that currency.

The exchange risk associated with a foreign denominated instrument is a key element in foreign investment. This risk flows from differential monetary policy and growth in real productivity, which results in differential inflation rates.

a. Tracking error
b. Market risk
c. Credit risk
d. Currency risk

18. _________ is a type of risk faced by investors, corporations, and governments. It is a risk that can be understood and managed with proper aforethought and investment.

Broadly, _________ refers to the complications businesses and governments may face as a result of what are commonly referred to as political decisions--or 'any political change that alters the expected outcome and value of a given economic action by changing the probability of achieving business objectives.' .

a. Capital asset
b. Single-index model
c. Mid price
d. Political risk

19. In business and accounting, _________s are everything of value that is owned by a person or company. The balance sheet of a firm records the monetary value of the _________s owned by the firm. The two major _________ classes are tangible _________s and intangible _________s.

a. Accounts payable
b. EBITDA
c. Income
d. Asset

20. In finance, _________ is the process of estimating the potential market value of a financial asset or liability. they can be done on assets (for example, investments in marketable securities such as stocks, options, business enterprises, or intangible assets such as patents and trademarks) or on liabilities (e.g., Bonds issued by a company.) _________s are required in many contexts including investment analysis, capital budgeting, merger and acquisition transactions, financial reporting, taxable events to determine the proper tax liability, and in litigation.

a. Valuation
b. Share
c. Procter ' Gamble
d. Margin

21. _________ is the planning process used to determine whether a firm's long term investments such as new machinery, replacement machinery, new plants, new products, and research development projects are worth pursuing. It is budget for major capital, or investment, expenditures.

Many formal methods are used in _________, including the techniques such as

- Net present value
- Profitability index
- Internal rate of return
- Modified Internal Rate of Return
- Equivalent annuity

These methods use the incremental cash flows from each potential investment, or project. Techniques based on accounting earnings and accounting rules are sometimes used - though economists consider this to be improper - such as the accounting rate of return, and 'return on investment.' Simplified and hybrid methods are used as well, such as payback period and discounted payback period.

a. Capital budgeting
b. Shareholder value
c. Preferred stock
d. Financial distress

22. _________ means the inability to pay one's debts as they fall due. Usually used in Business terms, _________ refers to the inability for a 'limited liability' company to pay off debts.

This is defined in two different ways:

Cash flow _________ -

Unable to pay debts as they fall due.

Balance sheet _________ -

Having negative net assets: liabilities exceed assets; or net liabilities.

a. AAB
b. A Random Walk Down Wall Street
c. Interest
d. Insolvency

23. A _________ is a situation that involves losing one quality or aspect of something in return for gaining another quality or aspect. It implies a decision to be made with full comprehension of both the upside and downside of a particular choice.

In economics the term is expressed as opportunity cost, referring the most preferred alternative given up.

a. Trade-off
b. Capital outflow
c. Total revenue
d. Break-even point

24. In accounting, _________ are considered liabilities of the business that are to be settled in cash within the fiscal year or the operating cycle, whichever period is longer.

For example accounts payable for goods, services or supplies that were purchased for use in the operation of the business and payable within a normal period of time would be _________.

Bonds, mortgages and loans that are payable over a term exceeding one year would be fixed liabilities.

a. Net income
b. Closing entries
c. Gross sales
d. Current liabilities

25. _________ or financing is to provide capital (funds), which means money for a project, a person, a business or any other private or public institutions.

Those funds can be allocated for either short term or long term purposes. The health fund is a new way of _________ private healthcare centers.

a. Proxy fight
b. Product life cycle
c. Synthetic CDO
d. Funding

26. In economic models, the _________ time frame assumes no fixed factors of production. Firms can enter or leave the marketplace, and the cost (and availability) of land, labor, raw materials, and capital goods can be assumed to vary. In contrast, in the short-run time frame, certain factors are assumed to be fixed, because there is not sufficient time for them to change.

a. Short-run
b. 529 plan
c. 4-4-5 Calendar
d. Long-run

27. _________ is a financial transaction whereby a business sells its accounts receivable (i.e., invoices) at a discount. _________ differs from a bank loan in three main ways. First, the emphasis is on the value of the receivables (essentially a financial asset), not the firm's credit worthiness.

a. Debt-for-equity swap
b. Credit card balance transfer
c. Financial Literacy Month
d. Factoring

28. The _________ is an equation that equals the cost of goods sold divided by the average inventory. Average inventory equals beginning inventory plus ending inventory divided by 2.

The formula for _________:

$$\text{Inventory Turnover} = \frac{\text{Cost of Goods Sold}}{\text{Average Inventory}}$$

The formula for average inventory:

$$\text{Average Inventory} = \frac{\text{Beginning inventory} + \text{Ending inventory}}{2}$$

A low turnover rate may point to overstocking, obsolescence, or deficiencies in the product line or marketing effort.

a. Operating leverage
b. Inventory turnover
c. Earnings yield
d. Information ratio

29. A _________ is the system of organizations, people, technology, activities, information and resources involved in moving a product or service from supplier to customer. _________ activities transform natural resources, raw materials and components into a finished product that is delivered to the end customer. In sophisticated _________ systems, used products may re-enter the _________ at any point where residual value is recyclable.

a. Supply chain
b. 4-4-5 Calendar
c. 7-Eleven
d. 529 plan

30. _________, in bookkeeping, refers to assets, liabilities, income, and expenses recorded on individual pages of the so called book of final entry or ledger. Changes in _________ value are made by chronologically posting debit (DR) and credit (CR) entries to its page. Examples of _________s are cash, _________s receivable, mortgages, loans, land and buildings, common stock, sales, services provided, wages, and payroll overhead.

a. Accretion
b. Alpha
c. Option
d. Account

31. _________ is one of a series of accounting transactions dealing with the billing of customers who owe money to a person, company or organization for goods and services that have been provided to the customer. In most business entities this is typically done by generating an invoice and mailing or electronically delivering it to the customer, who in turn must pay it within an established timeframe called credit or payment terms.

An example of a common payment term is Net 30, meaning payment is due in the amount of the invoice 30 days from the date of invoice.

a. Impaired asset
b. Income
c. Accounts receivable
d. Accounting methods

32. _________ is a file or account that contains money that a person or company owes to suppliers, but hasn't paid yet (a form of debt.) When you receive an invoice you add it to the file, and then you remove it when you pay. Thus, the A/P is a form of credit that suppliers offer to their purchasers by allowing them to pay for a product or service after it has already been received.

a. Outstanding balance
b. Earnings before interest, taxes, depreciation and amortization
c. Accrual
d. Accounts payable

33. In marketing, _________ refers to the total cost of holding inventory. This includes warehousing costs such as rent, utilities and salaries, financial costs such as opportunity cost, and inventory costs related to perishibility, shrinkage and insurance.

a. 4-4-5 Calendar
b. 529 plan
c. 7-Eleven
d. Carrying cost

34. _________ is the level of inventory that minimizes the total inventory holding costs and ordering costs. The framework used to determine this order quantity is also known as Wilson _________ Model. The model was developed by F. W. Harris in 1913.

a. Economic order quantity
b. A Random Walk Down Wall Street
c. AAB
d. ABN Amro

35. _________ refers to a business or organization attempting to acquire goods or services to accomplish the goals of the enterprise. Though there are several organizations that attempt to set standards in the _________ process, processes can vary greatly between organizations. Typically the word '_________' is not used interchangeably with the word 'procurement', since procurement typically includes Expediting, Supplier Quality, and Traffic and Logistics (T'L) in addition to _________.

a. 7-Eleven
b. 4-4-5 Calendar
c. 529 plan
d. Purchasing

36. A _________ is an employee within a company, business or other organization who is responsible at some level for buying or approving the acquisition of goods and services needed by the company. The position responsibilities may be the same as that of a buyer or purchasing agent, or may include wider supervisory or managerial responsibilities. A _________ may oversee the acquisition of materials needed for production, general supplies for offices and facilities, equipment, or construction contracts.

a. Day trader
b. Stockbroker
c. Financial analyst
d. Purchasing manager

37. In economics, business, and accounting, a _________ is the value of money that has been used up to produce something, and hence is not available for use anymore. In business, the _________ may be one of acquisition, in which case the amount of money expended to acquire it is counted as _________. In this case, money is the input that is gone in order to acquire the thing.

a. Marginal cost
b. Sliding scale fees
c. Cost
d. Fixed costs

38. The _________ is the level of inventory when a fresh order should be made with suppliers to bring the inventory up by the Economic order quantity ('EOQ'.)

The _________ for replenishment of stock occurs when the level of inventory drops down to zero. In view of instantaneous replenishment of stock the level of inventory jumps to the original level from zero level.

a. Reorder point
b. 7-Eleven
c. 4-4-5 Calendar
d. 529 plan

39. In economics, and cost accounting, _________ describes the total economic cost of production and is made up of variable costs, which vary according to the quantity of a good produced and include inputs such as labor and raw materials, plus fixed costs, which are independent of the quantity of a good produced and include inputs (capital) that cannot be varied in the short term, such as buildings and machinery. _________ in economics includes the total opportunity cost of each factor of production in addition to fixed and variable costs.

The rate at which _________ changes as the amount produced changes is called marginal cost.

a. Total cost
b. 4-4-5 Calendar
c. 529 plan
d. 7-Eleven

40. _________ is an inventory strategy implemented to improve the return on investment of a business by reducing in-process inventory and its associated carrying costs. In order to achieve _________ the process must have signals of what is going on elsewhere within the process. This means that the process is often driven by a series of signals, which can be Kanban, that tell production processes when to make the next part.

a. Greed and fear
b. Pac-Man defense
c. Just-in-time
d. Debtor-in-possession financing

41. _________ is a term used by inventory specialists to describe a level of extra stock that is maintained below the cycle stock to buffer against stockouts. _________ exists to counter uncertainties in supply and demand. _________ is defined as extra units of inventory carried as protection against possible stockouts .(shortfall in raw material or packaging.)

a. Safety stock
b. Golden parachute
c. Counting house
d. Funding

42. In lending agreements, _________ is a borrower's pledge of specific property to a lender, to secure repayment of a loan. The _________ serves as protection for a lender against a borrower's risk of default - that is, a borrower failing to pay the principal and interest under the terms of a loan obligation. If a borrower does default on a loan (due to insolvency or other event), that borrower forfeits (gives up) the property pledged as _________ *ollateral* - and the lender then becomes the owner of the _________.

a. Nominal value
b. Future-oriented
c. Refinancing risk
d. Collateral

43. _________ is a measurement of corporate or economic size equal to the share price times the number of shares outstanding of a public company. As owning stock represents owning the company, including all its equity, capitalization could represent the public opinion of a company's net worth and is a determining factor in stock valuation. Likewise, the capitalization of stock markets or economic regions may be compared to other economic indicators.

a. Synthetic CDO
b. Market capitalization
c. Proxy fight
d. Just-in-time

44. _________ is a type of private equity capital typically provided to early-stage, high-potential, growth companies in the interest of generating a return through an eventual realization event such as an IPO or trade sale of the company. _________ investments are generally made as cash in exchange for shares in the invested company. It is typical for _________ investors to identify and back companies in high technology industries such as biotechnology and ICT.

a. Probability distribution
b. Treasury Inflation-Protected Securities
c. Venture capital
d. Tail risk

45. The _________ is the rate that a company is expected to pay to finance its assets. WACC is the minimum return that a company must earn on existing asset base to satisfy its creditors, owners, and other providers of capital.

Companies raise money from a number of sources: common equity, preferred equity, straight debt, convertible debt, exchangeable debt, warrants, options, pension liabilities, executive stock options, governmental subsidies, and so on.

a. Cost of capital
b. Capital intensity
c. 4-4-5 Calendar
d. Weighted average cost of capital

46. _________ are costs incurred on the purchase of land, buildings, construction and equipment to be used in the production of goods or the rendering of services. In other words, the total cost needed to bring a project to a commercially operable status. However, _________ are not limited to the initial construction of a factory or other business.

a. Capital costs
b. Trade-off
c. Defined contribution plan
d. Capital outflow

47. The _________ is an expected return that the provider of capital plans to earn on their investment.

Capital (money) used for funding a business should earn returns for the capital providers who risk their capital. For an investment to be worthwhile, the expected return on capital must be greater than the _________.

a. Weighted average cost of capital
b. Capital intensity
c. Cost of capital
d. 4-4-5 Calendar

48. In economics and finance, _________ is the change in total cost that arises when the quantity produced changes by one unit. It is the cost of producing one more unit of a good. Mathematically, the _________ function is expressed as the first derivative of the total cost (TC) function with respect to quantity (Q). Note that the _________ may change with volume, and so at each level of production, the _________ is the cost of the next unit produced.

A typical _________ Curve

a. Sliding scale fees
b. Cost accounting
c. Fixed costs
d. Marginal cost

49. _________ is the difference between price and the costs of bringing to market whatever it is that is accounted as an enterprise (whether by harvest, extraction, manufacture, or purchase) in terms of the component costs of delivered goods and/or services and any operating or other expenses.

A key difficulty in measuring profit is in defining costs. Pure economic monetary profits can be zero or negative even in competitive equilibrium when accounted monetized costs exceed monetized price.

a. Accounting profit
b. AAB
c. Economic profit
d. A Random Walk Down Wall Street

50. _________ is one of the accounting liquidity ratios, a financial ratio. This ratio measures the number of times, on average, receivables (e.g. Accounts Receivable) are collected during the period. A popular variant of the _________ is to convert it into an Average Collection Period in terms of days.

a. Return on equity
b. Sharpe ratio
c. PEG ratio
d. Receivables turnover ratio

51. _________ are expenses that change in proportion to the activity of a business. In other words, _________ are the sum of marginal costs. It can also be considered normal costs. Along with fixed costs, _________ make up the two components of total cost. Direct Costs, however, are costs that can be associated with a particular cost object.

a. Fixed costs
b. Variable costs
c. Cost accounting
d. Transaction cost

52. In accounting and finance, _________ is the portion of receivables that can no longer be collected, typically from accounts receivable or loans. _________ in accounting is considered an expense.

There are two methods to account for _________:

1. Direct write off method (Non - GAAP)

A receivable which is not considered collectible is charged directly to the income statement.

1. Allowance method (GAAP)

An estimate is made at the end of each fiscal year of the amount of _________. This is then accumulated in a provision which is then used to reduce specific receivable accounts as and when necessary.

a. Bad debt
b. 529 plan
c. 4-4-5 Calendar
d. Tax expense

53. _________ is that which is owed; usually referencing assets owed, but the term can cover other obligations. In the case of assets, _________ is a means of using future purchasing power in the present before a summation has been earned. Some companies and corporations use _________ as a part of their overall corporate finance strategy.

a. Partial Payment
b. Credit cycle
c. Cross-collateralization
d. Debt

54. In banking and finance, _________ denotes all activities from the time a commitment is made for a transaction until it is settled. _________ is necessary because the speed of trades is much faster than the cycle time for completing the underlying transaction.

In its widest sense _________ involves the management of post-trading, pre-settlement credit exposures, to ensure that trades are settled in accordance with market rules, even if a buyer or seller should become insolvent prior to settlement.

a. Clearing
b. Share
c. Clearing house
d. Procter ' Gamble

55. The free _________ of a public company is an estimate of the proportion of shares that are not held by large owners and that are not stock with sales restrictions (restricted stock that cannot be sold until they become unrestricted stock.)

The free _________ or a public _________ is usually defined as being all shares held by investors other than:

- shares held by owners owning more than 5% of all shares (those could be institutional investors, 'strategic shareholders,' founders, executives, and other insiders' holdings)
- restricted stocks (granted to executives that can be, but don't have to be, registered insiders)
- insider holdings (it is assumed that insiders hold stock for the very long term)

The free _________ is an important criterion in quoting a share on the stock market.

To _________ a company means to list its shares on a public stock exchange through an initial public offering (or 'flotation'.)

- Open market
- Outstanding shares
- Market capitalization
- Public _________ *loat*
- Reverse takeover

.

a. Golden parachute
b. Synthetic CDO
c. Trade finance
d. Float

56. _________ is the transfer of funds from diverse accounts into a central account to improve the efficiency of cash management. The consolidation of cash into a single account allows a company to maintain smaller cash balances overall, and to identify excess cash available for short term investments. The cash available in different bank accounts are pooled into a master account.The advantages of _________ are 1) Cash control 2) Cash visibility .

a. Cash concentration
b. Conditional prepayment rate
c. Capitalization rate
d. Profitability index

57. A _________ is a financial services company that provides clearing and settlement services for financial transactions, usually on a futures exchange, and often acts as central counterparty (the payor actually pays the _________, which then pays the payee). A _________ may also offer novation, the substitution of a new contract or debt for an old, or other credit enhancement services to its members.

The term is also used for banks like Suffolk Bank that acted as a restraint on the over-issuance of private bank notes.

a. Warrant
b. Clearing house
c. Bucket shop
d. Valuation

58. In the global money market, _________ is an unsecured promissory note with a fixed maturity of one to 270 days. _________ is a money-market security issued (sold) by large banks and corporations to get money to meet short term debt obligations (for example, payroll), and is only backed by an issuing bank or corporation's promise to pay the face amount on the maturity date specified on the note. Since it is not backed by collateral, only firms with excellent credit ratings from a recognized rating agency will be able to sell their _________ at a reasonable price.

a. Book building
b. Trade-off theory
c. Commercial paper
d. Financial distress

59. _________s are deposits denominated in United States dollars at banks outside the United States, and thus are not under the jurisdiction of the Federal Reserve. Consequently, such deposits are subject to much less regulation than similar deposits within the United States, allowing for higher margins. There is nothing 'European' about _________ deposits; a US dollar-denominated deposit in Tokyo or Caracas would likewise be deemed _________ deposits.

a. A Random Walk Down Wall Street
b. AAB
c. Eurodollar
d. ABN Amro

60. _________ is the term used to describe deposits residing in banks that are located outside the borders of the country that issues the currency the deposit is denominated in. For example a deposit denominated in US dollars residing in a Japanese bank is a _________ deposit, or more specifically a Eurodollar deposit.

Key points are the location of the bank and the denomination of the currency, not the nationality of the bank or the owner of the deposit/loan.

a. Eurocurrency
b. A Random Walk Down Wall Street
c. ABN Amro
d. AAB

61. The _________ (NYSE: FNM), commonly known as Fannie Mae, is a stockholder-owned corporation chartered by Congress in 1968 as a government sponsored enterprise (GSE), but founded in 1938 during the Great Depression. The corporation's purpose is to purchase and securitize mortgages in order to ensure that funds are consistently available to the institutions that lend money to home buyers.

On September 7, 2008, James Lockhart, director of the Federal Housing Finance Agency (FHFA), announced that Fannie Mae and Freddie Mac were being placed into conservatorship of the FHFA.

a. SPDR
b. The Depository Trust ' Clearing Corporation
c. General partnership
d. Federal National Mortgage Association

62. In finance, the _________ is the global financial market for short-term borrowing and lending. It provides short-term liquidity funding for the global financial system. The _________ is where short-term obligations such as Treasury bills, commercial paper and bankers' acceptances are bought and sold.

a. Cramdown
b. Debt-for-equity swap
c. Consumer debt
d. Money market

63. A _________ allows a borrower to use a financial security as collateral for a cash loan at a fixed rate of interest. In a repo, the borrower agrees to immediately sell a security to a lender and also agrees to buy the same security from the lender at a fixed price at some later date. A repo is equivalent to a cash transaction combined with a forward contract.

a. Repurchase agreement
b. Volatility arbitrage
c. Total return swap
d. Contango

64. _________ mature in one year or less. Like zero-coupon bonds, they do not pay interest prior to maturity; instead they are sold at a discount of the par value to create a positive yield to maturity. Many regard _________ as the least risky investment available to U.S. investors.

a. Treasury securities
b. 4-4-5 Calendar
c. Treasury Inflation Protected Securities
d. Treasury bills

65. _________ are government bonds issued by the United States Department of the Treasury through the Bureau of the Public Debt. They are the debt financing instruments of the U.S. Federal government, and they are often referred to simply as Treasuries or Treasurys. There are four types of marketable _________: Treasury bills, Treasury notes, Treasury bonds, and Treasury Inflation Protected Securities (TIPS.)

a. Treasury Inflation Protected Securities
b. Treasury Inflation-Protected Securities
c. 4-4-5 Calendar
d. Treasury securities

66. A _________ s a time deposit, a financial product commonly offered to consumers by banks, thrift institutions, and credit unions.

They are similar to savings accounts in that they are insured and thus virtually risk-free; they are 'money in the bank'. They are different from savings accounts in that they have a specific, fixed term (often three months, six months, or one to five years), and, usually, a fixed interest rate.

a. Certificate of deposit
b. Time deposit
c. Variable rate mortgage
d. Reserve requirement

67. In finance, a _________ is a type of bond that can be converted into shares of stock in the issuing company, usually at some pre-announced ratio. It is a hybrid security with debt- and equity-like features. Although it typically has a low coupon rate, the holder is compensated with the ability to convert the bond to common stock, usually at a substantial discount to the stock's market value.

a. Convertible bond
b. Corporate bond
c. Bond fund
d. Gilts

68. A _________ is a professionally managed type of collective investment scheme that pools money from many investors and invests it in stocks, bonds, short-term money market instruments, and/or other securities. The _________ will have a fund manager that trades the pooled money on a regular basis. Currently, the worldwide value of all _________s totals more than $26 trillion.

Since 1940, there have been three basic types of investment companies in the United States: open-end funds, also known in the US as _________s; unit investment trusts (UITs); and closed-end funds.

a. Financial intermediary
b. Trust company
c. Mutual fund
d. Net asset value

69. In finance, the term _________ describes the amount in cash that returns to the owners of a security. Normally it does not include the price variations, at the difference of the total return. _________ applies to various stated rates of return on stocks (common and preferred, and convertible), fixed income instruments (bonds, notes, bills, strips, zero coupon), and some other investment type insurance products (e.g. annuities.)

a. Macaulay duration
b. Yield to maturity
c. 4-4-5 Calendar
d. Yield

70. The institution most often referenced by the word '_________' is a public or publicly traded _________, the shares of which are traded on a public stock exchange (e.g., the New York Stock Exchange or Nasdaq in the United States) where shares of stock of _________s are bought and sold by and to the general public. Most of the largest businesses in the world are publicly traded _________s. However, the majority of _________s are said to be closely held, privately held or close _________s, meaning that no ready market exists for the trading of shares.

a. Depository Trust Company
b. Protect
c. Federal Home Loan Mortgage Corporation
d. Corporation

71. A _________ is the price of a single share of a no. of saleable stocks of the company. Once the stock is purchased, the owner becomes a shareholder of the company that issued the share.

a. Trading curb
b. Stock split
c. Share price
d. Whisper numbers

72. In finance, _________ refers to the way a corporation finances its assets through some combination of equity, debt, or hybrid securities. A firm's _________ is then the composition or 'structure' of its liabilities. For example, a firm that sells $20 billion in equity and $80 billion in debt is said to be 20% equity-financed and 80% debt-financed.

a. Market for corporate control
b. Capital structure
c. Rights issue
d. Book building

1. _________, in bookkeeping, refers to assets, liabilities, income, and expenses recorded on individual pages of the so called book of final entry or ledger. Changes in _________ value are made by chronologically posting debit (DR) and credit (CR) entries to its page. Examples of _________s are cash, _________s receivable, mortgages, loans, land and buildings, common stock, sales, services provided, wages, and payroll overhead.

a. Accretion
b. Option
c. Alpha
d. Account

2. _________ is a file or account that contains money that a person or company owes to suppliers, but hasn't paid yet (a form of debt.) When you receive an invoice you add it to the file, and then you remove it when you pay. Thus, the A/P is a form of credit that suppliers offer to their purchasers by allowing them to pay for a product or service after it has already been received.

a. Accounts payable
b. Earnings before interest, taxes, depreciation and amortization
c. Outstanding balance
d. Accrual

3. In lending agreements, _________ is a borrower's pledge of specific property to a lender, to secure repayment of a loan. The _________ serves as protection for a lender against a borrower's risk of default - that is, a borrower failing to pay the principal and interest under the terms of a loan obligation. If a borrower does default on a loan (due to insolvency or other event), that borrower forfeits (gives up) the property pledged as _________ *ollateral* - and the lender then becomes the owner of the _________.

a. Refinancing risk
b. Nominal value
c. Future-oriented
d. Collateral

4. In the global money market, _________ is an unsecured promissory note with a fixed maturity of one to 270 days. _________ is a money-market security issued (sold) by large banks and corporations to get money to meet short term debt obligations (for example, payroll), and is only backed by an issuing bank or corporation's promise to pay the face amount on the maturity date specified on the note. Since it is not backed by collateral, only firms with excellent credit ratings from a recognized rating agency will be able to sell their _________ at a reasonable price.

a. Book building
b. Financial distress
c. Trade-off theory
d. Commercial paper

5. In accounting, _________ are considered liabilities of the business that are to be settled in cash within the fiscal year or the operating cycle, whichever period is longer.

For example accounts payable for goods, services or supplies that were purchased for use in the operation of the business and payable within a normal period of time would be _________.

Bonds, mortgages and loans that are payable over a term exceeding one year would be fixed liabilities.

a. Current liabilities
b. Gross sales
c. Net income
d. Closing entries

6. In economics, the concept of the _________ refers to the decision-making time frame of a firm in which at least one factor of production is fixed. Costs which are fixed in the _________ have no impact on a firms decisions. For example a firm can raise output by increasing the amount of labour through overtime.

a. 529 plan
b. 4-4-5 Calendar
c. Long-run
d. Short-run

7. _________ is the provision of resources (such as granting a loan) by one party to another party where that second party does not reimburse the first party immediately, thereby generating a debt, and instead arranges either to repay or return those resources (or material(s) of equal value) at a later date. The first party is called a creditor, also known as a lender, while the second party is called a debtor, also known as a borrower.

Movements of financial capital are normally dependent on either _________ or equity transfers.

a. Clearing house
b. Warrant
c. Comparable
d. Credit

8. A _________ is a fungible, negotiable instrument representing financial value. They are broadly categorized into debt securities (such as banknotes, bonds and debentures), and equity securities; e.g., common stocks. The company or other entity issuing the _________ is called the issuer.

a. Security
b. Securities lending
c. Book entry
d. Tracking stock

9. The _________ measures how long an investment with suppliers deprives a firm of cash -- it is (in the generic case of a retailer) the time between disbursement for inventory and collection on its sale. Thus, the _________ measures how risky it would be to increase this investment with suppliers in the course of expanding customer sales. However, shortening the _________ creates its own risks: while a firm could even achieve a negative _________ by collecting from customers before paying suppliers, a policy of strict collections and lax payments is not always sustainable.

a. Price/cash flow ratio
b. Return on sales
c. Return on capital employed
d. Cash conversion cycle

10. _________ or financing is to provide capital (funds), which means money for a project, a person, a business or any other private or public institutions.

Those funds can be allocated for either short term or long term purposes. The health fund is a new way of _________ private healthcare centers.

a. Synthetic CDO
b. Proxy fight
c. Product life cycle
d. Funding

11. An _________ or bill is a commercial document issued by a seller to the buyer, indicating the products, quantities, and agreed prices for products or services the seller has provided the buyer. An _________ indicates the buyer must pay the seller, according to the payment terms.

In the rental industry, an _________ must include a specific reference to the duration of the time being billed, so rather than quantity, price and discount the invoicing amount is based on quantity, price, discount and duration.

a. AAB
b. ABN Amro
c. A Random Walk Down Wall Street
d. Invoice

12. In economics, business, and accounting, a _________ is the value of money that has been used up to produce something, and hence is not available for use anymore. In business, the _________ may be one of acquisition, in which case the amount of money expended to acquire it is counted as _________. In this case, money is the input that is gone in order to acquire the thing.

a. Cost
b. Sliding scale fees
c. Marginal cost
d. Fixed costs

13. A '_________' is a 'Charge' that is paid to obtain the right to delay a payment. Essentially, the payer purchases the right to make a given payment in the future instead of in the Present. The '_________', or 'Charge' that must be paid to delay the payment, is simply the difference between what the payment amount would be if it were paid in the present and what the payment amount would be paid if it were paid in the future.

a. Risk aversion
b. Value at risk
c. Risk modeling
d. Discount

14. _________ can be regarded as an outcome of mental processes (cognitive process) leading to the selection of a course of action among several alternatives. Every _________ process produces a final choice. The output can be an action or an opinion of choice.

a. 529 plan
b. Decision making
c. 4-4-5 Calendar
d. 7-Eleven

15. Accrual, in accounting, describes the accounting method known as _________, whereby revenues and expenses are recognized when they are accrued, i.e. accumulated (earned or incurred), regardless when the actual cash is received or paid out.

E.g. a company delivers a product to a customer who will pay for it 30 days later in the next fiscal year starting a week after the delivery. The company recognizes the proceeds as a revenue in its current income statement still for the fiscal year of the delivery, even though it will get paid in cash during the following accounting period.

a. AAB
b. ABN Amro
c. A Random Walk Down Wall Street
d. Accrual basis

16. _________ is that which is owed; usually referencing assets owed, but the term can cover other obligations. In the case of assets, _________ is a means of using future purchasing power in the present before a summation has been earned. Some companies and corporations use _________ as a part of their overall corporate finance strategy.

a. Debt
b. Credit cycle
c. Partial Payment
d. Cross-collateralization

17. The _________, effective annual interest rate, Annual Equivalent Rate (AER) or simply effective rate is the interest rate on a loan or financial product restated from the nominal interest rate as an interest rate with annual compound interest. It is used to compare the annual interest between loans with different compounding terms (daily, monthly, annually, or other.)

The _________ differs in two important respects from the annual percentage rate (APR):

1. the _________ generally does not incorporate one-time charges such as front-end fees;
2. the _________ is (generally) not defined by legal or regulatory authorities (as APR is in many jurisdictions.)

By contrast, the 'effective APR' is used as a legal term, where front-fees and other costs can be included, as defined by local law.

Annual Percentage Yield or effective annual yield is the analogous concept used for savings or investment products, such as a certificate of deposit.

a. AAB
b. Effective interest rate
c. A Random Walk Down Wall Street
d. ABN Amro

18. _________ is a fee paid on borrowed assets. It is the price paid for the use of borrowed money , or, money earned by deposited funds . Assets that are sometimes lent with _________ include money, shares, consumer goods through hire purchase, major assets such as aircraft, and even entire factories in finance lease arrangements.

a. Interest
b. A Random Walk Down Wall Street
c. AAB
d. Insolvency

19. _________ is a term applied in many countries to a reference interest rate used by banks. The term originally indicated the rate of interest at which banks lent to favored customers, i.e., those with high credibility, though this is no longer always the case. Some variable interest rates may be expressed as a percentage above or below _________.

a. Time deposit
b. Credit bureau
c. Reserve requirement
d. Prime rate

20. An _________ is the price a borrower pays for the use of money they do not own, and the return a lender receives for deferring the use of funds, by lending it to the borrower. _________s are normally expressed as a percentage rate over the period of one year.

_________s targets are also a vital tool of monetary policy and are used to control variables like investment, inflation, and unemployment.

a. AAB
b. ABN Amro
c. Interest rate
d. A Random Walk Down Wall Street

21. _________ is a life of security. It may also refer to the final payment date of a loan or other financial instrument, at which point all remaining interest and principal is due to be paid.

1, 3, 6 months _________ band can be calculated by using 30-day per month periods.

a. False billing
b. Replacement cost
c. Primary market
d. Maturity

22. _________ are formal records of a business' financial activities.

_________ provide an overview of a business' financial condition in both short and long term. There are four basic _________:

1. **Balance sheet**: also referred to as statement of financial position or condition, reports on a company's assets, liabilities, and net equity as of a given point in time.
2. **Income statement**: also referred to as Profit and Loss statement (or a 'P'L'), reports on a company's income, expenses, and profits over a period of time.
3. **Statement of retained earnings**: explains the changes in a company's retained earnings over the reporting period.
4. **Statement of cash flows**: reports on a company's cash flow activities, particularly its operating, investing and financing activities.

a. Statement on Auditing Standards No. 70: Service Organizations
b. Financial statements
c. Statement of retained earnings
d. Notes to the Financial Statements

23. A _________ is the maximum amount of credit that a financial institution or other lender will extend to a debtor for a particular line of credit. For example, the maximum that a credit card company will allow a card holder to borrow at any given point on a specific card.

This limit is based on a variety of factors ranging from an individual's ability to make interest payments, an organization's cashflow and/or ability to repay the principal, to the credit standards employed by the lender.

a. 4-4-5 Calendar
b. 529 plan
c. 7-Eleven
d. Credit limit

24. A _________ is any credit facility extended to a business by a bank or financial institution. A _________ may take several forms such as cash credit, overdraft, demand loan, export packing credit, term loan, discounting or purchase of commercial bills etc. It is like an account that can readily be tapped into if the need arises or not touched at all and saved for emergencies.

a. Debt-snowball method
b. Cash credit
c. Default Notice
d. Line of credit

25. _________ is a type of credit that does not have a fixed number of payments, in contrast to installment credit. Examples of _________s used by consumers include credit cards. Corporate _________ facilities are typically used to provide liquidity for a company's day-to-day operations.

a. Commercial finance
b. Package loan
c. Reverse stock split
d. Revolving credit

26. _________, in finance and accounting, means stated value or face value. From this comes the expressions at par (at the _________), over par (over _________) and under par (under _________.)

The term '_________' has several meanings depending on context and geography.

a. Global Squeeze
b. Sinking fund
c. FIDC
d. Par value

27. In finance, the _________ between two currencies specifies how much one currency is worth in terms of the other. For example an _________ of 102 Japanese yen to the United States dollar means that JPY 102 is worth the same as USD 1. The foreign exchange market is one of the largest markets in the world.

a. ABN Amro
b. A Random Walk Down Wall Street
c. AAB
d. Exchange rate

28. _________ is a form of risk that arises from the change in price of one currency against another. Whenever investors or companies have assets or business operations across national borders, they face _________ if their positions are not hedged.

- Transaction risk is the risk that exchange rates will change unfavourably over time. It can be hedged against using forward currency contracts;
- Translation risk is an accounting risk, proportional to the amount of assets held in foreign currencies. Changes in the exchange rate over time will render a report inaccurate, and so assets are usually balanced by borrowings in that currency.

The exchange risk associated with a foreign denominated instrument is a key element in foreign investment. This risk flows from differential monetary policy and growth in real productivity, which results in differential inflation rates.

a. Currency risk
b. Credit risk
c. Tracking error
d. Market risk

29. A _________, in business matters, is an entity that is controlled by a bigger and more powerful entity. The controlled entity is called a company, corporation, or limited liability company, and the controlling entity is called its parent (or the parent company.) The reason for this distinction is that a lone company cannot be a _________ of any organization; only an entity representing a legal fiction as a separate entity can be a _________.

a. 4-4-5 Calendar
b. 529 plan
c. Joint stock company
d. Subsidiary

30. _________ is the term used to describe deposits residing in banks that are located outside the borders of the country that issues the currency the deposit is denominated in. For example a deposit denominated in US dollars residing in a Japanese bank is a _________ deposit, or more specifically a Eurodollar deposit.

Key points are the location of the bank and the denomination of the currency, not the nationality of the bank or the owner of the deposit/loan.

a. ABN Amro
b. AAB
c. A Random Walk Down Wall Street
d. Eurocurrency

31. _________ is exchange of capital, goods, and services across international borders or territories. In most countries, it represents a significant share of gross domestic product (GDP.) While _________ has been present throughout much of history , its economic, social, and political importance has been on the rise in recent centuries.

a. Index number
b. United States Treasury security
c. OTC Bulletin Board
d. International trade

32. A standard, commercial _________ is a document issued mostly by a financial institution, used primarily in trade finance, which usually provides an irrevocable payment undertaking.

The _________ can also be the source of payment for a transaction, meaning that redeeming the _________ will pay an exporter. Letters of credit are used primarily in international trade transactions of significant value, for deals between a supplier in one country and a customer in another.

a. Bond indenture
b. McFadden Act
c. Duty of loyalty
d. Letter of credit

33. In accounting, a _________ is an asset on the balance sheet which is expected to be sold or otherwise used up in the near future, usually within one year, or one business cycle - whichever is longer. Typical _________s include cash, cash equivalents, accounts receivable, inventory, the portion of prepaid accounts which will be used within a year, and short-term investments.

On the balance sheet, assets will typically be classified into _________s and long-term assets.

a. Long-term liabilities
b. Historical cost
c. Write-off
d. Current asset

34. The _________ of a stock is a measure of the price paid for a share relative to the annual income or profit earned by the firm per share. It is a financial ratio used for valuation: a higher _________ means that investors are paying more for each unit of income, so the stock is more expensive compared to one with lower _________.

The _________ has units of years, which can be interpreted as 'number of years of earnings to pay back purchase price'.

a. Sustainable growth rate
b. P/E ratio
c. Quick ratio
d. Return of capital

35. In business and accounting, _________s are everything of value that is owned by a person or company. The balance sheet of a firm records the monetary value of the _________s owned by the firm. The two major _________ classes are tangible _________s and intangible _________s.

a. EBITDA
b. Accounts payable
c. Income
d. Asset

36. In the United States, _________ is the function of offering loans to businesses. Commercial financing is generally offered by a bank or other lender. Most commercial banks offer commercial financing, and the loans are either secured by business assets or alternatively can be unsecured, where the lender relies of the cash flows of the business to repay the facility.

a. Bonus share
b. Commercial finance
c. Normative economics
d. Volatility clustering

37. _________ is a financial transaction whereby a business sells its accounts receivable (i.e., invoices) at a discount. _________ differs from a bank loan in three main ways. First, the emphasis is on the value of the receivables (essentially a financial asset), not the firm's credit worthiness.

a. Credit card balance transfer
b. Debt-for-equity swap
c. Financial Literacy Month
d. Factoring

38. _________ is one of a series of accounting transactions dealing with the billing of customers who owe money to a person, company or organization for goods and services that have been provided to the customer. In most business entities this is typically done by generating an invoice and mailing or electronically delivering it to the customer, who in turn must pay it within an established timeframe called credit or payment terms.

An example of a common payment term is Net 30, meaning payment is due in the amount of the invoice 30 days from the date of invoice.

a. Accounts receivable
b. Impaired asset
c. Income
d. Accounting methods

39. In law, a _________ is a form of security interest granted over an item of property to secure the payment of a debt or performance of some other obligation. The owner of the property, who grants the _________, is referred to as the lienor and the person who has the benefit of the _________ is referred to as the _________ee.

The etymological root is: Anglo-French _________, loyen bond, restraint, from Latin ligamen, from ligare to bind.

a. Lien
b. Sarbanes-Oxley Act
c. Family and Medical Leave Act
d. Joint venture

40. _________ is a list for goods and materials held available in stock by a business. It is also used for a list of the contents of a household and for a list for testamentary purposes of the possessions of someone who has died. In accounting _________ is considered an asset.

a. ABN Amro
b. AAB
c. A Random Walk Down Wall Street
d. Inventory

41. In finance, the _________ is used to determine a theoretically appropriate required rate of return of an asset, if that asset is to be added to an already well-diversified portfolio, given that asset's non-diversifiable risk. The model takes into account the asset's sensitivity to non-diversifiable risk (also known as systemic risk or market risk), often represented by the quantity beta (β) in the financial industry, as well as the expected return of the market and the expected return of a theoretical risk-free asset.

The model was introduced by Jack Treynor (1961, 1962), William Sharpe (1964), John Lintner (1965a,b) and Jan Mossin (1966) independently, building on the earlier work of Harry Markowitz on diversification and modern portfolio theory.

a. Cox-Ingersoll-Ross model
b. Hull-White model
c. Random walk hypothesis
d. Capital asset pricing model

42. The institution most often referenced by the word '_________' is a public or publicly traded _________, the shares of which are traded on a public stock exchange (e.g., the New York Stock Exchange or Nasdaq in the United States) where shares of stock of _________s are bought and sold by and to the general public. Most of the largest businesses in the world are publicly traded _________s. However, the majority of _________s are said to be closely held, privately held or close _________s, meaning that no ready market exists for the trading of shares.

a. Federal Home Loan Mortgage Corporation
b. Depository Trust Company
c. Protect
d. Corporation

43. A _________ is the price of a single share of a no. of saleable stocks of the company. Once the stock is purchased, the owner becomes a shareholder of the company that issued the share.

a. Whisper numbers
b. Trading curb
c. Stock split
d. Share price

44. In finance, _________ refers to the way a corporation finances its assets through some combination of equity, debt, or hybrid securities. A firm's _________ is then the composition or 'structure' of its liabilities. For example, a firm that sells $20 billion in equity and $80 billion in debt is said to be 20% equity-financed and 80% debt-financed.

a. Rights issue
b. Market for corporate control
c. Book building
d. Capital structure

45. A _________ is a property interest created by agreement or by operation of law over assets to secure the performance of an obligation, usually the payment of a debt. It gives the beneficiary of the _________ certain preferential rights in the disposition of secured assets. Such rights vary according to the type of _________, but in most cases, a holder of the _________ is entitled to seize, and usually sell, the property to discharge the debt that the _________ secures.

a. Netting
b. FIDC
c. Retention ratio
d. Security interest

1. In finance, a _________ is a type of bond that can be converted into shares of stock in the issuing company, usually at some pre-announced ratio. It is a hybrid security with debt- and equity-like features. Although it typically has a low coupon rate, the holder is compensated with the ability to convert the bond to common stock, usually at a substantial discount to the stock's market value.

a. Bond fund
b. Gilts
c. Corporate bond
d. Convertible bond

2. A _________ is a financial contract whose value is derived from the value of something else (known as the underlying.) The underlying on which a _________ is based can be an asset, weather conditions bonds or other forms of credit.

a. Derivative
b. 4-4-5 Calendar
c. 7-Eleven
d. 529 plan

3. Leasing is a process by which a firm can obtain the use of a certain fixed assets for which it must pay a series of contractual, periodic, tax deductable payments. The lessee is the receiver of the services or the assets under the lease contract and the lessor is the owner of the assets. The relationship between the tenant and the landlord is called a _________, and can be for a fixed or an indefinite period of time (called the term of the lease.)

a. Real Estate Investment Trust
b. Real estate investing
c. REIT
d. Tenancy

4. An _________ is a contract written by a seller that conveys to the buyer the right -- but not the obligation -- to buy (in the case of a call _________) or to sell (in the case of a put _________) a particular asset, such as a piece of property such as, among others, a futures contract. In return for granting the _________, the seller collects a payment (the premium) from the buyer.

For example, buying a call _________ provides the right to buy a specified quantity of a security at a set strike price at some time on or before expiration, while buying a put _________ provides the right to sell.

a. AT'T Mobility LLC
b. Option
c. Annuity
d. Amortization

5. A _________ is a fungible, negotiable instrument representing financial value. They are broadly categorized into debt securities (such as banknotes, bonds and debentures), and equity securities; e.g., common stocks. The company or other entity issuing the _________ is called the issuer.

a. Security
b. Book entry
c. Securities lending
d. Tracking stock

6. In finance, a _________ is a security that entitles the holder to buy stock of the company that issued it at a specified price, which is usually higher than the stock price at time of issue.

_________s are frequently attached to bonds or preferred stock as a sweetener, allowing the issuer to pay lower interest rates or dividends. They can be used to enhance the yield of the bond, and make them more attractive to potential buyers.

a. Clearing
b. Warrant
c. Clearing house
d. Credit

7. _________ is a process by which a firm can obtain the use of a certain fixed assets for which it must pay a series of contractual, periodic, tax deductable payments. The lessee is the receiver of the services or the assets under the lease contract and the lessor is the owner of the assets. The relationship between the tenant and the landlord is called a tenancy, and can be for a fixed or an indefinite period of time (called the term of the lease).

a. Royalties
b. Foreign Corrupt Practices Act
c. Quiet period
d. Leasing

8. _________ is the value on a given date of a future payment or series of future payments, discounted to reflect the time value of money and other factors such as investment risk. _________ calculations are widely used in business and economics to provide a means to compare cash flows at different times on a meaningful 'like to like' basis.

The most commonly applied model of the time value of money is compound interest.

a. Negative gearing
b. Net present value
c. Present value
d. Present value of benefits

9. A finance lease or _________ is a type of lease. It is a commercial arrangement where:

- the lessee (customer or borrower) will select an asset (equipment, vehicle, software);
- the lessor (finance company) will purchase that asset;
- the lessee will have use of that asset during the lease;
- the lessee will pay a series of rentals or installments for the use of that asset;
- the lessor will recover a large part or all of the cost of the asset plus earn interest from the rentals paid by the lessee;
- the lessee has the option to acquire ownership of the asset (e.g. paying the last rental, or bargain option purchase price);

The finance company is the legal owner of the asset during duration of the lease.

However the lessee has control over the asset providing them the benefits and risks of (economic) ownership.

A finance lease differs from an operating lease in that:

- in a finance lease the lessee has use of the asset over most of its economic life and beyond (generally by making small 'peppercorn' payments at the end of the lease term.)

In an operating lease the lessee only uses the asset for some of the asset's life.

- in a finance lease the lessor will recover all or most of the cost of the equipment from the rentals paid by the lessee.

In an operating lease the lessor will have a substantial investment or residual value on completion of the lease.

- in a finance lease the lessee has the benefits and risks of economic ownership of the asset (e.g. risk of obsolescence, paying for maintenance, claiming capital allowances/depreciation.)

In an operating lease the lessor has the benefits and risks of owning the asset.

The U.S. Financial Accounting Standards Board and the International Accounting Standards Board announced in 2006 a joint project to comprehensively review lease accounting standards.

a. Capitalization rate
b. Cash management
c. Cash concentration
d. Capital lease

10. An _________ is a lease whose term is short compared to the useful life of the asset or piece of equipment (an airliner, a ship etc.) being leased. An _________ is commonly used to acquire equipment on a relatively short-term basis.

a. ABN Amro
b. A Random Walk Down Wall Street
c. AAB
d. Operating lease

11. The _________ is a private, not-for-profit organization whose primary purpose is to develop generally accepted accounting principles (GAAP) within the United States in the public's interest. The Securities and Exchange Commission (SEC) designated the _________ as the organization responsible for setting accounting standards for public companies in the U.S. It was created in 1973, replacing the Accounting Principles Board and the Committee on Accounting Procedure of the American Institute of Certified Public Accountants. The _________'s mission is 'to establish and improve standards of financial accounting and reporting for the guidance and education of the public, including issuers, auditors, and users of financial information.'

The _________ is not a governmental body.

a. PlaNet Finance
b. Credit karma
c. MRU Holdings
d. FASB

12. A _________ is a lease in which the lessor puts up some of the money required to purchase the asset and borrows the rest from a lender. The lender is given a senior secured interest on the asset and an assignment of the lease and lease payments. The lessee makes payments to the lessor, who makes payments to the lender.

a. Leveraged lease
b. Collection agency
c. Debt buyer
d. Guaranteed consumer funding

13. _________ is the provision of resources (such as granting a loan) by one party to another party where that second party does not reimburse the first party immediately, thereby generating a debt, and instead arranges either to repay or return those resources (or material(s) of equal value) at a later date. The first party is called a creditor, also known as a lender, while the second party is called a debtor, also known as a borrower.

Movements of financial capital are normally dependent on either _________ or equity transfers.

a. Comparable
b. Clearing house
c. Warrant
d. Credit

14. _________ or net present worth (NPW) is defined as the total present value (PV) of a time series of cash flows. It is a standard method for using the time value of money to appraise long-term projects. Used for capital budgeting, and widely throughout economics, it measures the excess or shortfall of cash flows, in present value terms, once financing charges are met.

a. Tax shield
b. Negative gearing
c. Net present value
d. Present value of costs

15. An _________ can be defined as a contract which provides an income stream in return for an initial payment.

An immediate _________ is an _________ for which the time between the contract date and the date of the first payment is not longer than the time interval between payments. A common use for an immediate _________ is to provide a pension to a retired person or persons.

a. Intrinsic value
b. AT'T Inc.
c. Amortization
d. Annuity

16. In business, _________ is income that a company receives from its normal business activities, usually from the sale of goods and services to customers. Some companies also receive _________ from interest, dividends or royalties paid to them by other companies. _________ may refer to business income in general, or it may refer to the amount, in a monetary unit, received during a period of time, as in 'Last year, Company X had _________ of $32 million.'

In many countries, including the UK, _________ is referred to as turnover.

a. Matching principle
b. Bottom line
c. Furniture, Fixtures and Equipment
d. Revenue

17. The role of the _________ is to issue accounting standards in the United Kingdom. It is recognised for that purpose under the Companies Act 1985. It took over the task of setting accounting standards from the Accounting Standards Committee (ASC) in 1990.

a. AAB
b. ABN Amro
c. A Random Walk Down Wall Street
d. Accounting Standards Board

18. _________ is the field of accountancy concerned with the preparation of financial statements for decision makers, such as stockholders, suppliers, banks, employees, government agencies, owners, and other stakeholders. The fundamental need for _________ is to reduce principal-agent problem by measuring and monitoring agents' performance and reporting the results to interested users.

_________ is used to prepare accounting information for people outside the organization or not involved in the day to day running of the company.

a. 7-Eleven
b. 529 plan
c. 4-4-5 Calendar
d. Financial Accounting

19. The _________ is a private, not-for-profit organization whose primary purpose is to develop generally accepted accounting principles (GAAP) within the United States in the public's interest. The Securities and Exchange Commission (SEC) designated the _________ as the organization responsible for setting accounting standards for public companies in the U.S. It was created in 1973, replacing the Accounting Principles Board and the Committee on Accounting Procedure of the American Institute of Certified Public Accountants. The _________'s mission is 'to establish and improve standards of financial accounting and reporting for the guidance and education of the public, including issuers, auditors, and users of financial information.'

The _________ is not a governmental body.

a. Financial Accounting Standards Board
b. World Congress of Accountants
c. KPMG
d. Federal Deposit Insurance Corporation

20. _________ or financing is to provide capital (funds), which means money for a project, a person, a business or any other private or public institutions.

Those funds can be allocated for either short term or long term purposes. The health fund is a new way of _________ private healthcare centers.

a. Proxy fight
b. Synthetic CDO
c. Product life cycle
d. Funding

21. _________ is a legally declared inability or impairment of ability of an individual or organization to pay their creditors. Creditors may file a _________ petition against a debtor ('involuntary _________') in an effort to recoup a portion of what they are owed or initiate a restructuring. In the majority of cases, however, _________ is initiated by the debtor (a 'voluntary _________' that is filed by the bankrupt individual or organization.)

a. Bankruptcy
b. 4-4-5 Calendar
c. 529 plan
d. Debt settlement

22. In economics, business, and accounting, a _________ is the value of money that has been used up to produce something, and hence is not available for use anymore. In business, the _________ may be one of acquisition, in which case the amount of money expended to acquire it is counted as _________. In this case, money is the input that is gone in order to acquire the thing.

a. Sliding scale fees
b. Marginal cost
c. Fixed costs
d. Cost

23. In finance, a _________ or accounting ratio is a ratio of two selected numerical values taken from an enterprise's financial statements. There are many standard ratios used to try to evaluate the overall financial condition of a corporation or other organization. They may be used by managers within a firm, by current and potential shareholders (owners) of a firm, and by a firm's creditors. Security analysts use these to compare the strengths and weaknesses in various companies.

a. Price/cash flow ratio
b. Return on capital employed
c. Sustainable growth rate
d. Financial ratio

24. _________ is a measure of the ability of a debtor to pay their debts as and when they fall due. It is usually expressed as a ratio or a percentage of current liabilities.

For a corporation with a published balance sheet there are various ratios used to calculate a measure of liquidity.

a. Operating profit margin
b. Invested capital
c. Operating leverage
d. Accounting liquidity

25. A _________, in its most general sense, is a solemn promise to engage in or refrain from a specified action.

More specifically, a _________, in contrast to a contract, is a one-way agreement whereby the _________er is the only party bound by the promise. A _________ may have conditions and prerequisites that qualify the undertaking, including the actions of second or third parties, but there is no inherent agreement by such other parties to fulfill those requirements.

a. Clayton Antitrust Act
b. Partnership
c. Federal Trade Commission Act
d. Covenant

26. In finance, a _________ is a debt security, in which the authorized issuer owes the holders a debt and, depending on the terms of the _________, is obliged to pay interest (the coupon) and/or to repay the principal at a later date, termed maturity.

Thus a _________ is a loan: the issuer is the borrower, the _________ holder is the lender, and the coupon is the interest. _________s provide the borrower with external funds to finance long-term investments, or, in the case of government _________s, to finance current expenditure.

a. Puttable bond
b. Bond
c. Catastrophe bonds
d. Convertible bond

27. A _________ is defined as a certificate of agreement of loans which is given under the company's stamp and carries an undertaking that the _________ holder will get a fixed return (fixed on the basis of interest rates) and the principal amount whenever the _________ matures.

In finance, a _________ is a long-term debt instrument used by governments and large companies to obtain funds. It is defined as 'a debt secured only by the debtor's earning power, not by a lien on any specific asset.' It is similar to a bond except the securitization conditions are different.

a. Collection agency
b. Debenture
c. Partial Payment
d. Collateral Management

28. Straight-line depreciation is the simplest and most-often-used technique, in which the company estimates the _________ of the asset at the end of the period during which it will be used to generate revenues (useful life) and will expense a portion of original cost in equal increments over that period. The _________ is an estimate of the value of the asset at the time it will be sold or disposed of; it may be zero or even negative. _________ is scrap value, by another name.

a. Fixed investment
b. Net profit
c. Depreciation
d. Salvage value

29. In business and accounting, _________s are everything of value that is owned by a person or company. The balance sheet of a firm records the monetary value of the _________s owned by the firm. The two major _________ classes are tangible _________s and intangible _________s.

a. EBITDA
b. Accounts payable
c. Income
d. Asset

30. In business and finance, a _________ (also referred to as equity _________) of stock means a _________ of ownership in a corporation (company.) In the plural, stocks is often used as a synonym for _________s especially in the United States, but it is less commonly used that way outside of North America.

In the United Kingdom, South Africa, and Australia, stock can also refer to completely different financial instruments such as government bonds or, less commonly, to all kinds of marketable securities.

a. Procter ' Gamble
b. Margin
c. Bucket shop
d. Share

31. _________, in finance and accounting, means stated value or face value. From this comes the expressions at par (at the _________), over par (over _________) and under par (under _________.)

The term '_________' has several meanings depending on context and geography.

a. Global Squeeze
b. Sinking fund
c. Par value
d. FIDC

32. _________ is typically a higher ranking stock than voting shares, and its terms are negotiated between the corporation and the investor.

_________ usually carry no voting rights, but may carry superior priority over common stock in the payment of dividends and upon liquidation. _________ may carry a dividend that is paid out prior to any dividends to common stock holders.

a. Trade-off theory
b. Follow-on offering
c. Second lien loan
d. Preferred stock

33. _________ is a form of corporation equity ownership represented in the securities. It is dangerous in comparison to preferred shares and some other investment options, in that in the event of bankruptcy, _________ investors receive their funds after preferred stockholders, bondholders, creditors, etc. On the other hand, common shares on average perform better than preferred shares or bonds over time.

a. Stock market bubble
b. Common stock
c. Stop-limit order
d. Stock split

34. _________ is the difference between price and the costs of bringing to market whatever it is that is accounted as an enterprise (whether by harvest, extraction, manufacture, or purchase) in terms of the component costs of delivered goods and/or services and any operating or other expenses.

A key difficulty in measuring profit is in defining costs. Pure economic monetary profits can be zero or negative even in competitive equilibrium when accounted monetized costs exceed monetized price.

a. A Random Walk Down Wall Street
b. Accounting profit
c. Economic profit
d. AAB

35. A mutual shareholder or _________ is an individual or company (including a corporation) that legally owns one or more shares of stock in a joint stock company. A company's shareholders collectively own that company. Thus, the typical goal of such companies is to enhance shareholder value.

a. Limit order
b. Stock market bubble
c. Trading curb
d. Stockholder

36. _________, in accrual accounting, is any account where the asset or liability is not realized until a future date, e.g. annuities, charges, taxes, income, etc. The _________ item may be carried, dependent on type of deferral, as either an asset or liability.See also: accrual

_________ is also used in the university admissions process. It is the action by which a school rejects a student for early admission but still opts to review that student in the general admissions pool.

a. Current asset
b. Net profit
c. Revenue
d. Deferred

37. _________ is the price at which an asset would trade in a competitive Walrasian auction setting. _________ is often used interchangeably with open _________, fair value or fair _________, although these terms have distinct definitions in different standards, and may differ in some circumstances.

International Valuation Standards defines _________ as 'the estimated amount for which a property should exchange on the date of valuation between a willing buyer and a willing seller in an arm'e;s-length transaction after proper marketing wherein the parties had each acted knowledgeably, prudently, and without compulsion.'

_________ is a concept distinct from market price, which is 'e;the price at which one can transact'e;, while _________ is 'e;the true underlying value'e; according to theoretical standards.

a. T-Model
b. Debt restructuring
c. Wrap account
d. Market value

38. The _________ is a financial market where participants buy and sell debt securities, usually in the form of bonds. As of 2006, the size of the international _________ is an estimated $45 trillion, of which the size of the outstanding U.S. _________ debt was $25.2 trillion.

Nearly all of the $923 billion average daily trading volume in the U.S. _________ takes place between broker-dealers and large institutions in a decentralized, over-the-counter market.

a. Fixed income
b. 529 plan
c. 4-4-5 Calendar
d. Bond Market

39. In options, the _________ is a key variable in a derivatives contract between two parties. Where the contract requires delivery of the underlying instrument, the trade will be at the _________, regardless of the spot price (market price) of the underlying instrument at that time.

Definition - The fixed price at which the owner of an option can purchase, in the case of a call in the case of a put, the underlying security or commodity.

a. Naked put
b. Swaption
c. Moneyness
d. Strike price

40. A _________, securities exchange or (in Europe) bourse is a corporation or mutual organization which provides 'trading' facilities for stock brokers and traders, to trade stocks and other securities. _________s also provide facilities for the issue and redemption of securities as well as other financial instruments and capital events including the payment of income and dividends. The securities traded on a _________ include: shares issued by companies, unit trusts and other pooled investment products and bonds.

a. 4-4-5 Calendar
b. 529 plan
c. Stock Exchange
d. 7-Eleven

41. A _________ is a financial contract between two parties, the buyer and the seller of this type of option. Often it is simply labeled a 'call'. The buyer of the option has the right, but not the obligation to buy an agreed quantity of a particular commodity or financial instrument (the underlying instrument) from the seller of the option at a certain time (the expiration date) for a certain price (the strike price.)

a. Bull spread
b. Bear call spread
c. Call option
d. Bear spread

42. A _________ is a financial contract between two parties, the seller (writer) and the buyer of the option. The put allows its buyer the right but not the obligation to sell a commodity or financial instrument (the underlying instrument) to the writer (seller) of the option at a certain time for a certain price (the strike price.) The writer (seller) has the obligation to purchase the underlying asset at that strike price, if the buyer exercises the option.

a. Debit spread
b. Bear spread
c. Put option
d. Bear call spread

43. The _________ is an American financial and commodity derivative exchange based in Chicago. The _________ was founded in 1898 as the Chicago Butter and Egg Board. Originally, the exchange was a non-profit organization.

a. Public Company Accounting Oversight Board
b. Financial Crimes Enforcement Network
c. Chicago Mercantile Exchange
d. Gamelan Council

44. The phrase _________ refers to the aspect of corporate strategy, corporate finance and management dealing with the buying, selling and combining of different companies that can aid, finance, or help a growing company in a given industry grow rapidly without having to create another business entity.

An acquisition, also known as a takeover, is the buying of one company (the 'target') by another. An acquisition may be friendly or hostile.

a. 529 plan
b. 4-4-5 Calendar
c. 7-Eleven
d. Mergers and acquisitions

45. The institution most often referenced by the word '_________' is a public or publicly traded _________, the shares of which are traded on a public stock exchange (e.g., the New York Stock Exchange or Nasdaq in the United States) where shares of stock of _________s are bought and sold by and to the general public. Most of the largest businesses in the world are publicly traded _________s. However, the majority of _________s are said to be closely held, privately held or close _________s, meaning that no ready market exists for the trading of shares.

a. Corporation
b. Depository Trust Company
c. Federal Home Loan Mortgage Corporation
d. Protect

46. A _________ is the price of a single share of a no. of saleable stocks of the company. Once the stock is purchased, the owner becomes a shareholder of the company that issued the share.

a. Whisper numbers
b. Trading curb
c. Stock split
d. Share price

47. In finance, _________ refers to the way a corporation finances its assets through some combination of equity, debt, or hybrid securities. A firm's _________ is then the composition or 'structure' of its liabilities. For example, a firm that sells $20 billion in equity and $80 billion in debt is said to be 20% equity-financed and 80% debt-financed.

a. Rights issue
b. Market for corporate control
c. Capital structure
d. Book building

1. _________ is a legally declared inability or impairment of ability of an individual or organization to pay their creditors. Creditors may file a _________ petition against a debtor ('involuntary _________') in an effort to recoup a portion of what they are owed or initiate a restructuring. In the majority of cases, however, _________ is initiated by the debtor (a 'voluntary _________' that is filed by the bankrupt individual or organization.)

a. Debt settlement
b. 529 plan
c. 4-4-5 Calendar
d. Bankruptcy

2. In finance and economics, _________ or divestiture is the reduction of some kind of asset for either financial goals or ethical objectives. A _________ is the opposite of an investment.

Often the term is used as a means to grow financially in which a company sells off a business unit in order to focus their resources on a market it judges to be more profitable, or promising.

a. Portfolio investment
b. Divestment
c. Certificate in Investment Performance Measurement
d. Late trading

3. A _________ occurs when a financial sponsor acquires a controlling interest in a company's equity and where a significant percentage of the purchase price is financed through leverage (borrowing.) The assets of the acquired company are used as collateral for the borrowed capital, sometimes with assets of the acquiring company. The bonds or other paper issued for _________s are commonly considered not to be investment grade because of the significant risks involved.

a. Limited partnership
b. Pension fund
c. Leverage
d. Leveraged buyout

4. The phrase _________ refers to the aspect of corporate strategy, corporate finance and management dealing with the buying, selling and combining of different companies that can aid, finance, or help a growing company in a given industry grow rapidly without having to create another business entity.

An acquisition, also known as a takeover, is the buying of one company (the 'target') by another. An acquisition may be friendly or hostile.

a. 529 plan
b. 7-Eleven
c. 4-4-5 Calendar
d. Mergers and acquisitions

5. In economics, a _________ is the combination of two or more firms competing in the same market with the same good or service.

a. Horizontal merger
b. Passive income
c. 4-4-5 Calendar
d. Fixed exchange rate system

6. _________ or amalgamation is the act of merging many things into one. In business, it often refers to the mergers or acquisitions of many smaller companies into much larger ones. The financial accounting term of _________ refers to the aggregated financial statements of a group company as consolidated account.

a. Retained earnings
b. Consolidation
c. Write-off
d. Cost of goods sold

7. A _________ is a company that owns other companies' outstanding stock. It usually refers to a company which does not produce goods or services itself, rather its only purpose is owning shares of other companies. They allow the reduction of risk for the owners and can allow the ownership and control of a number of different companies.

a. Privately held company
b. Federal National Mortgage Association
c. MRU Holdings
d. Holding company

8. A _________, in business matters, is an entity that is controlled by a bigger and more powerful entity. The controlled entity is called a company, corporation, or limited liability company, and the controlling entity is called its parent (or the parent company.) The reason for this distinction is that a lone company cannot be a _________ of any organization; only an entity representing a legal fiction as a separate entity can be a _________.

a. 529 plan
b. Joint stock company
c. 4-4-5 Calendar
d. Subsidiary

9. _________ is the corporate management term for the act of reorganizing the legal, ownership, operational, or other structures of a company for the purpose of making it more profitable or better organized for its present needs. Alternate reasons for restructing include a change of ownership or ownership structure, demerger repositioning debt _________ and financial _________.

a. Day trading
b. Concentrated stock
c. Cross-border leasing
d. Restructuring

10. In finance, a _________ (non-investment grade bond, speculative grade bond or junk bond) is a bond that is rated below investment grade at the time of purchase. These bonds have a higher risk of default or other adverse credit events, but typically pay higher yields than better quality bonds in order to make them attractive to investors.

a. Sharpe ratio
b. Private equity
c. Volatility
d. High yield bond

11. _________ is a corporate finance term denoting a type of takeover bid. The _________ is a public, open offer or invitation (usually announced in a newspaper advertisement) by a prospective acquirer to all stockholders of a publicly traded corporation (the target corporation) to tender their stock for sale at a specified price during a specified time, subject to the tendering of a minimum and maximum number of shares. In a _________, the bidder contacts shareholders directly; the directors of the company may or may not have endorsed the _________ proposal.

a. Follow-on offering
b. Tender offer
c. Shareholder value
d. Cash is king

12. _________ is a diversified financial services company with operations around the world. Wells Fargo is the fourth largest bank in the US by assets and the second largest bank by market cap.

a. Holding company
b. Federal Deposit Insurance Corporation
c. Gold exchange-traded fund
d. Wells Fargo ' Co.

13. In finance, a _________ is a debt security, in which the authorized issuer owes the holders a debt and, depending on the terms of the _________, is obliged to pay interest (the coupon) and/or to repay the principal at a later date, termed maturity.

Thus a _________ is a loan: the issuer is the borrower, the _________ holder is the lender, and the coupon is the interest. _________s provide the borrower with external funds to finance long-term investments, or, in the case of government _________s, to finance current expenditure.

a. Bond
b. Convertible bond
c. Catastrophe bonds
d. Puttable bond

14. In economics, a _________ is a mechanism that allows people to easily buy and sell (trade) financial securities (such as stocks and bonds), commodities (such as precious metals or agricultural goods), and other fungible items of value at low transaction costs and at prices that reflect the efficient-market hypothesis.

_________s have evolved significantly over several hundred years and are undergoing constant innovation to improve liquidity.

Both general markets (where many commodities are traded) and specialized markets (where only one commodity is traded) exist.

a. Secondary market
b. Delta hedging
c. Cost of carry
d. Financial market

15. _________ or financing is to provide capital (funds), which means money for a project, a person, a business or any other private or public institutions.

Those funds can be allocated for either short term or long term purposes. The health fund is a new way of _________ private healthcare centers.

a. Product life cycle
b. Funding
c. Synthetic CDO
d. Proxy fight

16. In business, a _________ is the purchase of one company (the target) by another (the acquirer or bidder). In the UK the term refers to the acquisition of a public company whose shares are listed on a stock exchange, in contrast to the acquisition of a private company.

Before a bidder makes an offer for another company, it usually first informs that company's board of directors.

a. 529 plan
b. Takeover
c. Stock swap
d. 4-4-5 Calendar

17. _________ in finance is a risk management technique, related to hedging, that mixes a wide variety of investments within a portfolio. Because the fluctuations of a single security have less impact on a diverse portfolio, _________ minimizes the risk from any one investment.

A simple example of _________ is the following: On a particular island the entire economy consists of two companies: one that sells umbrellas and another that sells sunscreen.

a. 7-Eleven
b. 529 plan
c. 4-4-5 Calendar
d. Diversification

18. In business and finance, a _________ (also referred to as equity _________) of stock means a _________ of ownership in a corporation (company.) In the plural, stocks is often used as a synonym for _________s especially in the United States, but it is less commonly used that way outside of North America.

In the United Kingdom, South Africa, and Australia, stock can also refer to completely different financial instruments such as government bonds or, less commonly, to all kinds of marketable securities.

a. Share
b. Margin
c. Bucket shop
d. Procter ' Gamble

19. _________ is the difference between price and the costs of bringing to market whatever it is that is accounted as an enterprise (whether by harvest, extraction, manufacture, or purchase) in terms of the component costs of delivered goods and/or services and any operating or other expenses.

A key difficulty in measuring profit is in defining costs. Pure economic monetary profits can be zero or negative even in competitive equilibrium when accounted monetized costs exceed monetized price.

a. Accounting profit
b. A Random Walk Down Wall Street
c. Economic profit
d. AAB

20. A mutual shareholder or _________ is an individual or company (including a corporation) that legally owns one or more shares of stock in a joint stock company. A company's shareholders collectively own that company. Thus, the typical goal of such companies is to enhance shareholder value.

a. Trading curb
b. Limit order
c. Stock market bubble
d. Stockholder

21. _________ is a measure of the ability of a debtor to pay their debts as and when they fall due. It is usually expressed as a ratio or a percentage of current liabilities.

For a corporation with a published balance sheet there are various ratios used to calculate a measure of liquidity.

a. Accounting liquidity
b. Invested capital
c. Operating leverage
d. Operating profit margin

22. The term _________ has three unrelated technical definitions, and is also used in a variety of non-technical ways.

- In financial economics, it refers to any asset used to make money, as opposed to assets used for personal enjoyment or consumption. This is an important distinction because two people can disagree sharply about the value of personal assets, one person might think a sports car is more valuable than a pickup truck, another person might have the opposite taste. But if an asset is held for the purpose of making money, taste has nothing to do with it, only differences of opinion about how much money the asset will produce. With the further assumption that people agree on the probability distribution of future cash flows, it is possible to have an objective _________ pricing model. Even without the assumption of agreement, it is possible to set rational limits on _________ value.
- In governmental accounting, it is defined as any asset used in operations with an initial useful life extending beyond one reporting period. Generally, government managers have a 'stewardship' duty to maintain _________s under their control. See International Public Sector Accounting Standards for details.
- In US tax accounting, it is defined as any property other than a list of exceptions. The main exceptions are anything held for sale, and any real estate or depreciable property used in business. Almost everything you own and use for personal purposes, pleasure or investment is a _________. If something is a _________ for tax purposes, gains or losses on sale or disposition are capital gains or capital losses. For individuals, however, capital losses on property held for personal use are generally not deductible. See the IRS publication Tax Facts about Capital Gains and Losses for details.

A well-known financial accounting textbook advises that the term be avoided except in tax accounting because it is used in so many different senses, not all of them well-defined. For example it is often used as a synonym for fixed assets or for investments in securities.

A common non-technical usage occurs when people ask that employees or the environment or something else be treated as a _________.

a. Settlement date
b. Solvency
c. Capital asset
d. Political risk

23. In finance, the _________ is used to determine a theoretically appropriate required rate of return of an asset, if that asset is to be added to an already well-diversified portfolio, given that asset's non-diversifiable risk. The model takes into account the asset's sensitivity to non-diversifiable risk (also known as systemic risk or market risk), often represented by the quantity beta (β) in the financial industry, as well as the expected return of the market and the expected return of a theoretical risk-free asset.

The model was introduced by Jack Treynor (1961, 1962), William Sharpe (1964), John Lintner (1965a,b) and Jan Mossin (1966) independently, building on the earlier work of Harry Markowitz on diversification and modern portfolio theory.

a. Cox-Ingersoll-Ross model
b. Hull-White model
c. Random walk hypothesis
d. Capital asset pricing model

24. A _________ is officially defined as being 'any merger that is not horizontal or vertical; in general, it is the combination of firms in different industries or firms operating in different geographic areas'. _________s can serve various purposes, including extending corporate territories and extending a product range. One example of a _________ was the merger between the Walt Disney Company and the American Broadcasting Company.

a. Refunding
b. Volatility clustering
c. Redemption value
d. Conglomerate merger

25. In finance, _________ occurs when a debtor has not met its legal obligations according to the debt contract, e.g. it has not made a scheduled payment, or has violated a loan covenant (condition) of the debt contract. _________ may occur if the debtor is either unwilling or unable to pay their debt. This can occur with all debt obligations including bonds, mortgages, loans, and promissory notes.

a. Credit crunch
b. Vendor finance
c. Debt validation
d. Default

26. _________ is the risk of loss due to a debtor's non-payment of a loan or other line of credit (either the principal or interest (coupon) or both)

Most lenders employ their own models (credit scorecards) to rank potential and existing customers according to risk, and then apply appropriate strategies. With products such as unsecured personal loans or mortgages, lenders charge a higher price for higher risk customers and vice versa. With revolving products such as credit cards and overdrafts, risk is controlled through careful setting of credit limits.

a. Credit risk
b. Transaction risk
c. Market risk
d. Liquidity risk

27. In finance, the _________ between two currencies specifies how much one currency is worth in terms of the other. For example an _________ of 102 Japanese yen to the United States dollar means that JPY 102 is worth the same as USD 1. The foreign exchange market is one of the largest markets in the world.

a. ABN Amro
b. A Random Walk Down Wall Street
c. AAB
d. Exchange rate

28. _________ is a form of risk that arises from the change in price of one currency against another. Whenever investors or companies have assets or business operations across national borders, they face _________ if their positions are not hedged.

- Transaction risk is the risk that exchange rates will change unfavourably over time. It can be hedged against using forward currency contracts;
- Translation risk is an accounting risk, proportional to the amount of assets held in foreign currencies. Changes in the exchange rate over time will render a report inaccurate, and so assets are usually balanced by borrowings in that currency.

The exchange risk associated with a foreign denominated instrument is a key element in foreign investment. This risk flows from differential monetary policy and growth in real productivity, which results in differential inflation rates.

a. Credit risk
b. Market risk
c. Currency risk
d. Tracking error

29. _________ is a type of risk faced by investors, corporations, and governments. It is a risk that can be understood and managed with proper aforethought and investment.

Broadly, _________ refers to the complications businesses and governments may face as a result of what are commonly referred to as political decisions--or 'any political change that alters the expected outcome and value of a given economic action by changing the probability of achieving business objectives.' .

a. Single-index model
b. Mid price
c. Capital asset
d. Political risk

30. In business and accounting, _________s are everything of value that is owned by a person or company. The balance sheet of a firm records the monetary value of the _________s owned by the firm. The two major _________ classes are tangible _________s and intangible _________s.

a. Income
b. EBITDA
c. Accounts payable
d. Asset

31. In finance, _________ is the process of estimating the potential market value of a financial asset or liability. they can be done on assets (for example, investments in marketable securities such as stocks, options, business enterprises, or intangible assets such as patents and trademarks) or on liabilities (e.g., Bonds issued by a company.) _________s are required in many contexts including investment analysis, capital budgeting, merger and acquisition transactions, financial reporting, taxable events to determine the proper tax liability, and in litigation.

a. Share
b. Margin
c. Procter ' Gamble
d. Valuation

32. _________ is the planning process used to determine whether a firm's long term investments such as new machinery, replacement machinery, new plants, new products, and research development projects are worth pursuing. It is budget for major capital, or investment, expenditures.

Many formal methods are used in _________, including the techniques such as

- Net present value
- Profitability index
- Internal rate of return
- Modified Internal Rate of Return
- Equivalent annuity

These methods use the incremental cash flows from each potential investment, or project. Techniques based on accounting earnings and accounting rules are sometimes used - though economists consider this to be improper - such as the accounting rate of return, and 'return on investment.' Simplified and hybrid methods are used as well, such as payback period and discounted payback period.

a. Preferred stock
b. Capital budgeting
c. Shareholder value
d. Financial distress

33. A _________ is a form of partnership similar to a general partnership, except that in addition to one or more general partners (GPs), there are one or more limited partners (_________s). It is a partnership in which only one partner is required to be a general partner.

The GPs are, in all major respects, in the same legal position as partners in a conventional firm, i.e. they have management control, share the right to use partnership property, share the profits of the firm in predefined proportions, and have joint and several liability for the debts of the partnership.

a. Fund of funds
b. Limited liability company
c. Leverage
d. Limited partnership

34. A _________ is a type of business entity in which partners (owners) share with each other the profits or losses of the business undertaking in which all have invested. _________s are often favored over corporations for taxation purposes, as the _________ structure does not generally incur a tax on profits before it is distributed to the partners (i.e. there is no dividend tax levied.) However, depending on the _________ structure and the jurisdiction in which it operates, owners of a _________ may be exposed to greater personal liability than they would as shareholders of a corporation.

a. Fiduciary
b. National Securities Markets Improvement Act of 1996
c. Clayton Antitrust Act
d. Partnership

35. The institution most often referenced by the word '_________' is a public or publicly traded _________, the shares of which are traded on a public stock exchange (e.g., the New York Stock Exchange or Nasdaq in the United States) where shares of stock of _________s are bought and sold by and to the general public. Most of the largest businesses in the world are publicly traded _________s. However, the majority of _________s are said to be closely held, privately held or close _________s, meaning that no ready market exists for the trading of shares.

a. Federal Home Loan Mortgage Corporation
b. Protect
c. Depository Trust Company
d. Corporation

36. A _________ is a new organization or entity formed by a split from a larger one, such as a television series based on a pre-existing one, or a new company formed from a university research group or business incubator. In literature, especially in milieu-based popular fictional book series like mysteries, westerns, fantasy, or science fiction, the term sub-series is generally used instead of _________, but with essentially the same meaning.

_________s as a descriptive term can also include a dissenting faction of a membership organization, a sect of a cult, or a denomination of a church.

a. 529 plan
b. 4-4-5 Calendar
c. Spin-off
d. 7-Eleven

37. In probability theory and statistics, _________ indicates the strength and direction of a linear relationship between two random variables. That is in contrast with the usage of the term in colloquial speech, which denotes any relationship, not necessarily linear. In general statistical usage, _________ or co-relation refers to the departure of two random variables from independence.

a. Variance
b. Geometric mean
c. Probability distribution
d. Correlation

38. The term _________ is a term applied to practices that are perfunctory, or seek to satisfy the minimum requirements or to conform to a convention or doctrine. It has different meanings in different fields.

In accounting, _________ earnings are those earnings of companies in addition to actual earnings calculated under the Generally Accepted Accounting Principles (GAAP) in their quarterly and yearly financial reports.

a. Deferred financing costs
b. Deferred income
c. Pro forma
d. Long-term liabilities

39. _________, refers to consumption opportunity gained by an entity within a specified time frame, which is generally expressed in monetary terms. However, for households and individuals, '_________ is the sum of all the wages, salaries, profits, interests payments, rents and other forms of earnings received... in a given period of time.' For firms, _________ generally refers to net-profit: what remains of revenue after expenses have been subtracted.

a. Annual report
b. OIBDA
c. Income
d. Accrual

40. An _________ is a financial statement for companies that indicates how Revenue is transformed into net income The purpose of the _________ is to show managers and investors whether the company made or lost money during the period being reported.

The important thing to remember about an _________ is that it represents a period of time.

a. AAB
b. ABN Amro
c. A Random Walk Down Wall Street
d. Income statement

41. A _________ is a business takeover or acquisition in which the acquiring company uses its own stock to pay for the acquired company. Each shareholder of the newly acquired company receives a certain number of shares of the acquiring company's stock for each share of stock they previously held in the acquired company. Sometimes some shareholders are required to wait for an agreed-upon period of time before they are allowed to sell their new shares of stock.

a. 4-4-5 Calendar
b. 529 plan
c. Stock swap
d. Takeover

42. In finance, a _________ is a derivative in which two counterparties agree to exchange one stream of cash flows against another stream. These streams are called the legs of the _________.

The cash flows are calculated over a notional principal amount, which is usually not exchanged between counterparties.

a. Local volatility
b. Volatility arbitrage
c. Volatility swap
d. Swap

43. _________ is a company's earnings per share (EPS) calculated using fully diluted shares outstanding (i.e. including the impact of stock option grants and convertible bonds.) Diluted EPS indicates a 'worst case' scenario, one in which everyone who could have received stock without purchasing it directly for the full market value did so.

To find diluted EPS, basic EPS is calculated for each of the categories on the income statement first.

a. Financial ratio
b. Net assets
c. Price/cash flow ratio
d. Diluted Earnings Per Share

44. The _________ of a stock is a measure of the price paid for a share relative to the annual income or profit earned by the firm per share. It is a financial ratio used for valuation: a higher _________ means that investors are paying more for each unit of income, so the stock is more expensive compared to one with lower _________.

The _________ has units of years, which can be interpreted as 'number of years of earnings to pay back purchase price'.

a. Return of capital
b. P/E ratio
c. Sustainable growth rate
d. Quick ratio

45. _________ is an economic concept with commonplace familiarity. It is the price that a good or service is offered at, or will fetch, in the marketplace. It is of interest mainly in the study of microeconomics.

a. Market price
b. Convertible arbitrage
c. Central Securities Depository
d. Delta hedging

46. A _________ or bank is a financial institution whose primary activity is to act as a payment agent for customers and to borrow and lend money.

The first modern bank was founded in Italy in Genoa in 1406, its name was Banco di San Giorgio (Bank of St. George.)

Many other financial activities were added over time.

a. Banker
b. Bought deal
c. Black Sea Trade and Development Bank
d. 4-4-5 Calendar

47. A _________ is an agreement between a company and an employee (usually upper executive) specifying that the employee will receive certain significant benefits if employment is terminated. Sometimes, certain conditions, typically a change in company ownership, must be met, but often the cause of termination is unspecified. These benefits may include severance pay, cash bonuses, stock options, or other benefits.

a. Debtor-in-possession financing
b. Golden parachute
c. Market capitalization
d. Trade finance

48. _________ is money paid by a company (or allied company or individual) to acquire its own shares of stock from a shareholder who is threatening to take control of, or unwanted influence of, the company.

The term is a neologism combining the terms greenback and blackmail, invented by journalists and commentators who saw the practices of corporate raiders as a form of blackmail. The target company is financially held hostage, and is legally forced to pay the _________er to go away.

a. Greenmail
b. Stock swap
c. 529 plan
d. 4-4-5 Calendar

49. In corporate finance, a _________ is a change of the capital structure of the company--usually to substitute debt for equity.

_________s are used by privately held companies as a means of refinancing, generally to provide returns to the shareholders while not requiring a total sale of the company. These types of recapitalizations can be minor adjustments to the capital structure or may involve a change of control.

a. Leveraged recapitalization
b. Modern portfolio theory
c. Median
d. Bed Bath ' Beyond Inc.

50. In finance, _________ (or gearing) is borrowing money to supplement existing funds for investment in such a way that the potential positive or negative outcome is magnified and/or enhanced. It generally refers to using borrowed funds, or debt, so as to attempt to increase the returns to equity. Deleveraging is the action of reducing borrowings.

a. Pension fund
b. Financial endowment
c. Leverage
d. Limited partnership

51. _________ is the imposition of two or more taxes on the same income (in the case of income taxes), asset (in the case of capital taxes), or financial transaction (in the case of sales taxes.) It refers to two distinct situations:

- taxation of dividend income without relief or credit for taxes paid by the company paying the dividend on the income from which the dividend is paid. This arises in the so-called 'classical' system of corporate taxation, used in the United States.
- taxation by two or more countries of the same income, asset or transaction, for example income paid by an entity of one country to a resident of a different country. The double liability is often mitigated by tax treaties between countries.

It is not unusual for a business or individual who is resident in one country to make a taxable gain (earnings, profits) in another. This person may find that he is obliged by domestic laws to pay tax on that gain locally and pay again in the country in which the gain was made. Since this is inequitable, many nations make bilateral _________ agreements with each other.

a. 529 plan
b. 4-4-5 Calendar
c. 7-Eleven
d. Double taxation

52. In economics, business, and accounting, a _________ is the value of money that has been used up to produce something, and hence is not available for use anymore. In business, the _________ may be one of acquisition, in which case the amount of money expended to acquire it is counted as _________. In this case, money is the input that is gone in order to acquire the thing.

a. Fixed costs
b. Marginal cost
c. Cost
d. Sliding scale fees

53. _________ means the inability to pay one's debts as they fall due. Usually used in Business terms, _________ refers to the inability for a 'limited liability' company to pay off debts.

This is defined in two different ways:

Cash flow _________ -

Unable to pay debts as they fall due.

Balance sheet _________ -

Having negative net assets: liabilities exceed assets; or net liabilities.

a. Interest
b. Insolvency
c. AAB
d. A Random Walk Down Wall Street

54. _________ is a financial measure used to determine the attractiveness of an investment. It is generally used as part of a capital budgeting process to rank various alternative choices. It is a modification of the Internal Rate of Return (IRR).

_________ ranks project efficiency consistently with the present worth ratio (variant of NPV/Discounted Negative Cash Flow), considered the gold standard in many finance textbooks.

MIRR is calculated as follows:

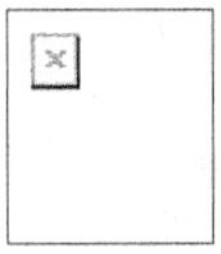
width=747 border=0>

where n is the number of (equal) periods in which the cash flows occur.

a. Black-Scholes
b. Binomial options pricing model
c. Current yield
d. Modified Internal Rate of Return

55. _________ is a life of security. It may also refer to the final payment date of a loan or other financial instrument, at which point all remaining interest and principal is due to be paid.

1, 3, 6 months _________ band can be calculated by using 30-day per month periods.

a. Replacement cost
b. False billing
c. Primary market
d. Maturity

56. A _________ is a party (e.g. person, organization, company, or government) that has a claim to the services of a second party. The first party, in general, has provided some property or service to the second party under the assumption (usually enforced by contract) that the second party will return an equivalent property or service. The second party is frequently called a debtor or borrower.

a. NOPLAT
b. Redemption value
c. Creditor
d. False billing

57. In law, _________ refers to the process by which a company (or part of a company) is brought to an end, and the assets and property of the company redistributed. _________ can also be referred to as winding-up or dissolution, although dissolution technically refers to the last stage of _________. The process of _________ also arises when customs, an authority or agency in a country responsible for collecting and safeguarding customs duties, determines the final computation or ascertainment of the duties or drawback accruing on an entry.

a. 529 plan
b. 4-4-5 Calendar
c. Debt settlement
d. Liquidation

58. In finance, _________ refers to the way a corporation finances its assets through some combination of equity, debt, or hybrid securities. A firm's _________ is then the composition or 'structure' of its liabilities. For example, a firm that sells $20 billion in equity and $80 billion in debt is said to be 20% equity-financed and 80% debt-financed.

a. Market for corporate control
b. Rights issue
c. Book building
d. Capital structure

59. The _________, was a law enacting several significant changes to the U.S. Bankruptcy Code. Referred to colloquially as the 'New Bankruptcy Law', the Act of Congress attempts to, among other things, make it more difficult for some consumers to file bankruptcy under Chapter 7; some of these consumers may instead utilize Chapter 13.

a. Bankruptcy Abuse Prevention and Consumer Protection Act of 2005
b. Foreclosure
c. Covenant
d. Personal property

60. In economics a _________ is simply an entity that owes a debt to someone else, the entity could be an individual, a firm, a government, or an organization. The counterparty of this arrangement is called a creditor. When the counterparty of this debt arrangement is a bank, the _________ is more often referred to as a borrower.

a. Biweekly Mortgage
b. Tick size
c. Financial rand
d. Debtor

61. _________ is the likely price of an asset when it is allowed insufficient time to sell on the open market, thereby reducing its exposure to potential buyers. _________ is typically lower than fair market value. Unlike cash or securities, certain illiquid assets, like real estate, often require a period of several months in order to obtain their fair market value in a sale, and will generally sell for a significantly lower price if a sale is forced to occur in a shorter time period.

a. Liquidation value
b. Real estate investing
c. Tenancy
d. REIT

62. A _________ is a fungible, negotiable instrument representing financial value. They are broadly categorized into debt securities (such as banknotes, bonds and debentures), and equity securities; e.g., common stocks. The company or other entity issuing the _________ is called the issuer.

a. Securities lending
b. Tracking stock
c. Book entry
d. Security

63. A _________ is the price of a single share of a no. of saleable stocks of the company. Once the stock is purchased, the owner becomes a shareholder of the company that issued the share.

a. Whisper numbers
b. Trading curb
c. Share price
d. Stock split

1. _________ is the term used to describe deposits residing in banks that are located outside the borders of the country that issues the currency the deposit is denominated in. For example a deposit denominated in US dollars residing in a Japanese bank is a _________ deposit, or more specifically a Eurodollar deposit.

Key points are the location of the bank and the denomination of the currency, not the nationality of the bank or the owner of the deposit/loan.

a. AAB
b. A Random Walk Down Wall Street
c. ABN Amro
d. Eurocurrency

2. _________ are formal records of a business' financial activities.

_________ provide an overview of a business' financial condition in both short and long term. There are four basic _________:

1. **Balance sheet**: also referred to as statement of financial position or condition, reports on a company's assets, liabilities, and net equity as of a given point in time.
2. **Income statement**: also referred to as Profit and Loss statement (or a 'P'L'), reports on a company's income, expenses, and profits over a period of time.
3. **Statement of retained earnings**: explains the changes in a company's retained earnings over the reporting period.
4. **Statement of cash flows**: reports on a company's cash flow activities, particularly its operating, investing and financing activities.

a. Statement of retained earnings
b. Notes to the Financial Statements
c. Statement on Auditing Standards No. 70: Service Organizations
d. Financial statements

3. _________ in its classic form is defined as a company from one country making a physical investment into building a factory in another country. It is the establishment of an enterprise by a foreigner. Its definition can be extended to include investments made to acquire lasting interest in enterprises operating outside of the economy of the investor.

a. MicroPlace
b. Public company
c. Dow Jones ' Company
d. Foreign direct investment

4. The phrase _________ refers to the aspect of corporate strategy, corporate finance and management dealing with the buying, selling and combining of different companies that can aid, finance, or help a growing company in a given industry grow rapidly without having to create another business entity.

An acquisition, also known as a takeover, is the buying of one company (the 'target') by another. An acquisition may be friendly or hostile.

a. 529 plan
b. 7-Eleven
c. 4-4-5 Calendar
d. Mergers and acquisitions

5. The _________ is the market for securities, where companies and governments can raise longterm funds. The _________ includes the stock market and the bond market. Financial regulators, such as the U.S. Securities and Exchange Commission, oversee the _________s in their designated countries to ensure that investors are protected against fraud.

a. Forward market
b. Delta neutral
c. Spot rate
d. Capital market

6. When companies conduct business across borders, they must deal in foreign currencies. Companies must exchange foreign currencies for home currencies when dealing with receivables, and vice versa for payables. This is done at the current exchange rate between the two countries. _________ is the risk that the exchange rate will change unfavorably before the currency is exchanged.

a. Foreign exchange risk
b. Lower of cost or market rule
c. 4-4-5 Calendar
d. 529 plan

7. _________ is a legally declared inability or impairment of ability of an individual or organization to pay their creditors. Creditors may file a _________ petition against a debtor ('involuntary _________') in an effort to recoup a portion of what they are owed or initiate a restructuring. In the majority of cases, however, _________ is initiated by the debtor (a 'voluntary _________' that is filed by the bankrupt individual or organization.)

a. Bankruptcy
b. Debt settlement
c. 529 plan
d. 4-4-5 Calendar

8. _________ is a type of trade policy that allows traders to act and transact without interference from government. Thus, the policy permits trading partners mutual gains from trade, with goods and services produced according to the theory of comparative advantage.

Under a _________ policy, prices are a reflection of true supply and demand, and are the sole determinant of resource allocation.

a. Seasoned equity offering
b. Free Trade
c. Yield spread
d. Monte Carlo methods

9. The _________ is a trilateral trade bloc in North America created by the governments of the United States, Canada, and Mexico. The agreement creating the trade bloc came into force on January 1, 1994. It superseded the Canada-United States Free Trade Agreement between the U.S. and Canada.

a. 7-Eleven
b. 4-4-5 Calendar
c. 529 plan
d. North American Free Trade Agreement

10. The _________ is an important selective, mainly private, international organization designed by its founders to supervise and liberalize international trade. The organization officially commenced on 1 January 1995, under the Marrakesh Agreement, succeeding the 1947 General Agreement on Tariffs and Trade (GATT.)

The _________ deals with regulation of trade between participating countries; it provides a framework for negotiating and formalising trade agreements, and a dispute resolution process aimed at enforcing participants' adherence to _________ agreements which are signed by representatives of member governments and ratified by their parliaments.

a. Gamelan Council
b. Financial Crimes Enforcement Network
c. World Trade Organization
d. Public Company Accounting Oversight Board

11. _________ refers to a tax levied by various jurisdictions on the profits made by companies or associations. It is a tax on the value of the corporation's profits.

The measure of taxable profits varies from country to country.

a. Proxy fight
b. Corporate tax
c. First-mover advantage
d. Trade finance

12. A _________ is an entity formed between two or more parties to undertake economic activity together. The parties agree to create a new entity by both contributing equity, and they then share in the revenues, expenses, and control of the enterprise. The venture can be for one specific project only, or a continuing business relationship such as the Sony Ericsson _________.

a. Lien
b. Fair Debt Collection Practices Act
c. Pre-emption right
d. Joint venture

13. A _________ is a payment made by a corporation to its shareholder members. When a corporation earns a profit or surplus, that money can be put to two uses: it can either be re-invested in the business (called retained earnings), or it can be paid to the shareholders as a _________. Many corporations retain a portion of their earnings and pay the remainder as a _________.

a. Dividend yield
b. Dividend
c. Dividend puzzle
d. Special dividend

14. _________ is the portion of income that is the subject of taxation according to the laws that determine what is income and the taxation rate for that income. Generally, _________ refers to an individual's (or corporation's) gross income, adjusted for various deductions allowable by statute. The main questions put by most individuals in any jurisdiction are 'what makes up my _________' and what tax rates should be applied such that I can work out my tax liability to the state.

a. 7-Eleven
b. Taxable income
c. 4-4-5 Calendar
d. 529 plan

15. _________, refers to consumption opportunity gained by an entity within a specified time frame, which is generally expressed in monetary terms. However, for households and individuals, '_________ is the sum of all the wages, salaries, profits, interests payments, rents and other forms of earnings received... in a given period of time.' For firms, _________ generally refers to net-profit: what remains of revenue after expenses have been subtracted.

a. OIBDA
b. Accrual
c. Income
d. Annual report

16. An _________ is a tax levied on the financial income of people, corporations, or other legal entities. Various _________ systems exist, with varying degrees of tax incidence. Income taxation can be progressive, proportional, or regressive.

a. Income tax
b. ABN Amro
c. A Random Walk Down Wall Street
d. AAB

17. In economics, a _________ is a mechanism that allows people to easily buy and sell (trade) financial securities (such as stocks and bonds), commodities (such as precious metals or agricultural goods), and other fungible items of value at low transaction costs and at prices that reflect the efficient-market hypothesis.

_________s have evolved significantly over several hundred years and are undergoing constant innovation to improve liquidity.

Both general markets (where many commodities are traded) and specialized markets (where only one commodity is traded) exist.

a. Cost of carry
b. Secondary market
c. Delta hedging
d. Financial market

18. A _________ is an international bond that is denominated in a currency not native to the country where it is issued. It can be categorised according to the currency in which it is issued. London is one of the centers of the _________ market, but _________s may be traded throughout the world - for example in Singapore or Tokyo.

a. Economic entity
b. Education production function
c. Interest rate option
d. Eurobond

19. The _________ is a bank that provides financial and technical assistance to developing countries for development programs (e.g. bridges, roads, schools, etc.) with the stated goal of reducing poverty.

The _________ differs from the _________ Group, in that the _________ comprises only two institutions:

- International Bank for Reconstruction and Development (IBRD)
- International Development Association (IDA)

Whereas the latter incorporates these two in addition to three more:

- International Finance Corporation (IFC)
- Multilateral Investment Guarantee Agency (MIGA)
- International Centre for Settlement of Investment Disputes (ICSID)

John Maynard Keynes (right) represented the UK at the conference, and Harry Dexter White represented the US.

The _________ was created following the ratification of the United Nations Monetary and Financial Conference | Bretton Woods agreement. The concept was originally conceived in July 1944 at the United Nations Monetary and Financial Conference.

a. 7-Eleven
b. World Bank
c. 4-4-5 Calendar
d. 529 plan

20. _________ or amalgamation is the act of merging many things into one. In business, it often refers to the mergers or acquisitions of many smaller companies into much larger ones. The financial accounting term of _________ refers to the aggregated financial statements of a group company as consolidated account.

a. Cost of goods sold
b. Consolidation
c. Write-off
d. Retained earnings

21. The role of the _________ is to issue accounting standards in the United Kingdom. It is recognised for that purpose under the Companies Act 1985. It took over the task of setting accounting standards from the Accounting Standards Committee (ASC) in 1990.

a. AAB
b. A Random Walk Down Wall Street
c. Accounting Standards Board
d. ABN Amro

22. _________ is the field of accountancy concerned with the preparation of financial statements for decision makers, such as stockholders, suppliers, banks, employees, government agencies, owners, and other stakeholders. The fundamental need for _________ is to reduce principal-agent problem by measuring and monitoring agents' performance and reporting the results to interested users.

_________ is used to prepare accounting information for people outside the organization or not involved in the day to day running of the company.

a. 7-Eleven
b. 529 plan
c. 4-4-5 Calendar
d. Financial Accounting

23. The _________ is a private, not-for-profit organization whose primary purpose is to develop generally accepted accounting principles (GAAP) within the United States in the public's interest. The Securities and Exchange Commission (SEC) designated the _________ as the organization responsible for setting accounting standards for public companies in the U.S. It was created in 1973, replacing the Accounting Principles Board and the Committee on Accounting Procedure of the American Institute of Certified Public Accountants. The _________'s mission is 'to establish and improve standards of financial accounting and reporting for the guidance and education of the public, including issuers, auditors, and users of financial information.'

The _________ is not a governmental body.

a. KPMG
b. Federal Deposit Insurance Corporation
c. World Congress of Accountants
d. Financial Accounting Standards Board

24. _________ is the monetary unit of account of the principal economic environment in which an economic entity operates.

Statement of Financial Standards No. 52 (SFAS 52) is the primary source of GAAP for translation of foreign currency financial statements.

a. Functional currency
b. Reserve currency
c. Devaluation
d. Currency board

25. _________ is the standard framework of guidelines for financial accounting used in the United States of America. It includes the standards, conventions, and rules accountants follow in recording and summarizing transactions, and in the preparation of financial statements. _________ are now issued by the Financial Accounting Standards Board (FASB).

a. Generally accepted accounting principles
b. Depreciation
c. Revenue
d. Net income

26. _________ is the difference between price and the costs of bringing to market whatever it is that is accounted as an enterprise (whether by harvest, extraction, manufacture, or purchase) in terms of the component costs of delivered goods and/or services and any operating or other expenses.

A key difficulty in measuring profit is in defining costs. Pure economic monetary profits can be zero or negative even in competitive equilibrium when accounted monetized costs exceed monetized price.

a. A Random Walk Down Wall Street
b. Economic profit
c. AAB
d. Accounting profit

27. In financial accounting, the term _________ is most commonly used to describe any part of shareholders' equity, except for basic share capital. Sometimes, the term is used instead of the term provision; such a use, however, is inconsistent with the terminology suggested by International Accounting Standards Board. For more information about provisions, see provision (accounting.)

a. Closing entries
b. Reserve
c. Treasury stock
d. FIFO and LIFO accounting

28. _________, in bookkeeping, refers to assets, liabilities, income, and expenses recorded on individual pages of the so called book of final entry or ledger. Changes in _________ value are made by chronologically posting debit (DR) and credit (CR) entries to its page. Examples of _________s are cash, _________s receivable, mortgages, loans, land and buildings, common stock, sales, services provided, wages, and payroll overhead.

a. Accretion
b. Account
c. Option
d. Alpha

29. The term _________ has three unrelated technical definitions, and is also used in a variety of non-technical ways.

- In financial economics, it refers to any asset used to make money, as opposed to assets used for personal enjoyment or consumption. This is an important distinction because two people can disagree sharply about the value of personal assets, one person might think a sports car is more valuable than a pickup truck, another person might have the opposite taste. But if an asset is held for the purpose of making money, taste has nothing to do with it, only differences of opinion about how much money the asset will produce. With the further assumption that people agree on the probability distribution of future cash flows, it is possible to have an objective _________ pricing model. Even without the assumption of agreement, it is possible to set rational limits on _________ value.
- In governmental accounting, it is defined as any asset used in operations with an initial useful life extending beyond one reporting period. Generally, government managers have a 'stewardship' duty to maintain _________s under their control. See International Public Sector Accounting Standards for details.
- In US tax accounting, it is defined as any property other than a list of exceptions. The main exceptions are anything held for sale, and any real estate or depreciable property used in business. Almost everything you own and use for personal purposes, pleasure or investment is a _________. If something is a _________ for tax purposes, gains or losses on sale or disposition are capital gains or capital losses. For individuals, however, capital losses on property held for personal use are generally not deductible. See the IRS publication Tax Facts about Capital Gains and Losses for details.

A well-known financial accounting textbook advises that the term be avoided except in tax accounting because it is used in so many different senses, not all of them well-defined. For example it is often used as a synonym for fixed assets or for investments in securities.

A common non-technical usage occurs when people ask that employees or the environment or something else be treated as a _________.

a. Settlement date
b. Political risk
c. Solvency
d. Capital asset

30. In finance, the _________ is used to determine a theoretically appropriate required rate of return of an asset, if that asset is to be added to an already well-diversified portfolio, given that asset's non-diversifiable risk. The model takes into account the asset's sensitivity to non-diversifiable risk (also known as systemic risk or market risk), often represented by the quantity beta (β) in the financial industry, as well as the expected return of the market and the expected return of a theoretical risk-free asset.

The model was introduced by Jack Treynor (1961, 1962), William Sharpe (1964), John Lintner (1965a,b) and Jan Mossin (1966) independently, building on the earlier work of Harry Markowitz on diversification and modern portfolio theory.

a. Random walk hypothesis
b. Cox-Ingersoll-Ross model
c. Hull-White model
d. Capital asset pricing model

31. In finance, _________ occurs when a debtor has not met its legal obligations according to the debt contract, e.g. it has not made a scheduled payment, or has violated a loan covenant (condition) of the debt contract. _________ may occur if the debtor is either unwilling or unable to pay their debt. This can occur with all debt obligations including bonds, mortgages, loans, and promissory notes.

a. Debt validation
b. Vendor finance
c. Credit crunch
d. Default

32. _________ is the risk of loss due to a debtor's non-payment of a loan or other line of credit (either the principal or interest (coupon) or both)

Most lenders employ their own models (credit scorecards) to rank potential and existing customers according to risk, and then apply appropriate strategies. With products such as unsecured personal loans or mortgages, lenders charge a higher price for higher risk customers and vice versa. With revolving products such as credit cards and overdrafts, risk is controlled through careful setting of credit limits.

a. Credit risk
b. Transaction risk
c. Market risk
d. Liquidity risk

33. In finance, the _________ between two currencies specifies how much one currency is worth in terms of the other. For example an _________ of 102 Japanese yen to the United States dollar means that JPY 102 is worth the same as USD 1. The foreign exchange market is one of the largest markets in the world.

a. ABN Amro
b. AAB
c. A Random Walk Down Wall Street
d. Exchange rate

34. _________ is a form of risk that arises from the change in price of one currency against another. Whenever investors or companies have assets or business operations across national borders, they face _________ if their positions are not hedged.

- Transaction risk is the risk that exchange rates will change unfavourably over time. It can be hedged against using forward currency contracts;
- Translation risk is an accounting risk, proportional to the amount of assets held in foreign currencies. Changes in the exchange rate over time will render a report inaccurate, and so assets are usually balanced by borrowings in that currency.

The exchange risk associated with a foreign denominated instrument is a key element in foreign investment. This risk flows from differential monetary policy and growth in real productivity, which results in differential inflation rates.

a. Credit risk
b. Market risk
c. Currency risk
d. Tracking error

35. _________, refers to a globally traded currency that can serve as a reliable and stable store of value. Factors contributing to a currency's hard status can include political stability, low inflation, consistent monetary and fiscal policies, backing by reserves of precious metals, and long-term stable or upward-trending valuation against other currencies on a trade-weighted basis.

As of 2008, _________ could be argued to include the United States dollar, euro, Swiss franc, British pound sterling, Norwegian krone, Swedish krona, Canadian dollar, Japanese yen, and Australian dollar.

a. Reserve currency
b. Devaluation
c. Petrodollar recycling
d. Hard currency

36. _________ is a type of risk faced by investors, corporations, and governments. It is a risk that can be understood and managed with proper aforethought and investment.

Broadly, _________ refers to the complications businesses and governments may face as a result of what are commonly referred to as political decisions--or 'any political change that alters the expected outcome and value of a given economic action by changing the probability of achieving business objectives.' .

a. Capital asset
b. Single-index model
c. Mid price
d. Political risk

37. In business and accounting, _________s are everything of value that is owned by a person or company. The balance sheet of a firm records the monetary value of the _________s owned by the firm. The two major _________ classes are tangible _________s and intangible _________s.
a. Accounts payable
b. EBITDA
c. Income
d. Asset

38. In finance, _________ is the process of estimating the potential market value of a financial asset or liability. they can be done on assets (for example, investments in marketable securities such as stocks, options, business enterprises, or intangible assets such as patents and trademarks) or on liabilities (e.g., Bonds issued by a company.) _________s are required in many contexts including investment analysis, capital budgeting, merger and acquisition transactions, financial reporting, taxable events to determine the proper tax liability, and in litigation.
a. Procter ' Gamble
b. Margin
c. Share
d. Valuation

39. _________ is the planning process used to determine whether a firm's long term investments such as new machinery, replacement machinery, new plants, new products, and research development projects are worth pursuing. It is budget for major capital, or investment, expenditures.

Many formal methods are used in _________, including the techniques such as

- Net present value
- Profitability index
- Internal rate of return
- Modified Internal Rate of Return
- Equivalent annuity

These methods use the incremental cash flows from each potential investment, or project. Techniques based on accounting earnings and accounting rules are sometimes used - though economists consider this to be improper - such as the accounting rate of return, and 'return on investment.' Simplified and hybrid methods are used as well, such as payback period and discounted payback period.

a. Preferred stock
b. Financial distress
c. Shareholder value
d. Capital budgeting

40. The _________ or spot rate of a commodity, a security or a currency is the price that is quoted for immediate (spot) settlement (payment and delivery.) Spot settlement is normally one or two business days from trade date. This is in contrast with the forward price established in a forward contract or futures contract, where contract terms (price) are set now, but delivery and payment will occur at a future date.

a. Cost of carry
b. Spot price
c. Central Securities Depository
d. Market price

41. In economics, _________ is a rise in the general level of prices of goods and services in an economy over a period of time. The term '_________' once referred to increases in the money supply (monetary _________); however, economic debates about the relationship between money supply and price levels have led to its primary use today in describing price _________. _________ can also be described as a decline in the real value of money--a loss of purchasing power in the medium of exchange which is also the monetary unit of account.

a. A Random Walk Down Wall Street
b. Inflation
c. ABN Amro
d. AAB

42. _________ is the provision of resources (such as granting a loan) by one party to another party where that second party does not reimburse the first party immediately, thereby generating a debt, and instead arranges either to repay or return those resources (or material(s) of equal value) at a later date. The first party is called a creditor, also known as a lender, while the second party is called a debtor, also known as a borrower.

Movements of financial capital are normally dependent on either _________ or equity transfers.

a. Clearing house
b. Credit
c. Comparable
d. Warrant

43. _________ is a fee paid on borrowed assets. It is the price paid for the use of borrowed money , or, money earned by deposited funds . Assets that are sometimes lent with _________ include money, shares, consumer goods through hire purchase, major assets such as aircraft, and even entire factories in finance lease arrangements.

a. Insolvency
b. Interest
c. AAB
d. A Random Walk Down Wall Street

44. An _________ is a contract written by a seller that conveys to the buyer the right -- but not the obligation -- to buy (in the case of a call _________) or to sell (in the case of a put _________) a particular asset, such as a piece of property such as, among others, a futures contract. In return for granting the _________, the seller collects a payment (the premium) from the buyer.

For example, buying a call _________ provides the right to buy a specified quantity of a security at a set strike price at some time on or before expiration, while buying a put _________ provides the right to sell.

a. Annuity
b. Amortization
c. Option
d. AT'T Mobility LLC

45. _________ (or PwC) is one of the world's largest professional services firms. It was formed in 1998 from a merger between Price Waterhouse and Coopers ' Lybrand, both formed in London.

_________ earned aggregated worldwide revenues of $28 billion for fiscal 2008, and employed over 146,000 people in 150 countries.

a. Credit karma
b. Lending Club
c. Texas ratio
d. PricewaterhouseCoopers

46. _________ is the balance of the amounts of cash being received and paid by a business during a defined period of time, sometimes tied to a specific project. Measurement of _________ can be used

- to evaluate the state or performance of a business or project.
- to determine problems with liquidity. Being profitable does not necessarily mean being liquid. A company can fail because of a shortage of cash, even while profitable.
- to generate project rate of returns. The time of _________s into and out of projects are used as inputs to financial models such as internal rate of return, and net present value.
- to examine income or growth of a business when it is believed that accrual accounting concepts do not represent economic realities. Alternately, _________ can be used to 'validate' the net income generated by accrual accounting.

_________ as a generic term may be used differently depending on context, and certain _________ definitions may be adapted by analysts and users for their own uses. Common terms include operating _________ and free _________.

_________s can be classified into:

1. Operational _________s: Cash received or expended as a result of the company's core business activities.
2. Investment _________s: Cash received or expended through capital expenditure, investments or acquisitions.
3. Financing _________s: Cash received or expended as a result of financial activities, such as interests and dividends.

All three together - the net _________ - are necessary to reconcile the beginning cash balance to the ending cash balance. Loan draw downs or equity injections, that is just shifting of capital but no expenditure as such, are not considered in the net _________.

a. Shareholder value
b. Cash flow
c. Corporate finance
d. Real option

47. A '_________' is a 'Charge' that is paid to obtain the right to delay a payment. Essentially, the payer purchases the right to make a given payment in the future instead of in the Present. The '_________', or 'Charge' that must be paid to delay the payment, is simply the difference between what the payment amount would be if it were paid in the present and what the payment amount would be paid if it were paid in the future.

a. Value at risk
b. Risk aversion
c. Risk modeling
d. Discount

48. _________ or financing is to provide capital (funds), which means money for a project, a person, a business or any other private or public institutions.

Those funds can be allocated for either short term or long term purposes. The health fund is a new way of _________ private healthcare centers.

a. Synthetic CDO
b. Proxy fight
c. Product life cycle
d. Funding

49. _________ are made by investors and investment managers.

Investors commonly perform investment analysis by making use of fundamental analysis, technical analysis and gut feel.

_________ are often supported by decision tools.

a. Asset allocation
b. Investing online
c. Investment performance
d. Investment decisions

50. In economic models, the _________ time frame assumes no fixed factors of production. Firms can enter or leave the marketplace, and the cost (and availability) of land, labor, raw materials, and capital goods can be assumed to vary. In contrast, in the short-run time frame, certain factors are assumed to be fixed, because there is not sufficient time for them to change.

a. Long-run
b. Short-run
c. 529 plan
d. 4-4-5 Calendar

51. _________ is the price at which an asset would trade in a competitive Walrasian auction setting. _________ is often used interchangeably with open _________, fair value or fair _________, although these terms have distinct definitions in different standards, and may differ in some circumstances.

International Valuation Standards defines _________ as 'the estimated amount for which a property should exchange on the date of valuation between a willing buyer and a willing seller in an arm'e;s-length transaction after proper marketing wherein the parties had each acted knowledgeably, prudently, and without compulsion.'

_________ is a concept distinct from market price, which is 'e;the price at which one can transact'e;, while _________ is 'e;the true underlying value'e; according to theoretical standards.

a. Debt restructuring
b. T-Model
c. Wrap account
d. Market value

52. In financial accounting, a _________ or statement of cash flows is a financial statement that shows a company's flow of cash. The money coming into the business is called cash inflow, and money going out from the business is called cash outflow. The statement shows how changes in balance sheet and income accounts affect cash and cash equivalents, and breaks the analysis down to operating, investing, and financing activities.

a. 4-4-5 Calendar
b. 7-Eleven
c. 529 plan
d. Cash flow statement

53. In economics, business, and accounting, a _________ is the value of money that has been used up to produce something, and hence is not available for use anymore. In business, the _________ may be one of acquisition, in which case the amount of money expended to acquire it is counted as _________. In this case, money is the input that is gone in order to acquire the thing.

a. Sliding scale fees
b. Fixed costs
c. Cost
d. Marginal cost

54. _________ is a life of security. It may also refer to the final payment date of a loan or other financial instrument, at which point all remaining interest and principal is due to be paid.

1, 3, 6 months _________ band can be calculated by using 30-day per month periods.

a. Primary market
b. Replacement cost
c. False billing
d. Maturity

55. In finance, _________ refers to the way a corporation finances its assets through some combination of equity, debt, or hybrid securities. A firm's _________ is then the composition or 'structure' of its liabilities. For example, a firm that sells $20 billion in equity and $80 billion in debt is said to be 20% equity-financed and 80% debt-financed.

a. Market for corporate control
b. Capital structure
c. Book building
d. Rights issue

56. In finance, a _________ is a debt security, in which the authorized issuer owes the holders a debt and, depending on the terms of the _________, is obliged to pay interest (the coupon) and/or to repay the principal at a later date, termed maturity.

Thus a _________ is a loan: the issuer is the borrower, the _________ holder is the lender, and the coupon is the interest. _________s provide the borrower with external funds to finance long-term investments, or, in the case of government _________s, to finance current expenditure.

a. Convertible bond
b. Puttable bond
c. Bond
d. Catastrophe bonds

57. _________ is that which is owed; usually referencing assets owed, but the term can cover other obligations. In the case of assets, _________ is a means of using future purchasing power in the present before a summation has been earned. Some companies and corporations use _________ as a part of their overall corporate finance strategy.

a. Cross-collateralization
b. Debt
c. Partial Payment
d. Credit cycle

58. _________ in finance is a risk management technique, related to hedging, that mixes a wide variety of investments within a portfolio. Because the fluctuations of a single security have less impact on a diverse portfolio, _________ minimizes the risk from any one investment.

A simple example of _________ is the following: On a particular island the entire economy consists of two companies: one that sells umbrellas and another that sells sunscreen.

a. 529 plan
b. 7-Eleven
c. 4-4-5 Calendar
d. Diversification

59. A _________ is a foreign exchange agreement between two parties to exchange principal and fixed rate interest payments on a loan in one currency for principal and fixed rate interest payments on an equal (regarding net present value) loan in another currency. They are motivated by comparative advantage.

a. Currency swap
b. Forex swap
c. Currency pair
d. Foreign exchange market

60. An _________ is the price a borrower pays for the use of money they do not own, and the return a lender receives for deferring the use of funds, by lending it to the borrower. _________s are normally expressed as a percentage rate over the period of one year.

_________s targets are also a vital tool of monetary policy and are used to control variables like investment, inflation, and unemployment.

a. A Random Walk Down Wall Street
b. ABN Amro
c. Interest rate
d. AAB

61. An _________ is a derivative in which one party exchanges a stream of interest payments for another party's stream of cash flows. _________s can be used by hedgers to manage their fixed or floating assets and liabilities. They can also be used by speculators to replicate unfunded bond exposures to profit from changes in interest rates.

a. International Swaps and Derivatives Association
b. Implied volatility
c. Equity swap
d. Interest rate swap

62. _________ refers to financial institutions that have been established (or chartered) by more than one country, and hence are subjects of international law. Their owners or shareholders are generally national governments, although other international institutions and other organisations occasionally figure as shareholders. The most prominent _________ are creations of multiple nations, although some bilateral financial institutions (created by two countries) exist and are technically _________.

a. AAB
b. A Random Walk Down Wall Street
c. International financial institutions
d. ABN Amro

63. In accounting and finance, _________ is the portion of receivables that can no longer be collected, typically from accounts receivable or loans. _________ in accounting is considered an expense.

There are two methods to account for _________:

1. Direct write off method (Non - GAAP)

A receivable which is not considered collectible is charged directly to the income statement.

1. Allowance method (GAAP)

An estimate is made at the end of each fiscal year of the amount of _________. This is then accumulated in a provision which is then used to reduce specific receivable accounts as and when necessary.

a. 4-4-5 Calendar
b. Bad debt
c. 529 plan
d. Tax expense

64. In financial accounting, _________s are precautions for which the amount or probability of occurrence are not known. Typical examples are _________s for warranty costs and _________ for taxes the term reserve is used instead of term _________; such a use, however, is inconsistent with the terminology suggested by International Accounting Standards Board.

a. Money measurement concept
b. Momentum Accounting and Triple-Entry Bookkeeping
c. Petty cash
d. Provision

65. In finance, a _________ is a derivative in which two counterparties agree to exchange one stream of cash flows against another stream. These streams are called the legs of the _________.

The cash flows are calculated over a notional principal amount, which is usually not exchanged between counterparties.

a. Volatility swap
b. Volatility arbitrage
c. Local volatility
d. Swap

66. _________ is the incidence or process of transferring ownership of a business, enterprise, agency or public service from the public sector (government) to the private sector (business.) In a broader sense, _________ refers to transfer of any government function to the private sector including governmental functions like revenue collection and law enforcement.

The term '_________' also has been used to describe two unrelated transactions. The first is a buyout, by the majority owner, of all shares of a public corporation or holding company's stock, privatizing a publicly traded stock. The second is a demutualization of a mutual organization or cooperative to form a joint stock company.

a. 4-4-5 Calendar
b. 529 plan
c. 7-Eleven
d. Privatization

67. A _________ is a private or public market for the trading of company stock and derivatives of company stock at an agreed price; these are securities listed on a stock exchange as well as those only traded privately.

The size of the world _________ is estimated at about $36.6 trillion US at the beginning of October 2008 . The world derivatives market has been estimated at about $480 trillion face or nominal value, 12 times the size of the entire world economy.

a. Anton Gelonkin
b. Stock market
c. Adolph Coors
d. Andrew Tobias

68. The _________, effective annual interest rate, Annual Equivalent Rate (AER) or simply effective rate is the interest rate on a loan or financial product restated from the nominal interest rate as an interest rate with annual compound interest. It is used to compare the annual interest between loans with different compounding terms (daily, monthly, annually, or other.)

The _________ differs in two important respects from the annual percentage rate (APR):

1. the _________ generally does not incorporate one-time charges such as front-end fees;
2. the _________ is (generally) not defined by legal or regulatory authorities (as APR is in many jurisdictions.)

By contrast, the 'effective APR' is used as a legal term, where front-fees and other costs can be included, as defined by local law.

Annual Percentage Yield or effective annual yield is the analogous concept used for savings or investment products, such as a certificate of deposit.

a. ABN Amro
b. AAB
c. A Random Walk Down Wall Street
d. Effective interest rate

69. _________ is a term applied in many countries to a reference interest rate used by banks. The term originally indicated the rate of interest at which banks lent to favored customers, i.e., those with high credibility, though this is no longer always the case. Some variable interest rates may be expressed as a percentage above or below _________.

a. Time deposit
b. Prime rate
c. Credit bureau
d. Reserve requirement

70. In economics, the concept of the _________ refers to the decision-making time frame of a firm in which at least one factor of production is fixed. Costs which are fixed in the _________ have no impact on a firms decisions. For example a firm can raise output by increasing the amount of labour through overtime.

a. Short-run
b. 4-4-5 Calendar
c. 529 plan
d. Long-run

71. In United States banking, _________ is a marketing term for certain services offered primarily to larger business customers. It may be used to describe all bank accounts (such as checking accounts) provided to businesses of a certain size, but it is more often used to describe specific services such as cash concentration, zero balance accounting, and automated clearing house facilities. Sometimes, private banking customers are given _________ services.

a. Capitalization rate
b. Global tactical asset allocation
c. Profitability index
d. Cash management

72. A _________ is an agreement between two parties to buy or sell an asset at a specified point of time in the future. The price of the underlying instrument, in whatever form, is paid before control of the instrument changes. This is one of the many forms of buy/sell orders where the time of trade is not the time where the securities themselves are exchanged.

a. Derivatives markets
b. Constant maturity credit default swap
c. Loan Credit Default Swap Index
d. Forward contract

73. In finance, a _________ is a standardized contract, to buy or sell a specified commodity of standardized quality at a certain date in the future, at a market determined price (the futures price.)

The price is determined by the instantaneous equilibrium between the forces of supply and demand among competing buy and sell orders on the exchange at the time of the purchase or sale of the contract.

In many cases, the items may be such non-traditional 'commodities' as foreign currencies, commercial or government paper [e.g., bonds], or 'baskets' of corporate equity ['stock indices'] or other financial instruments.

a. Financial future
b. Futures contract
c. Repurchase agreement
d. Heston model

74. _________ means regulating, adapting or settling in a variety of contexts:

In commercial law, _________ means the settlement of a loss incurred on insured goods. The calculation of the amounts of compensation to be paid by or to the several interests is a complicated matter. It involves much detail and arithmetic, and requires a full and accurate knowledge of the principles of the subject.

a. Adjustment
b. Intelligent investor
c. Asset recovery
d. Equity method

75. A _________ is an exchange of promises between two or more parties to do an act which is enforceable in a court of law. It is where an unqualified offer meets a qualified acceptance and the parties reach Consensus ad Idem. The parties must have the necessary capacity to _________ and the _________ must not be either trifling, indeterminate, impossible or illegal.

a. 7-Eleven
b. 529 plan
c. 4-4-5 Calendar
d. Contract

76. _________ is a list for goods and materials held available in stock by a business. It is also used for a list of the contents of a household and for a list for testamentary purposes of the possessions of someone who has died. In accounting _________ is considered an asset.

a. AAB
b. A Random Walk Down Wall Street
c. ABN Amro
d. Inventory

Chapter 1

1. b	2. b	3. d	4. d	5. d	6. d	7. d	8. d	9. d	10. c
11. d	12. c	13. d	14. d	15. b	16. a	17. d	18. d	19. a	20. b
21. d	22. a	23. b	24. d	25. d	26. d	27. a	28. d	29. a	30. d
31. d	32. d	33. b	34. c	35. d	36. a	37. d	38. d	39. a	40. b
41. c	42. a	43. d	44. d	45. c	46. d	47. c	48. c	49. d	50. a
51. a	52. d	53. b	54. d	55. c	56. c	57. a	58. d	59. c	60. b
61. d	62. b	63. c	64. d	65. a	66. d	67. a	68. d	69. a	70. d
71. b	72. d	73. d	74. c	75. b	76. b	77. d	78. d	79. a	80. d

Chapter 2

1. a	2. a	3. c	4. d	5. c	6. d	7. d	8. d	9. d	10. d
11. a	12. a	13. d	14. d	15. c	16. d	17. c	18. a	19. d	20. d
21. c	22. d	23. a	24. d	25. a	26. d	27. b	28. c	29. d	30. d
31. d	32. b	33. c	34. d	35. d	36. d	37. d	38. b	39. a	40. c
41. d	42. b	43. b	44. d	45. b	46. a	47. c	48. d	49. d	50. d
51. d	52. b	53. d	54. d	55. d	56. a	57. b	58. d	59. d	60. d
61. c	62. c	63. d	64. c	65. d	66. d	67. d	68. d	69. a	70. d
71. c	72. a	73. b	74. d	75. b	76. d	77. d	78. d	79. b	80. a

Chapter 3

1. b	2. d	3. d	4. a	5. d	6. d	7. a	8. d	9. d	10. d
11. a	12. d	13. d	14. a	15. d	16. d	17. a	18. b	19. c	20. d
21. d	22. d	23. b	24. a	25. c	26. d	27. b	28. d	29. d	30. b
31. d	32. d	33. d	34. d	35. d	36. d	37. a	38. c	39. b	40. c
41. a									

Chapter 4

1. d	2. c	3. d	4. d	5. c	6. b	7. c	8. d	9. d	10. d
11. d	12. d	13. d	14. d	15. d	16. a	17. d	18. c	19. b	20. c
21. d	22. d	23. b	24. d	25. d	26. d	27. d	28. d	29. d	30. b
31. a	32. d	33. a							

Chapter 5

1. a	2. b	3. d	4. d	5. c	6. d	7. d	8. d	9. c	10. d
11. d	12. c	13. d	14. a	15. c	16. c	17. c	18. d	19. c	20. a
21. b	22. b	23. c	24. d	25. c	26. a	27. c	28. a	29. a	30. d
31. d	32. c	33. c	34. b	35. d	36. c	37. c	38. d	39. c	40. d
41. c	42. d	43. d	44. d	45. d					

Chapter 6

1. d	2. d	3. a	4. d	5. d	6. d	7. b	8. b	9. d	10. b
11. d	12. c	13. c	14. a	15. b	16. d	17. c	18. d	19. d	20. d
21. d	22. b	23. d	24. c	25. d	26. b	27. d	28. d	29. d	30. a
31. a	32. b	33. d	34. d	35. a	36. c	37. d	38. b	39. c	40. d
41. b	42. d	43. d	44. d	45. c	46. d	47. c	48. b	49. a	50. c
51. c	52. d	53. d	54. b	55. c	56. d	57. c	58. d	59. d	60. d
61. d	62. c	63. b	64. b	65. d	66. d	67. a	68. b		

Chapter 7

1. d	2. c	3. a	4. a	5. d	6. b	7. d	8. d	9. d	10. d
11. d	12. b	13. b	14. c	15. a	16. c	17. a	18. b	19. d	20. b
21. b	22. d	23. c	24. a	25. d	26. a	27. d	28. d	29. a	30. d
31. d	32. d	33. d	34. d	35. d	36. a	37. d	38. d	39. d	40. b
41. d	42. b	43. a	44. d	45. a	46. b	47. d	48. d	49. a	50. b
51. d	52. c	53. a	54. d	55. a	56. d	57. c	58. c	59. a	60. d
61. d	62. d	63. d	64. b	65. a	66. d	67. d	68. c	69. d	70. d
71. d	72. c	73. a	74. b	75. d	76. b	77. d	78. d	79. a	80. d
81. c	82. b	83. d	84. d	85. d					

Chapter 8

1. d	2. d	3. d	4. d	5. d	6. a	7. a	8. d	9. d	10. d
11. a	12. d	13. a	14. d	15. b	16. b	17. d	18. d	19. c	20. d
21. d	22. a	23. d	24. b	25. d	26. d	27. b	28. b	29. b	

Chapter 9

1. c	2. d	3. b	4. d	5. d	6. d	7. a	8. b	9. a	10. d
11. d	12. d	13. c	14. d	15. d	16. b	17. c	18. b	19. d	20. d

Chapter 10

1. b	2. c	3. d	4. d	5. d	6. d	7. d	8. c	9. d	10. d
11. d	12. d	13. d	14. d	15. d	16. b	17. c	18. a	19. c	20. a
21. c	22. d	23. a	24. a	25. d	26. c	27. b	28. b	29. a	30. a
31. c	32. d	33. d	34. d	35. b	36. b				

Chapter 11

1. c	2. d	3. a	4. a	5. c	6. d	7. b	8. c	9. a	10. b
11. a	12. d	13. a	14. a	15. d	16. c	17. a	18. c	19. d	20. c
21. c	22. d	23. c	24. d	25. a	26. b	27. d	28. d	29. b	30. d
31. c	32. a	33. d	34. b	35. b	36. d	37. c	38. b	39. c	40. d
41. d	42. a	43. b	44. d	45. d	46. d	47. c	48. d	49. d	50. d
51. b	52. b	53. c							

Chapter 12

1. a	2. b	3. a	4. d	5. b	6. d	7. d	8. a	9. d	10. a
11. d	12. c	13. a	14. d	15. d	16. c	17. d	18. d	19. b	20. b
21. b	22. d	23. d	24. b	25. d	26. d	27. b	28. a	29. a	30. d
31. b	32. c	33. c	34. b	35. d	36. d	37. b	38. d	39. a	40. d
41. d	42. b	43. d	44. a	45. c	46. d	47. b	48. b	49. a	

Chapter 13

1. c	2. c	3. d	4. d	5. d	6. c	7. b	8. d	9. b	10. a
11. d	12. a	13. d	14. a	15. d	16. b	17. d	18. d	19. d	20. b
21. d	22. c	23. d	24. d	25. d	26. d	27. d	28. a	29. c	30. d

Chapter 14

1. d	2. d	3. d	4. d	5. d	6. d	7. c	8. b	9. c	10. a
11. d	12. b	13. b	14. b	15. a	16. a	17. d	18. d	19. d	20. a
21. a	22. d	23. a	24. d	25. d	26. d	27. d	28. b	29. a	30. d
31. c	32. d	33. d	34. a	35. d	36. d	37. c	38. a	39. a	40. c
41. a	42. d	43. b	44. c	45. d	46. a	47. c	48. d	49. a	50. d
51. b	52. a	53. d	54. a	55. d	56. a	57. b	58. c	59. c	60. a
61. d	62. d	63. a	64. d	65. d	66. a	67. a	68. c	69. d	70. d
71. c	72. b								

Chapter 15

1. d	2. a	3. d	4. d	5. a	6. d	7. d	8. a	9. d	10. d
11. d	12. a	13. d	14. b	15. d	16. a	17. b	18. a	19. d	20. c
21. d	22. b	23. d	24. d	25. d	26. d	27. d	28. a	29. d	30. d
31. d	32. d	33. d	34. b	35. d	36. b	37. d	38. a	39. a	40. d
41. d	42. d	43. d	44. d	45. d					

Chapter 16

1. d	2. a	3. d	4. b	5. a	6. b	7. d	8. c	9. d	10. d
11. d	12. a	13. d	14. c	15. d	16. d	17. d	18. d	19. a	20. d
21. a	22. d	23. d	24. d	25. d	26. b	27. b	28. d	29. d	30. d
31. c	32. d	33. b	34. b	35. d	36. d	37. d	38. d	39. d	40. c
41. c	42. c	43. c	44. d	45. a	46. d	47. c			

Chapter 17

1. d	2. b	3. d	4. d	5. a	6. b	7. d	8. d	9. d	10. d
11. b	12. d	13. a	14. d	15. b	16. b	17. d	18. a	19. a	20. d
21. a	22. c	23. d	24. d	25. d	26. a	27. d	28. c	29. d	30. d
31. d	32. b	33. d	34. d	35. d	36. c	37. d	38. c	39. c	40. d
41. c	42. d	43. d	44. b	45. a	46. a	47. b	48. a	49. a	50. c
51. d	52. c	53. b	54. d	55. d	56. c	57. d	58. d	59. a	60. d
61. a	62. d	63. c							

Chapter 18

1. d	2. d	3. d	4. d	5. d	6. a	7. a	8. b	9. d	10. c
11. b	12. d	13. b	14. b	15. c	16. a	17. d	18. d	19. b	20. b
21. c	22. d	23. d	24. a	25. a	26. d	27. b	28. b	29. d	30. d
31. d	32. a	33. d	34. c	35. d	36. d	37. d	38. d	39. d	40. b
41. b	42. b	43. b	44. c	45. d	46. b	47. d	48. d	49. d	50. a
51. d	52. d	53. c	54. d	55. b	56. c	57. b	58. d	59. a	60. c
61. d	62. c	63. b	64. d	65. d	66. d	67. b	68. d	69. b	70. a
71. d	72. d	73. b	74. a	75. d	76. d				

www.ingramcontent.com/pod-product-compliance
Lightning Source LLC
Chambersburg PA
CBHW081351230426
43667CB00017B/2794
* 9 7 8 1 4 2 8 8 6 9 2 3 3 *